Essentials of Research Methods

Essentials of Research Methods

A Guide to Social Science Research

Janet M. Ruane

Blackwell
Publishing

© 2005 by Janet M. Ruane

BLACKWELL PUBLISHING
350 Main Street, Malden, MA 02148-5020, USA
108 Cowley Road, Oxford OX4 1JF, UK
550 Swanston Street, Carlton, Victoria 3053, Australia

The right of Janet M. Ruane to be identified as the Author of this Work has been asserted in accordance with the UK Copyright, Designs, and Patents Act 1988.

First published 2005 by Blackwell Publishing Ltd

Library of Congress Cataloging-in-Publication Data

Ruane, Janet M.,
   Essentials of research methods : a guide to social science research / Janet M. Ruane.
      p. cm.
Includes bibliographical references and index.
   ISBN 0–631–23048–3 (hardback : alk. paper) – ISBN 0–631–23049–1 (pbk.: alk. paper)
   1. Social sciences–Research. 2. Social sciences–Statistical methods. I. Title.

H62.R728 2004
300'.72—dc22

2003024690

A catalogue record for this title is available from the British Library.

The publisher's policy is to use permanent paper from mills that operate a sustainable forestry policy, and which has been manufactured from pulp processed using acid-free and elementary chlorine-free practices. Furthermore, the publisher ensures that the text paper and cover board used have met acceptable environmental accreditation standards.

Set in 10/13pt Palatino
by Kolam Information Services Pvt. Ltd, Pondicherry, India
Printed and bound in the United Kingdom
by MPG Books Ltd, Bodmin, Cornwall

For further information on
Blackwell Publishing, visit our website:
http://www.blackwellpublishing.com

Contents

Figures and Tables

Figures

Tables

Preface

Those who teach research methods often face a common dilemma – methods is frequently a required course and therefore filled with students who would rather be *anywhere* else. Furthermore, since most students don't envision themselves pursuing research careers, few believe the course will be of any use to them. This is the didactic challenge embraced by this book. *Essentials of Research Methods* is driven and informed by the belief that knowledge of research methods really does matter. *Essentials* is committed to making believers out of students!

One common and simple strategy has guided my teaching and guided the writing of this book: I work at finding timely illustrations and meaningful examples that will help students "see" the relevance of methods in their daily lives. Consequently, my methods "radar" is always on and the reader will find many examples of it throughout the pages of the book. The lessons of a bad sample are readily communicated via misleading movie trailers. Television commercials can be seen as exercises in persuasion that aggressively promote some product by taking full advantage of traditional, intuitive, authoritative or empirical knowledge. *Consumer Reports* can be seen as offering a crash course in measurement validity and reliability. Nightly news programs take advantage of the versatile survey as an efficient tool for keeping a finger on the pulse of the people. Our people-watching in airports or public places shows us the very natural side of fieldwork. Inquisitive two-year-olds offer convincing proof of our natural interest in causal analysis. My many years of teaching methods has convinced me that if you make such methods connections, students will come to realize just how much research methods permeate their lives and they will be that much more inclined to learn the essentials. Each chapter in this book has been "test-driven" over and over again in the classroom. Each chapter is the product of many tune-ups and even some major overhauls. I know that students do hear the messages being delivered in each chapter. I also know that students like what they hear. Each semester, to my absolute delight, students tell me how surprised they are to discover that they are actually enjoying the course!

In short, *Essentials of Research Methods* works very hard at engaging the reader. The book is *not* a methods reference book; it is *not* the definitive work or the last word on research methods. It is, instead, a work that offers the basics needed for developing a good, useful working knowledge of methods. The book intentionally avoids methods overkill, electing instead to give the readers a full helping of methods but in a way that encourages them to come back for more. Toward this end, each chapter offers readers leads on where they can go to further explore and expand the essentials. By following this model, the book strives to launch a new breed of methods students – students of research methods for life.

Acknowledgments

It takes a village to raise a child... and it takes very close to a village to write a book. There are many people in my Montclair village who deserve an "assist" on this project. My students deserve credit for encouraging me to make methods available to them. My former GA, Kathryn Hammond, reminded me of the importance of (and satisfaction derived from) connecting with students. My department colleagues Laura Kramer and Peter Freund consistently checked on my progress and thereby helped to keep me on schedule. The newest addition to my department village, Susan O'Neil, helped to make some of the last-minute manuscript deadline tasks more bearable. Dean Richard Gigliotti also supported this project through Montclair's FSIP program. I am most appreciative of all this general MSU village support. I also received great assistance from my professional village – several people took the time to read and comment on early drafts of this work. I am particularly grateful for the valuable feedback I received from my Blackwell reviewers. I also appreciate the strong support and astute guidance I received from my development editor, Ken Provencher, and desk editor, Anna Oxbury.

The job of sitting and writing a book also requires support from the local village. I sincerely thank my family and friends who expressed interest (real or otherwise, it doesn't matter!) in the project. I kept two members of my family in mind (Luci and Jonathan) as "touchstones" for the tone of the book. I am especially grateful to my wonderful mother and sisters (Mary, Anne and Mary Jane) who yielded family time on behalf of this book. I know there were too many visits and holidays cut short because of my writing schedule. I also know that this book would still be in the "discussion" phase if it weren't for Karen Cerulo. She was extremely generous with her time, her feedback and her overall encouragement. Truth be known, Karen offered a village-worth of support all by herself! A village-worth of thanks to Karen.

1 When Should We Trust What We Know? Why Research Methods?

We live in an information-dominated society. Every day, like it or not, we are bombarded by facts, figures, news, and opinions; we are connected to countless information sources about our local community, our society, and our world. Awakening to clock radios or morning TV, we start our days with the latest breaking news. On route to work, radios, cell phones, and amber alert systems sustain the information loop. Palm pilots, billboards, and information kiosks also keep us in the know. At work, many of us "log on" and ride the information highway. The journey can continue at lunch or dinner or at a happy hour as more and more cafeterias and diners and bars offer patrons a side dish of information in the form of streaming electronic message boards. Standing in food checkout lines gives us just enough time to catch up on the latest celebrity scoop. And we return home to find our mailboxes stuffed with letters, notices, and solicitations reminding us of local, national, and international issues and crises. Our nightly fix of television entertainment has an information edge to it as we tune into *48 Hours* or *Dateline* or *20/20*. If we haven't had enough by day's end, we can fall off to sleep watching a late-night talk show, an hour or more of politically correct and incorrect programming, or a rebroadcast of Oprah. If we're "up for it," the stream of information can go on 24/7.

In recent years, our information age has taken an alluring, perhaps compelling, "personal" turn. To a large extent, the personal computer and the Internet allow us (even encourage us) to customize the information that comes our way. Yahoo, for instance, will set up a personal stock quote page for us. We can arrange for daily emails about our favorite sports teams and figures. Lap top computers and the Internet can deliver just about any "personalized" piece of news or factoid. Want to know how much social security you'll receive by the time you retire? Go to http://www.ssa.gov/SSA_Home.html and click onto the "Plan Your Retirement" link. Want to estimate your chances of developing heart disease? Go to http://www.americanheart.org and follow the "Health Tools" link. Want to know how your congressman or senator voted on the latest piece of legislation? Try the following Library of Congress service site: http://thomas.loc.gov/. Want to know more about your family history? Go to http://www.genealogytoday.com. Have any question at all? You might find some answers at http://answer-point.ask.com/.

Given all the ways of knowing that are available to us, and given our growing ability to get exactly the information that *we* want, students of research methods may wonder why we need to learn the methodical and labor-intensive procedures of research methods? Can't we get the information we need from the radio, TV, or from newspapers and magazines? Given the wealth of information available on the Internet, can't we be satisfied to just sit and click?

Perhaps a recent Internet banner ad for the *New York Times* offers the best answer to the question: "What's the point of an information age without the right information?" Information is only useful if it's accurate.

The incredible amount of information that confronts us (and the relative ease of accessing it) makes us all the more vulnerable to misinformation. Consider three pieces of "information" that recently circulated on the Internet:

- The Federal Communications Commission (FCC) is trying to ban God from television programming.
- Congressman Schnell is proposing a five cent tax on emails to raise funds for postal services.
- Bananas from Costa Rica carry a flesh-eating bacteria.[1]

All of these assertions grabbed a lot of attention on the Internet. Yet, *none* of these statements is true; The Federal Communications Act prohibits the FCC from censoring broadcast materials; there is no Congressman Schnell in the House; the flesh-eating banana bacteria story is a hoax. Internet rumors, however, are particularly hard to squelch because individuals are quite willing to believe anything they learn from the "all-knowing" computer. Though false, these rumors still exact a price. The

---

1   CBS *Evening News*, WCBS New York City Broadcast, July 19, 2000.

FCC received a half million angry letters of complaint about banning God from the airwaves. Similarly, Congress reported an "impeachment level" volume of citizen complaints about the proposed email tax. A spokesperson for banana importers reports that the false banana rumor has cost the industry $30 million in lost sales.

When confronted by an information glut, how are we to know which information is the "right" information? How are we to decide which information to trust? To answer these questions, we need to give some thought to the various sources of knowledge that drive our information society. We need also to consider if some sources of knowledge are more worthy of our trust than others.

Time-Based Knowing: Traditional Knowledge

Consider a popular "fact" asserted by many in today's society: Gay soldiers have no legitimate place in the US military. Military grunts and brass, politicians and pundits speak knowingly about the threat gay soldiers pose to unit solidarity. Order and discipline are thought to be incompatible with allowing gays in military service. According to opponents of gays in the military, nothing less than national security is at risk when soldiers must worry about sexual advances from other same-sex soldiers. Advocates of this position are confident that their assertions are correct. In part this confidence is derived from the fact that this negative view of gays in the military is a long-standing one – as such, it represents a tenacious form of knowledge: i.e., traditional knowledge.

With traditional knowledge the mere passing of time is seen as the basis for making knowledgeable assertions about the world. In surviving the test of time, long-standing ideas or enduring assertions about the world are assumed to be true. One of the reasons that the rumor about the FCC banning God from TV is given credence is because it has been circulating for the last 25 years! When we hear the same thing over and over, we frequently conclude that there's got to be some truth to it. But herein rests the major flaw of tradition as a source of knowledge and information: The mere passing of time *does NOT in itself establish something as true*. Consider the fact that for thousands of years "everyone knew" that the earth was flat. Navigators chartered their trips to accommodate this fact. Mapmakers were content with two-dimensional maps. But claiming the earth was flat did not make it so. The mere passing of time did not verify the assertion. (If anything, the passing of time is exactly what showed this assertion to be unequivocally false.)

Similarly, until the fifteenth century, astronomers held that the earth was the center of the universe. It was unthinkable to challenge this fact. (Recall the fate of Galileo for bucking the system – he was excommunicated from the Catholic Church for promoting a sun-centered model of the universe.) Once again, however, thousands of years of asserting that all heavenly things revolved around the earth did not make it so. Most recently, the genetic mapping evidence of the genome project challenged the traditional view of race as a biologically determined category. Despite age-old arguments to the contrary, human races are not genetically distinct. Humans share 99.9 percent of their DNA. Racial similarities, not differences, are in our genes.

As these examples show, traditional knowledge with its unthinking acquiescence to the passing of time can be very risky knowledge. The "age" of an idea or a belief does not necessarily prove its accuracy or truth.

Credential-Based Knowing: Authoritative Knowledge

Now consider another widely held view today: After a long bullish ride, many financial experts predicted that the start of the new millennium would see a major correction in the stock market. Many investors took the correction warning to heart and changed their investment strategies. The stock market example illustrates another popular and frequently utilized way of knowing: authoritative knowledge. With authoritative knowledge, we defer to experts when looking for accurate assertions about the world. In trusting experts, we are deferring to their credentials and training. We accept as accurate and true that which experts tell us.

Our willingness to trust authorities has led some to observe that ours is a society of "authority addicts." Many of you may already be familiar with a rather famous study by Stanley Milgram (1974) that poignantly revealed our willingness to defer to authorities. In this study, Milgram discovered that ordinary civilians would administer electrical shocks to others when directed by authority figures to do so. (Participants were told to administer shocks to those who had failed at a learning task.) Indeed, in various replications of the study, Milgram found that a majority of study participants were willing to administer the electrical jolts even when they thought the shocks were causing others severe pain. Milgram's research indicated that humans are willing to accept uncritically an authority figure's perceptions and definitions of reality.

Our enamorment with expert knowledge is really a lifetime affair. Many of our parents raised us with a little bit of help from baby and child "experts." Since the 1940s, millions of parents have regarded Dr Benjamin Spock's advice as the gospel truth about childcare. Before Spock, parents of the 1920s were embracing the expert advice of the behaviorist John Watson. Our early schooling experience is largely about teaching students to defer to authority. In grade school and high school we learn to respect authoritative sources of information – i.e., teachers and textbooks. Interestingly enough, some students find college unsettling because the authority program changes somewhat. The college years are the first time that some students are encouraged to question and scrutinize what they've already learned. This can be an exercise in anxiety; many of us prefer the security and stability that comes from trusting authority. (Indeed a popular bumper sticker of the eighties was aimed at challenging our deep-rooted authority addiction. The sticker simply read "Question Authority.")

Our reliance on authoritative knowledge continues into our adult years. In the area of health, many of us wouldn't dream of second guessing our physicians. We hesitate to question whether the pharmacist has properly filled our prescriptions. In buying or selling homes, most of us will rely on the expertise of realtors. We take our cars in for "diagnostic" check-ups. At present, countless Americans are investing for their financial futures on the basis of the economic "facts" presented by stock market analysts. (We refuse to think about the fallout if the experts are wrong.) Many of us feel secure about the accuracy of any information if we've read it in *The New York Times*[2] or seen it on *World News Tonight*. There is no doubt about it – authoritative knowledge offers us a certain comfort zone and we like it that way.

As with traditional knowledge, however, authoritative knowledge can be wrong. Frequently our trust in experts is misplaced. Credentials don't always give experts the corner on truth. Most of us know this all too well from our first-hand experiences with such things as weather forecasts, election projections, or media hype. Meteorologists tell us to get ready for a soggy weekend and it turns out to be lovely and sunny. They warn of a severe snowstorm and we wind up with a dusting. During the 2000 presidential campaign, the Sunday morning "talking heads" predicted a Bush landslide in the New Hampshire Primary and then had to

---

2 Indeed some would argue that the recent Jayson Blair scandal (Blair was a Times reporter who plagiarized and fabricated news stories) is most troubling for *The New York Times* because it undermines the paper's greatest asset: its reputation (Sloan 2003).

scramble to explain a McCain victory. Despite critical acclaim, Spielberg and Cruise's *Minority Report* turned out to be a major disappointment at the box office. And let's not forget the millennium's Y2K bug – despite the big hoopla, media experts were essentially wrong about the expected calamity.

Of course, the stakes of our misplaced trust in experts can be higher than what's suggested by these last examples. Many financial experts, for instance, failed to foresee the famous stock market crash of 1929 – they were confident that stocks had achieved a new but safe high plateau. As a result, countless Americans who trusted the experts were financially ruined in the aftermath of Black Tuesday (October 29, 1929). In the three years following the crash, national income was cut in half and there were some 15 million unemployed Americans – up from 1.5 million in 1929 (Garraty & Gay 1972; Wiltz 1973).

Prior to 9/11, we might have thought that national security experts knew best about significant and credible threats to the safety of US citizens and territory. Yet post-9/11 reviews of "who knew what and when" suggest that experts had trouble connecting the dots that pointed to and forewarned us about the worst terrorist attack on US soil. FBI superiors elected to dismiss warnings from local agents in Minnesota and Arizona who were concerned about flight training activities of individuals under surveillance (Hirsch & Isikoff 2002). INS (Immigration and Naturalization Service) authorities failed to stop Mohamed Atta from entering the US despite the fact that he had an expired visa and links to known terrorists. On the very day of the attacks, airport security agents singled out nine of the terrorists for special scrutiny but did not prevent them from boarding the planes (*The New York Times* 2002). Our faith and trust in experts clearly failed us on this issue of homeland security. Why? Surely one of the reasons for the failure is that credentials don't automatically give people a corner on truth. Experts work with facts, information, and ideas *as they see them*. And as 9/11 painfully showed us, there isn't necessarily any common agreement regarding experts' perceptions of facts and information.

The previous discussion of child experts John Watson and Benjamin Spock provides yet another more mundane yet instructive example of how experts can offer very different "reads" of a social phenomenon. Both men were regarded as offering unassailable advice on childrearing. Yet the advice offered by the two experts was not at all compatible. Watson, a behaviorist, advocated a strict regime of childcare: Keep children on a four-hour feeding and sleeping schedule; resist cuddling or other signs of affection. Spock endorsed a much more child-friendly philosophy. He advocated love over rigid discipline and encouraged parents to treat children with respect. He even slipped Freudian ideas into his advice (but without letting the parents explicitly know this). Which expert really deserved the trust of parents? Note that some social critics charge that Spock was the "father of permissiveness" and helped raise a generation of hippies and war protestors who are now (mis)running the country (Whitall & Lawson 1998)!

Note too that authorities, however credentialed they are, can sometimes *intentionally* mislead us. Experts can distort information when it is in their vested interest to do so. For example, during the Vietnam War, military authorities obscured American participation in combat and doctored enemy casualty reports in order to offset resistance to the war. The efforts by President Johnson and military advisors to paint a positive picture of US involvement in the war eventually contributed to a serious "credibility gap" with the American public (Braestrup 2000). Or consider another exercise in expert deception – one that is now coming back to haunt an industry. In 1953, several CEOs of major tobacco companies created the Tobacco Industry Research Committee to counteract growing public concerns about the hazards of smoking. The tobacco industry spent the next several decades denying the health risks of cigarettes despite the fact that its own research efforts were showing the opposite to be true. As early as 1963, cigarette makers knew the addictive properties of nicotine but intentionally withheld the release of this damaging information. These cover-up efforts by the tobacco industry lasted decades, coming to light only in 1994 with the leak of a "smoking gun" (no pun intended). An anonymous "Mr Butts" released over 40 years' of internal company documents detailing how much tobacco industry experts knew but wouldn't tell about the dangers of its product (Zegart 2000).

On a less sinister note, authorities can also mislead us when they move outside their areas of training and expertise. Prior to the American Revolution, health care was a very risky enterprise. Why? Well perhaps it had something to do with the "medical experts" of the day. Most American medical practitioners were ship's surgeons, apothecaries, or clergy (Cockerham 1998). It was not until the early 1900s that the American Medical Association was able to effectively limit the practice of medicine to those with an MD degree (Starr 1982). Prior to the emergence of a secular worldview, legal rulings were also frequently left in the hands of religious authorities. Divinely ordained inquisitors were given the job of deciding a person's innocence or guilt on the basis of trials by ordeal (aka trials by torture). Presumably, the guilty would cry out damning admissions during their ordeal while the innocent, fortified by

God, would remain silent. In colonial America, accused witches had their legal fate determined by their ability to say the Lord's Prayer in public. A slip of the tongue was taken to be a sign that the accused was possessed by the devil (Pfohl 1994). A moment's reflection should help you see the risks entailed in moving beyond an authority's area of expertise. Our past reliance on questionable medical and legal "experts" no doubt cost some unfortunates their lives and liberty.

More Risky Knowledge Sources: Common Sense and Intuition

There are two additional knowledge sources worth mentioning: common sense and intuition. As with tradition and authority, each of these ways of knowing can be compelling. Common sense uses our personal experiences and the experiences of those we know as the source of "practical" knowledge. Common sense tells us that six-year-olds should not be in charge of family meal plans. Common sense tells us that adolescents should not supervise their own schedules or finances. And common sense tells us that if someone hits us before marriage, she or he is likely to hit us after marriage as well. Intuition can be thought of as "direct access" knowledge; it refers to a way of knowing that operates on "gut feelings" without the use of intellect. Intuition can be a powerful source of information – even a real lifesaver. (My intuition saved me from an assault and robbery when I was in graduate school.) Many of us have had occasions where our intuition has steered us away from making bad choices or steered us into "good bets." (My only winnings at the race-track have come from betting hunches.)

Still, as with traditional and authoritative knowledge, common sense and intuition are not error-free ways of knowing. Common sense places far too high a premium on personal experience as a basis for universal truths. Yet personal experience, because it is tied to the individual and unique circumstances, is not the best basis for generalized knowledge. Just imagine the health risks entailed when one person (say a husband) shares his prescription drugs for high blood pressure with another (say his wife). There is a rather high likelihood that the drugs that benefit one person could actually prove detrimental to another. (Small differences in our genes can greatly affect how we react to medicine. See http://www.nigms.nih.gov/funding/htm/diduno.html for additional information on why people can have wildly different reactions to medicines.) To paraphrase an old saying, one size experience doesn't fit all.

Intuition, because it operates outside the realm of intellect and reason, is often hard to understand. (In fact, there is an entire psychic industry that has evolved around the inability of most of us to listen to or "hear" our intuitive voice.) Our reliance on intuition is further complicated by our common sense. Common sense tells us to be suspicious of intuition. Common sense reminds us that while many of us eagerly broadcast times when our intuition has paid off, many of us will also conveniently forget all of the times when our hunches were wrong. (Think of all the *losing* horse and lottery bets that were placed because of hunches.)

Where does all of this leave us? Hopefully with a new found realization that much of the information that bombards us every day is based on some rather questionable knowledge sources. While many of our most familiar and comfortable ways of knowing may be fast and easy, they can also be risky, error-prone ways of knowing. Traditional and authoritative knowledge, common sense and intuition are all alike in that they encourage an uncritical acceptance of information. Ideas that have been around a long time, ideas that are presented by authorities, ideas that are practical or "feel right" can wind up being accepted as true *even when they are false*. Still, we need not despair; there is one way of knowing that is distinctively different from those we've just reviewed: science. Science and its research methods promote a critical assessment of information before that information is accepted as accurate.

Science as a Trustworthy Way of Knowing

If we are interested in obtaining the highest quality of information, we are well advised to engage scientific ways of knowing. An understanding of research methods allows us to become critical consumers of information. Understanding research methods allows us to assess the wealth of information we receive each day in light of some very discerning standards.

Science is distinctive in that it employs set methodical procedures that aim to reduce or control the amount of error that creeps into the process of knowing. For instance, the scientific approach demands **empirical evidence** to support any assertions about the world. Its empirical nature means that science places a high premium on the observation, direct and indirect, of concrete phenomena. Science also insists on our following **systematic, methodical "rules"** for gathering our empirical evidence. Evidence that is obtained in an unsystematic way is regarded as tainted or problematic; it is seen as less trustworthy. And science insists that the evidence we find in support of our assertions be **replicated** by other studies before it is considered trustworthy. This repetition of studies in search of the repetition of findings is an essential safeguard against our jumping to false conclusions. It is also an essential part of science's interest in discovering "laws" or regularities of both the physical and social worlds. Each of these standards is elaborated below.

Empirical evidence

Science as a way of knowing is not willing to accept assertions about the world at face value. In science, it is not sufficient, for instance, to maintain (as traditional knowledge does) that gays in the military are bad for soldier morale. It is not acceptable for us to believe that Costa Rican bananas are bad simply because an Internet communiqué tell us that. Science requires that assertions be backed by concrete, objective corroboration that shows or reveals the accuracy of the statements. In insisting on empirical evidence, science is asking for *sensory* evidence that we can see, smell, hear, or taste (Goode 2000). With this demand for empirical evidence, science is highlighting its inherently skeptical nature – unless we "show it" to be so (via the empirical world around us), claims about reality are merely that – "claims," nothing more. Science is not willing to trust a mere assertion – it demands empirical documentation.

Methodical rules

In the interest of curtailing error, science utilizes standardized procedures that guide our search for accurate information about the world around us. There are rules for developing and assessing the accuracy of the ways we try to document or measure social reality (i.e., criteria for establishing measurement validity). There are "rules" that govern our ability to draw causal connections between events or between characteristics and behaviors (i.e., criteria for establishing internal validity). There are rules that govern which people, things, or events we should focus on when studying the world around us (i.e., criteria for sampling). And there are rules that govern whether or not it is appropriate to generalize our research findings beyond our study at hand (i.e., criteria for establishing external validity). These rules constitute the heart of research methods. And while learning these rules is challenging work, they promise a benefit not offered by any other way of knowing. The methodical rules of research minimize the likelihood of error. In abiding by the discerning methodical rules of research, we gain confidence that our findings are accurate or error free.

Replication

To regard findings as true and reliable, science insists that those findings occur more than once. This insistence on repetition of studies and findings reveals a fundamentally conservative side to science. Replication is seen as a safeguard against our drawing premature and therefore possibly false conclusions about the world. Findings that can't be replicated arouse suspicion – isolated findings are regarded as flukes and are not considered worthy of our trust. (Recall the earlier discussion of Milgram's study of obedience to authority. He was not willing to draw any conclusions on the basis of just one study. Instead, he repeated the study over and over again to see if the findings continued to hold.) Indeed, the insistence on replication is simply the skeptical "show me" attitude of science coming full circle – if the findings are true, they should show up time after time under similar research conditions. One-time findings (like one-time sales offers) are usually too good to be true. Our confidence that our findings are accurate is further bolstered each time our findings are replicated by others employing the same rigorous methods of research.

Replication also serves science's interest in systematically explaining the world around us. The physical sciences are committed to discovering the invariable laws of nature. The social sciences are committed to discovering the regularities of social life. Sociology, my own academic discipline, pursues research to uncover general social patterns or forces that transcend particular characteristics of individuals and shape and influence our behaviors. Sociological research, for instance, consistently shows us that Americans follow the norms of homogamy when selecting marriage partners – i.e., we marry people who are very similar to us (McPherson et al. 2001; Ruane & Cerulo 2004), that suicide rates are inversely related to levels of social integration (Thorlindsson & Bjarnason 1998), and that poverty is quite detrimental to our mental, physical, and social well-being (Ruane & Cerulo 2004).

Goals of Research

The systematic, empirical standards of good research are often pursued in the name of four basic research goals: exploration, description, explanation, and evaluation. While a careful reading of a research article or report will likely reveal the underlying goal or motive for any research project, researchers will frequently explicitly state their purposes in the abstract or opening paragraphs of their writings.

Exploratory research is typically conducted in the interest of "getting to know" or increasing our understanding of a new or little researched setting, group, or phenomenon; it is used to gain insight into a research topic. Consequently, exploratory research tends to utilize relatively small samples of subjects that permit the researcher to get "up-close" first-hand information. To facilitate in-depth understanding, the researcher might engage in intensive one-on-one interviewing or pursue a participatory study that allows the researcher to "walk a mile" in the research subjects' shoes. Exploratory research often (though not exclusively) produces **qualitative data** – i.e., evidence presented in words, pictures, or some other narrative form that best captures the research subject's genuine experiences and understanding. For instance, in the 1980s, Palmer (1989) undertook a study of a newly emerging occupational specialty: the EMS (emergency medical systems) worker. In an effort to better understand the social context of this work, Palmer immersed himself in the world of paramedics by participating in and observing emergency runs and by interviewing emergency medical workers. His qualitative data consisted of the notes from his field observations and transcripts of the interviews with emergency personnel.

Descriptive research offers a detailed picture or account of some social phenomenon, setting, experience, group, etc. In painting a descriptive picture, this kind of research strives to be as accurate as possible. Consequently, descriptive research pays close attention to such issues as measurement and sampling. In effect, descriptive studies offers the research equivalent of a Joe Friday "just the facts" line of investigation – it seeks to find out what's going on and who is involved, the size of the group, and what the members look like, etc. In generating these basic facts, descriptive research aligns quite naturally (although again not inevitably) with quantitative methods. **Quantitative methods** document social variation in terms of *numerical* categories and rely on statistics to summarize large amounts of data. In recent years, for example, there has been a keen interest in knowing more about the fast growing population of Internet users. Since 2000, the *UCLA Internet Project* has been providing a yearly overview of a national sample of both Internet users and nonusers. The project also offers comparisons of new versus experienced Internet users. Current reports can be found at the UCLA Center for Communication Policy web site: www.ccp.ucla.edu. The quantitative nature of this research can readily be gleaned from the percentages and averages presented for the various groups of Internet users.

One question is noticeably overlooked in descriptive research – the *why* question. To understand the *why* or *how* of social phenomena, the researcher must pursue **explanatory research**. For example, descriptive research on domestic violence might seek to tell us about the prevalence of domestic violence, the most typical incidents, and the parties most likely to be involved in family violence. Explanatory research goes beyond these descriptive tasks. Explanatory research wants to know *why* some and not others resort to this family dynamic? *How* do violent events occur or unfold? Explanatory research makes a firm commitment to causal analysis. It confronts head on the challenges and difficulties of establishing causal order and connections. Explanatory research tries to identify the causes and/or effects of social phenomena. Some research on domestic violence, for instance, suggests that experiencing violence as a child increases one's tendency to resort to violence in subsequent relationships (Fitzpatrick 1997; McNeal & Amato 1998). Alcohol abuse has been cited as both a causal agent in producing violence (O'Farrell & Murphy 1995) as well as a consequence of victimization (El-Bassel et al. 1995; Plichita 1992).

Another goal of research that is closely related to explanatory research is achieved via evaluation research. **Evaluation research** seeks to judge the merits or efficacy of some social program or policy. If we want to know if an anger-management program "works," we would need to conduct some evaluation research. If we want to know if arresting abusive spouses is a good social control policy, evaluation research is in order. In the final analysis, evaluation research is interested in "outcomes" or results of some specific program or policy. Consequently, evaluation research must concern itself with the causal issues that are the hallmark of explanatory research. Evaluation research has a very practical, bottom-line orientation, however. In the present social climate of accountability, it is a "must do" area of research for many major social institutions (e.g., education, health care). It can also be a requirement for programs seeking program funding. In recent years, evaluation research of various drug prevention and/or rehabilitation programs has been in the media spotlight.

Using Research Methods to Become Critical Consumers of Information

While relatively few of us will be directly involved in the production of research, all of us will be involved in *consuming* such information. Thus, you might regard the learning of research methods as a matter of personal empowerment. We stand to gain by arming ourselves with scientific know-how. Our stakes in obtaining accurate information about our world are higher than ever. The sheer volume of information and the speed with which it travels carry grave ramifications concerning the consequences of misinformation. The damage of erroneous info can be as insidious as a computer virus. (Banana importers can offer 30 million reasons why this is true.) Consequently, the ability to evaluate information as more or less trustworthy is a crucial skill.

Our ability to evaluate information is directly tied to our knowledge of research methods. Information that is the product of carefully conducted scientific research is less likely to be in error, more deserving of our attention and trust. In the end, it may be your understanding of research methods that helps you make some critical life decisions. What's the most prudent diet or health regime for someone of your age, race, or gender? Which course of medical treatment is the best for you? What's the "safest" family vehicle? Do "red light cameras" really deter drivers from running red lights? Is there a real danger to using cell phones? Is there a good reason to pay higher prices for organic fruits and vegetables? Is home schooling the right choice for your family? Is your retirement fund safer in the hands of the government or in the hands of private investors? In large measure, your finding the right answers to these and other questions will depend on your ability to judge the quality of relevant information. In the end, your knowledge of research methods could very well be a life-enhancing, even a life-sustaining resource.

Expanding the Essentials

More information about persistent urban rumors and unfounded tales can be found at the About.com web site: http://www.about.com/

Internet Information – should we trust it or not? The query is prompted by the fact that information on the Internet is not screened for accuracy. Anyone, after all, can post anything on a web page. For a good tutorial on how to evaluate a web page, visit the following site maintained by the University of California, Berkeley: http://www.lib.Berkeley.edu/TeachingLib/Guides/Internet/. Scroll down and click on link to "Evaluating Web Pages: Why and How."

For any number of the topics covered in this text, you will find additional reader-friendly information at Bill Trochim's homepage: http://trochim. human.cornell.edu/. Once at the homepage, click on the Knowledge Base link, and then click the Contents link. Scroll down until you find the topic of interest to you. A good place to start would be with the links to "Language of Research" and "Five Big Words."

 Those wanting to delve further into the questions of knowing and truth and objective reality should take a look at the first few chapters in Babbie's *Observing Ourselves: Essays in Social Research* (1998).

Exercises

1   Visit the Urban Legends and Folklore link at About.com (see above). Review several of the legends and see if you can identify the "way of knowing" upon which they are based. Do you see any pattern?

2   Review a week or two of letters to the editor in your local newspapers. Identify the dominant knowledge source being used to support the claims/assertions made in the letters.

3   Carefully consider current print or television commercials. For each of the knowledge sources reviewed in this chapter, locate one or two ads/commercials that invoke these sources in order to convince us of the merits of their product claims. (E.g., a Hebrew National hot dog commercial has the voice of God telling us the product is good – this is clearly asking the consumer to defer to the ultimate authority.)

2 Ethics: It's the Right Thing To Do

While most of this book is concerned with introducing you to the logic and specific strategies of research methods, there is one issue that must be acknowledged as infusing all others: research ethics. Ultimately our research endeavors must abide by standards of professionalism and honesty; our efforts must strive to earn the respect and trust of both research participants and the public at large.

Concern over the issue of research ethics is a rather recent development. World War II provided one of our loudest wake-up calls regarding the ethics of research. Through the Nuremberg Trials, the world learned about concentration camp atrocities committed in the name of science. In 1946, 23 German physicians went on trial for crimes against prisoners of war. The crimes included experiments that exposed humans to extreme temperatures, the perpetration of mutilating surgeries, and the deliberate infection of prisoners with lethal pathogens (National Institutes of Health 1995).

But other ethics alerts have occurred more recently (and closer to home). In 1959, a Senate subcommittee investigated routine practices by pharmaceutical companies in their testing of new drugs. Drug companies would provide physicians with samples of experimental drugs not yet established as safe and pay the physicians to collect data on their unwitting patients. In 1963, the director of the National Institutes of Health exposed some troubling federally funded research being conducted by physicians at the Sloan-Kettering Cancer Research Institute. The physicians had injected live cancer cells into indigent elderly patients without their consent (Department of Energy 1995a).

In the 1970s the Senate held hearings on the Tuskegee Syphilis Study. In this research that began in the 1930s under the auspices of the US Public Health Service, approximately 400 black men in Tuskegee, Alabama, were involved without their knowledge in a longitudinal study of syphilis. In order to better understand the nature and course of the disease, the men in the study were denied penicillin even after it became the standard course of treatment for the disease. At least 28 research subjects died and 100 more suffered blindness and insanity from the effects of their untreated disease (or perhaps more to the point, from the effects of the study) (Department of Energy 1995a).

Most recently in the 1990s a Presidential Advisory Committee was formed to investigate ethically questionable government radiation experiments conducted in the United States between the late 1940s and early 1970s (Department of Energy 1995b). Toward the end of World War II, some Americans were injected with plutonium in order to study the element's effects on the human body. (The goal of the research was to gain information that would limit hazards to workers involved with the atom bomb project.) During the same time period radioactive oatmeal was reportedly fed to patients at a school for the retarded in Massachusetts. In the post-war period, the government sponsored research that entailed releasing radiation into the environment in Utah, New Mexico, Tennessee, and Washington without notifying the affected populations.

To be sure, the social sciences don't often entail the highly dramatic ethical issues encountered in medical or drug or nuclear research. Answering survey questions or being the focus of field studies may not pose serious threats to one's physical safety or well-being. Still the social science researcher would be ill advised to treat ethics as an irrelevant or secondary topic. Every research decision we make, from planning to the disclosure of results, should be made with an eye to ethics.

For our work to be ethically grounded, we must be prepared to evaluate our research plans and activities in light of generally accepted rules of conduct. For the sake of structuring this chapter, the discussion that follows will focus on several key ethical standards contained in the American Sociological Association's Code of Ethics. As you read through these principles, however, you will no doubt appreciate that they are not unique to the field of sociology. Rather the ethical principles that follow transcend any one specific discipline or field of study. Anyone embarking on the research path should be prepared to abide by these standards.

Research Should Not Cause Harm to Subjects

On first inspection, the "cause no harm" dictum may be the "no brainer" of all ethical guidelines for research. Any research activity that harms or poses unreasonable risks to subjects is incompatible with a fundamental ethical obligation to safeguard the physical, psychological and emotional well-being of participants. Research that carries the risk of subject harm without offering any clear benefits is ethically untenable. But even an obvious guideline like "cause no harm" can be a difficult rule to fully honor. It is sometimes hard to predict or know in advance the negative consequences of research. Research that appears safe and innocuous may have very different effects than those anticipated. Consider for instance the Cambridge-Somerville Youth Study of the 1930s. In 1939, Richard Cabot initiated an experimental treatment program for the prevention of delinquency among Boston youth. The research involved over 500 boys, half of whom were assigned to an experimental treatment group while the other half were assigned to a no treatment control group (Powers & Witmer 1951). In the mid 1970s, a research team led by Joan McCord conducted a follow-up assessment of the effectiveness of the program. Despite the honorable intentions of the original research program, McCord and her team found evidence that the boys in the treatment group may well have been harmed by their participation in the original study:

> Treated subjects were more likely than controls to evidence signs of alcoholism and serious mental illness, died at a younger age, suffered from more stress-related diseases, tended to be employed in lower-prestige occupations and were more likely to commit second crimes. (Kimmel 1988, p. 19)

As another example of just how hard it is for researchers to know in advance the consequences of their research, consider Haney et al.'s (1973) famous simulated prison experiment. These researchers carefully screened and selected 24 male college students for participation in a study of the behavior of "prisoners" and "guards" in a mock prison. The students knew they would be role-playing and they were paid for their participation. What *nobody* knew, however, was the impact the mock prison experience would have on the research subjects. Soon after the start of the study, some of the prisoners experienced depression, anxiety and psychosomatic symptoms. Some of the guards displayed abusive and aggressive behaviors. The study's investigators became so alarmed by what they witnessed that they canceled the experiment after only six days of its planned two-week run.

Clearly, without the ability to see into the future, it is impossible for researchers to know in advance all the possible or the final consequences of their research. Uncertainty about outcomes, however, shouldn't void or weaken the "do no harm" directive. The ethical obligation remains for researchers to anticipate likely outcomes and to take those steps that would mitigate the harm and maximize the benefits that might come to participants. One vehicle that allows researchers to better understand the consequences of participation is the **debriefing** session. In these post-study sessions, the researcher provides participants with more information about the study and elicits feedback on their thoughts, reactions and any negative aftereffects. Debriefing sessions are considered essential follow-ups to experiments where participants are often unaware of their exact study role (i.e., as experimental or control subjects) or of the intentional manipulation of the research conditions.

Researchers Should Obtain the Informed Consent of Subjects

The principle of **informed consent** is about the right of individuals to determine for themselves whether or not they want to be part of a research project. More specifically, informed consent refers to the right of research participants to be fully informed about all aspects of a research project that might influence their decision to participate. Consequently, freedom of choice and self-determination are at the heart of the informed consent principle. No one should be forced or duped into participating in a research endeavor. Informed consent forms should also remind respondents that they have the right to withdraw consent at any point in the study. Informed consent is such an important principle of ethical research that it is a required condition of any federally funded research project. That said, we must also acknowledge that informed consent is a principle that is all too frequently violated.

If we dissect the principle of informed consent, we will see that it really consists of four separate elements: the assumptions of competence, voluntarism, full information and comprehension (Paul Reynolds 1979). Understanding these elements provides some immediate insight into why it is that informed consent is so often violated.

Competence

This element of informed consent presumes that informed consent can only be given by competent individuals – i.e., individuals capable of deciding for themselves if participation in a study is in their best interest. Given the incredible diversity of social research topics and populations, research often involves subjects who lack the maturity or responsibility required for competent decision-making. The most obvious categories of those incapable of providing consent are children and mentally challenged individuals. To pursue research on these populations, informed consent must be obtained from parents or guardians. When honest sincere efforts are not made to do so, the principle of informed consent is violated. For instance, there had been a long standing complaint in education research that informed consent was all too frequently given little more than lip service. Informed consent would often be obtained via "passive" consent forms – forms that made consent the "no action" default position. For example, to obtain "passive" consent, forms might be sent home with elementary school students with the instructions that slips need only be returned if parents *objected* to their child's involvement. This tactic guaranteed higher consent rates since many children would either forget to present the slips to their parents or forget to return them to school officials. Clearly a procedure requiring clear and direct acknowledgment and consent by responsible parties is the better course of action.

Voluntarism

This element presumes that informed consent can only be given by individuals who are truly free to say yes or no to a research project. If any hint of coercion exists, the principle of informed consent is violated. Again, this presumption is not always so easy to satisfy. It is not hard to imagine conditions where research subjects might agree to a study for fear of negative consequences following their refusals. Charges of coercion, for instance, were levied against a long-term (1956–72) hepatitis study conducted at the Willowbrook State School for the Retarded on Staten Island (Department of Energy 1995a). Critics alleged that parents seeking to enroll their children in the school were offered "fast" admission to the school if they would consent to their children's involvement in the hepatitis study (wherein some of the children would be intentionally injected with the hepatitis serum).

An argument can easily be made that *any* research in institutional settings – hospitals, schools, prisons – has the potential to violate voluntarism. Institutional settings entail authority relationships that are inconsistent with true voluntarism. Following this reasoning, research participation that is a condition of fulfilling course requirements would be vulnerable to charges of coercion. Similarly, we must consider the possibility that any research that offers financial compensation to participants might have a coercive dimension. Indigent subjects may find it hard to say no to the offer of money as a participation inducement. Some have argued that for the element of voluntarism to be met, egalitarian relationships must exist between the researcher and participants. The fact that participants are so often regarded as research *subjects*, however, clearly indicates that any assumption of equality in a research endeavor is problematic. To stress the voluntary nature of consent, researchers might approach potential participants as valuable but autonomous "co-workers" in the research process.

Full information

This element presumes that research subjects will be given all the relevant information they will need to make an informed choice. But this standard is far from self-evident. How much information is enough? How relevant is relevant? Must every detail of a study be shared with participants? Will some details actually increase the chance of confusing respondents or biasing results? Some researchers contend that withholding select information is necessary in order to maintain the integrity of the study. This was certainly Milgram's position in his study of obedience to authority (1974). Milgram's research was intended to see if there were moral limits to what ordinary citizens could be ordered to do by authority figures. He did not, however, share this information with his research subjects. Instead, he simply told his participants that the study was about the effects of punishment on learning. In the course of the study, unwitting participants were "ordered" to administer electric shocks to individuals whenever they made mistakes in a learning exercise. In fact, the "learners" were never shocked, but the research participants did not know this. In retrospect we must now ask if Milgram's misleading explanation of his obedience study was ethical. Over the years, the standard that's been adopted is that of providing as much information as the "reasonable" person requires for decision-making. While this standard offers some guidance, it really doesn't completely clarify the issue. Indeed, our legal system has devoted much time and attention over the years to debating the reasonable man doctrine and such cases have shown that what is "reasonable" to one group may be "unreasonable" to another.

Comprehension

This element presumes that in order for individuals to provide informed consent, they must be able to *understand* the information received. By way of offering guidance, the Department of Health and Human Services advises that the consent document should be regarded as a *teaching* tool rather than as a legal instrument. At minimum, the comprehension aspect requires that research recruits be provided information in non-technical "lay language" (i.e., forms should not read like a contract!). Furthermore, to facilitate comprehension, participants should also be allowed to consult with others and to take some time between receiving information and making a decision about participation. Consequently, oral consent or consent procedures that don't give subjects any time to think over or reconsider their decision are really not fully abiding by the informed consent principle.

Researchers Should Respect Subjects' Privacy

The **right to privacy** refers to our ability to control when and under what conditions others will have access to information about us. Anyone familiar with the US culture and legal system should appreciate just how passionate people can be about this cherished principle. Since research is essentially a tool for "finding out," virtually any attempt to collect data from people can raise a red flag for the privacy issue. An invasion of privacy doesn't just occur when researchers sort through a town's garbage site or review private school records, it can also occur when a researcher poses questions the respondent considers "out of bounds." A subject's right to privacy requires the researcher to pay attention to three different privacy issues: (1) the sensitivity of the information being solicited, (2) the location or setting of the research, and (3) the disclosure of a study's findings (Diener & Crandall 1978).

Sensitivity of information

The privacy issue is undoubtedly complicated by the fact that any kind of personal information may be potentially threatening for some respondents. The greater the sensitivity of the research topic, the more safeguards are called for in order to protect the respondent's privacy. For instance, when surveys contain threatening questions, respondents should be forewarned and reassured about the steps that will be taken to protect their privacy. If sensitive topics are being covered in a person-to-person interview, researchers should consider resorting to an alternate "anonymous" format as a way to safeguard privacy (for a discussion of such a technique, see page 155 in Chapter 10).

Research setting

Just as the topics and populations of social research are extremely diverse, so too are the settings of social research. Research might be located in private homes, schools, work sites, neighborhood bars, street corners, and shopping malls to name but a few likely locations. In considering the privacy issue, the researcher should be prepared to evaluate the research site on a continuum of locations ranging from private to public. On first inspection, one might assume that locating sites on such a continuum would be a relatively easy task. But the extent to which a setting is private or public is not really all that obvious. Even the most public of settings may be perceived as an "off limits" private territory to the occupants. Consider, for instance, a public beach. Surely beach-goers understand that no one has a right to privacy on a public beach. Or do they? Think about the typical beach territory marking rituals we have all utilized. We mark off our territory with blankets and ice chests and with strategic placements of chairs and umbrellas. In effect, we are serving notice to other beach-goers that we've created a domain of privacy and woe to the person who ignores our privacy shields. Or think about your behaviors while driving your car on public streets. Despite the fact that we realize we are driving "in public" many of us will treat our cars as a "private" zone. We expect other drivers to engage in what Goffman (1963) called "civil inattention" – i.e., to pretend they don't see or hear us belting out a tune or yelling at our kids when we're stopped at traffic lights or tollbooths. In short, the privacy of a location is often problematic.

Determining whether a research site is private or not requires more than merely noting its spatial setting. This point becomes even more apparent when we consider the impact of technology on the privacy issue. Electronic surveillance is a fast growing segment of the security industry. While an overwhelming majority of the two million plus closed-circuit television systems currently used in the US are operated by private entities (Murphy 2002), interest in surveillance of public places has increased since 9/11. Surveillance tapes, of course, know no distinction between the private and public realms. The watchful eye of the security camera in a hospital parking lot will videotape vandals as well as those individuals stealing away for an afternoon rendezvous.

Electronic surveillance also sidesteps the notion of permission – the camera doesn't ask before recording. An international security company recently estimated that the average New Yorker is recorded on video approximately 75 times a day (Murphy 2002). With the expected expansion of technological surveillance and the growth of a "culture of surveillance" (Staples 1997), the social researcher will need to rethink how the lines between private and public are best drawn and how privacy of research subjects is best protected.

One of the most notorious examples of the privacy dilemma in a public research setting is offered by Laud Humphreys' study (1969) of tearooms (public restrooms used for impersonal homosexual encounters). Humphreys defended his selection of the research setting on the basis of the "democratic" nature of public restrooms. He felt that public restrooms would give him access to the most representative sample of tearoom patrons. What he failed to explicitly consider was that these very public locations were chosen by the patrons as a way to safeguard their own privacy. More private settings would be more restrictive in terms of access and would increase the chances of individuals' identities being or becoming known. Public restrooms allowed participants to enter under conditions of anonymity.[1]

Disseminating research findings

One clear way to violate a person's privacy is to go public with their personal information. While courts of law have ruled that certain groups that are "in the public eye" (e.g., politicians and celebrities) may forfeit some of their rights to privacy, the ordinary citizen should be able to enjoy this protection without qualification. Research poses a risk to privacy when findings are disclosed in a way that allows private information provided by individuals to be publicly linked to those individuals. Typically, researchers will offer protections of privacy by extending the guarantee of anonymity or confidentiality to research subjects.

To meet the promise of **anonymity**, the collection of data is structured so that the researcher cannot link specific information with the individuals

1 Ethical concerns are raised by the Humphreys study on still other fronts. Humphreys conducted follow-up in-home interviews with tearoom patrons. How was he able to do this? As individuals drove up to the public restrooms, Humphreys recorded the license plate numbers of their cars. He used this information to obtain home addresses. A year after his restroom observations, he changed his appearance and showed up at the patrons' homes posing as a health services interviewer.

who provide it. One way to accomplish anonymity in the research process is to purposely omit any self-identifiers during data collection. This is frequently a strategy employed on questionnaires where items that could identify the respondents are simply omitted – names, social security numbers, addresses, etc., are not requested. As a variation on this procedure respondents might be instructed to keep identifying information separate from the rest of their responses (i.e., they might be instructed to mail identifying information in one envelope and the actual survey in another). This procedure would allow the researcher to know that a respondent has returned a questionnaire but not be able to know which surveys belong to which respondents. Under conditions of anonymity, the names attached to specific data points can't be revealed because they simply aren't known.

The promise of **confidentiality** is an assurance by the researcher that the information provided by participants will never be linked to them publicly. Unlike anonymity, in confidential exchanges the researcher actually knows which names are linked to specific information but makes a promise not to go public with this information. In essence, the researcher agrees to a type of "secret-keeping" where he or he won't engage in any "he said/she said" revelations.

Once having made the offer, researchers clearly have an obligation to take the steps necessary to support their promises of anonymity and/or confidentiality. For instance, researchers should plan on assigning case numbers to replace any personal identification and to protect personal data. If lists that link case numbers with personal IDs exist, they should be kept in secure settings. Once data has been entered into computers for analysis, original surveys containing self-identifiers might be shredded.

On the face of it, the promises of anonymity and confidentiality would appear to be sufficient for safeguarding privacy. Revelations won't be made because we don't have names to reveal or because we promise not to do so. But the truth is that our guarantees of anonymity or confidentiality can be hard to keep. In the 1950s a rather telling privacy debacle occurred in Vidich and Bensman's (1958) field study of the political and social life of a small upstate New York town. The researchers thought they had adequately addressed the participants' privacy concerns with promises of anonymity and confidentiality. The researchers agreed to use fictitious names for both the town and the inhabitants when it came time to write up their findings. Unfortunately, the disguise of the town and townspeople was not effective. The locals could easily recognize themselves and their neighbors in the often critical and unflattering research narrative. Some concrete proof of the townspeople's dissatisfaction with the researchers' privacy guarantees can be gleaned from the fact that the town publicly lampooned the researchers at their annual Fourth of July parade (Kimmel 1988).

In making promises of confidentiality, researchers should also realize they actually may be promising more than they are prepared or willing to deliver. For instance, while we may offer the promise of confidentiality to research subjects, the courts have not always agreed that the exchanges between researchers and subjects are privileged communication. Consequently, social research data does not automatically enjoy the protection offered in other arenas: e.g., lawyer–client, doctor–patient, or clergy–penitent relationships. When push comes to shove, courts may subpoena research data and in so doing may publicize personal information about research participants. In failing to comply with court orders, the researcher is vulnerable to legal sanctions. Consequently, researchers who are embarking on projects that will gather sensitive information from respondents (e.g., gather information on sexual preferences or practices, on illegal activities, on psychological well-being, etc.) should consider obtaining a **certificate of confidentiality** for their projects. These certificates can be obtained through the National Institutes of Health and prevent forced disclosure of confidential research information. In the final analysis, researchers are well advised to explicitly state conditions of confidentiality (including any limits to confidentiality agreements) and to plan exactly how they will honor such agreements.

Researchers Should Avoid Conflicts of Interest

At first glance, an explicit dictum about conflict of interest may seem unnecessary in a research code of ethics. After all, researchers are dedicated to an objective and seemingly impartial collection of information. In truth, of course, researchers, like all social actors, are influenced by their social contexts. A context that can be extremely influential is that involving the corporate funding of research. For instance, corporate–campus liaisons are becoming more and more common as universities search for new sources of funding. These liaisons carry major implications for research. Corporate funders can dictate the direction and scope of research projects. They can also set the terms and conditions for publication of findings. In medical research, for instance, it is not uncommon for pharmaceuticals to place no-publishing clauses in contracts with university-based researchers. And it seems that corporate funders can also influence findings. A recent study by Danish researchers found that sources of funding affected researchers' findings in randomized clinical experiments. In a review of 159 articles published in the *British Medical Journal* between 1997 and 2001, researchers found that studies were more likely to show a positive result from an experimental intervention if the study was funded by a for-profit organization. Such positive results were missing from studies funded by non-profit organizations (Kjaergard & Als-Nielsen 2002).

Clearly researchers are within their rights when they align themselves with a cause or a research sponsor, or become the "hired gun" for a special interest group. In order to maintain the ethical high ground, however, they should make their allegiances known to their audience. Such acknowledgments put all on notice to possible biases in research efforts and findings. Indeed the authors of the previously cited study of randomized clinical trials maintain that their study clearly indicates the need for researchers to explicitly state their competing interests.

Ethical Reporting: The Whole Truth and Nothing but the Truth?

Researchers working as consultants or "hired guns" for corporations or special interest groups bring "front and center" one other area of ethical concern: fair and accurate reporting of research findings. Chapter 1 makes the case for empirical research being a trustworthy source of knowledge. With this point in mind, researchers need to be particularly mindful of the "power" of their research reports. Research findings, especially the statistics used to summarize those findings, can be quite persuasive. According to Joel Best in his book *Damned Lies and Statistics* (2001), the public has a tendency to treat statistics as "facts" beyond question. Curiously enough, we adopt this deferential stance toward statistics even though many of us seriously doubt our ability to process or critically assess numbers. It is a condition that Best refers to as "innumeracy" – i.e., mathematical illiteracy. Clearly, many social researchers are in a position where they can take advantage of innumeracy and play fast and loose with statistics.

Research findings and statistics are products of decisions made by researchers – decisions regarding measurement, sampling, research design, analysis, funding, etc. But findings, no matter how they are generated, can also be ammunition in political conflicts. This is especially likely to be the case when the researcher is working for a paying client or obligated to a funding agency. Research findings can be mobilized in ways to make or break, advance or block arguments. Researchers must make decisions regarding the findings and statistics they will report and feature. Featuring one set of statistics over another could lead to the construction of two very different stories based on the same data! As a simple example, consider that researchers have options when it comes to reporting averages – they might report the mean (a mathematically-based average), the median (a "middle position"-based average) or the mode (a frequency-based average). (See Chapter 12 for full discussion of each.) Now imagine a researcher who needs to report the average annual salary for a group of workers. Also imagine that there are a few extremely high salaries in the group that is otherwise dominated by low salaries. Indeed let's imagine that most of the workers are making the same low entry-level salary. Technically, all three averages – the mean, the median, and the mode – are "available" for reporting, but they would not all "tell" the same story. Given the conditions outlined above, reporting the mean salary would give an inflated picture of just how much the typical member of the group is actually earning (the mean is influenced by extreme values – i.e., the few extremely high salaries in our example). The more responsible average to report in such a scenario would be the median or mode (again see Chapter 12 for definitions of these terms and the logic of choosing one average over another).

When it comes to reporting their findings, the choices researchers make might well be influenced more by the story they want to tell (or are paid to tell) than by a fair and accurate rendering of the findings. This issue is no less of an ethical dilemma than the issues of informed consent, privacy, etc. Arguably it will be an increasing problem as more and more researchers seek and receive funding from organizations dedicated to their own research agendas. Researchers need to recognize their power to persuade and abide by standards of truthful, responsible reporting.

Reinforcing the Ethical Route: Institutional Review Boards

History has taught us the danger of allowing ethical considerations to be the sole responsibility of individual researchers. Consequently, to re-inforce the ethical behavior of researchers, most institutions involved in human research and all that receive federal funding have Institutional Review Boards (IRBs).[2] IRBs are charged with the ethical assessment of

2   The Department of Health and Human Services requires all institutions that receive federal research monies to establish IRBs in order to scrutinize all proposed studies sanctioned by the institutions. Furthermore, any researcher seeking federal support for their research must receive IRB approval before applying for federal monies.

proposals for all research projects under the institution's auspices. Today's Institutional Review Boards are byproducts of efforts to pass the National Research Act of 1974. In large measure, this act resulted from Congressional hearings on the Tuskegee study and other research abuses receiving public attention in the 1960s and 1970s. Both the National Research Act and IRBs are regarded as critical milestones in the development of federal standards for the protection of human research subjects. IRBs are generally composed of members with expertise in science and ethics as well as other non-scientific areas. The diversity of board members is seen as a strategic step for safeguarding the rights and welfare of research subjects. In assessing research proposals, IRBs invoke federal standards and regulations concerning the protection of human subjects.

Ethical Fusion

While we have anchored our review of research ethics in the American Sociological Association's code of ethics, the ethical standards of many professional associations are remarkably similar. (You should be able to find the codes of ethics for various professions on their official web pages.) Regardless of their specific discipline, researchers are generally charged with the responsibility of following rules of conduct that will safeguard the well-being of research subjects and treat them with dignity and respect. At the minimum, researchers should judge their planned research activity in terms of its potential benefits, the amount of risk it poses to participants, whether potential benefits outweigh the risks and whether or not adequate safeguards have been adopted to minimize any risks. In starting with these basic standards, researchers should be able to maintain the ethical high ground in their work.

Hopefully by the time you have worked your way to the end of this book, you will have learned much about the logic and techniques of social research. As you reach the end of this chapter, however, I hope that you have already realized that research needs to be conducted in an ethically responsible way. Troubling lessons of the past remind us that good research cannot afford to turn a blind eye to ethical standards. Good research demands that ethical concerns occupy a central place in the entire research process, from planning to data collection to reporting. Treating ethics as a secondary or marginal issue is an unjustifiably perilous path that will only serve to undercut the cause and value of research.

Expanding the Essentials

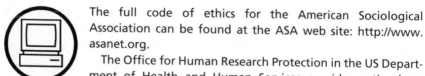

The full code of ethics for the American Sociological Association can be found at the ASA web site: http://www.asanet.org.

The Office for Human Research Protection in the US Department of Health and Human Services provides a tip sheet on informed consent: http://ohrp.osophs.dhhs.gov/humansubjects/guidance/ictips.htm.

Additional information about Certificates of Confidentiality can be obtained from the Confidentiality Kiosk at the National Institutes of Health web page: http://grants2.nih.gov/grants/policy/coc/index.htm.

A short but informative discussion of explicit vs. implicit confidentiality agreements as well as of the overall importance of confidential exchanges in social research can be found in Wes Jamison's article "Confidentiality in Social Science Research": http://www.wpi.edu/Academics/Projects/confidentiality.html.

A provocative discussion of the wisdom of promising absolute confidentiality in social research can be found in the January 2002 (vol. 32) issue of the electronic journal *Sociological Methodology*. Palys and Lowman in their article "Anticipating Law: Research Methods, Ethics and the Law of Privilege" advocate making very strong promises of confidentiality and detail design strategies to safeguard such promises. Articles by Lindgren and by Stone argue that the more prudent and even more ethical path is to offer conditional promises of confidentiality. http://search.epnet.com/direct.asp?an=7030958&db=aph.

For an interesting discussion of the special ethical issues that are common to Internet based research, see James Hamilton's article "The Ethics of Conducting Social-Science Research on the Internet" (2004).

Exercises

1   What ethical "red flags" might arise with the following research endeavors?

- observing people's routines at ATM machines,

- interviewing residents at an assisted living facility,

- conducting university sponsored research to assess student satisfaction.

2   Find out if your local university (or work) institution has an IRB. If so, see what you can learn about the board's procedures: e.g., who sits on the board; what is the time frame for the review process; does the board exempt any categories of research, etc.

3 Some Perfectly Valid Points: Measurement, Internal, and External Validity

As we saw in Chapter 1, science doesn't have a corner on the knowledge market. There are many different ways of knowing the world around us. Some of these alternate ways of knowing can be quite sufficient in satisfying our need to know. Your intuition may pay off at the racetrack. Your grandmother's sage advice may help you through a difficult family decision. Indeed every way of knowing has *something* to offer – that's what keeps them going and going and going. Still, science's systematic way of knowing does have a trump card to play. If we are interested in verifying the correctness of an assertion or claim about our social world, the scientific way of knowing has the edge. Valid knowledge – i.e., knowledge that is empirically correct – is best pursued via scientific research methods.[1]

Yet to say that science has an "edge" is not to say that science is infallible. Research procedures offer great safeguards against error, but error can still make its way into scientific findings. Humans can make mistakes in executing the methods of research – e.g., by contaminating evidence, selecting biased samples. Furthermore, "findings" don't speak for themselves. Humans must interpret them and in this process of interpretation there is plenty of room for questionable judgment calls and flat-out mistakes. This point was emphatically made in a recent case

1 As an interesting aside, in the summer of 2001 *Consumer Reports* declared the 2001 Mitsubishi Montero unsafe and recommended that consumers not buy it. Mitsubishi's response? The auto manufacturer dismissed *Consumer Reports'* methods as *unscientific* and unreliable.

showing the misuse of scientific evidence in criminal investigations. Since each of us has unique DNA, DNA evidence has become an extremely useful tool for solving crimes. A recent feature on *60 Minutes II*, however, provided a chilling reminder of the reality and gravity of "scientific mistakes" (Mabrey 2003). A Houston Texas crime lab misinterpreted the DNA evidence collected in a 1998 rape investigation focusing on a Houston teenager. The mistake resulted in an innocent 16-year-old being sentenced to 25 years in prison. (After spending four years in prison, the falsely convicted teenager's DNA was retested and found *not* to match the DNA obtained at the crime scene. The uncovering of this mistake has subsequently led to the review of close to 200 other DNA tests conducted by the Houston police department's crime lab. Seventeen of the cases involve men whose convictions have them facing the death sentence.) This example (and others like it) reminds us that even claims of scientific knowledge need to be met with a healthy dose of skepticism.[2] We should not blindly trust any claim to knowledge or truth but instead be ready to assess the accuracy or validity of *all* claims.

In our pursuit of valid knowledge, we are typically concerned with three "trust" issues. First, we want to know whether or not we can trust statements or claims of measurement. This concern raises the issue of measurement validity and requires us to take a long, hard look at the steps we take to empirically document reality. Second, we want to know whether or not we can trust causal statements about the world. This concern raises the issue of internal validity and requires us to take a long, hard look at research design. Last, we want to know whether we can trust our findings to apply beyond the study that produced them. This raises the issue of external validity and forces us to take a long, hard look at issues of sampling and replication.

Measurement Validity

Above all else, science is an empirical endeavor: it is concerned with using concrete, observable evidence to support its claims about the

---

2 To be sure, not all scientific mistakes are due to sub-standard workmanship (as alleged in the Houston police crime lab). Honest differences in interpreting scientific findings can lead to extended debates regarding reasonable conclusions supported by empirical evidence. Consider, for instance, that medical researchers are still at odds over the wisdom of following a high-fat, Atkins-style diet (Springen 2003; Taubes 2002). Similarly, medical researchers disagree in their interpretation of the evidence surrounding the link between autism and vaccines for childhood diseases (Allen 2002).

world. In the language of science, the evidence is derived via empirical *indicators* or *measures*. In focusing on the issue of measurement validity, the researcher is most concerned with critically evaluating the empirical indicators or measures used in our research efforts. When we claim **measurement validity**, we claim that we have been successful at measuring what we say we've measured. A few examples should help make the point.

Imagine you've just been through an outpatient surgical procedure. You will be cleared for release as soon as you are no longer running a temperature. In effect, your release is dependent on a measurement process – taking your temperature. An attending nurse uses a digital thermometer and finds your body temperature to be 100°F. You protest saying that you don't "feel" feverish, but the medical authorities decide not to release you. In trusting the results of the digital thermometer rather than your own self-assessment, your doctors and nurses are making a decision about measurement validity. That is, the medical authorities assumed that the measurement device (the thermometer) really did measure what it claimed to measure – your actual (and excessive) body temperature.

Or consider another rather common scenario today. Imagine you're in the process of buying a new home. Before proceeding with a contract, you've been advised to have the property tested for radon – a colorless, odorless, radioactive gas that can seep into homes. A home inspection service leaves radon detector canisters in the property for 48 hours. When you see the canisters – charcoal filled cans – you can't help but be skeptical. You wonder if these simple little devices measure anything, let alone radon. We could say you are having a measurement validity moment. That is, you are questioning if the canisters really do measure what they claim to measure – the presence of radon. You raise your concerns with a licensed engineer who assures you that the devices are government tested and approved for the job of radon detection.

As you can see from the above examples, decision-making is frequently tied to the issue of measurement validity. Indeed, measurement validity plays a central role in some of the most controversial social issues of our times. For instance, consider the long-standing debate in the legal system concerning the use of polygraph (lie-detector) tests. Advocates of the polygraph claim that this test (measure) is able to accurately detect if someone is being truthful or deceptive. Opponents challenge its truth detection capacity.

Certainly the potential value of the polygraph test in a criminal or civil trial is apparent. Seemingly countless hours of pretrial investigation or courtroom testimony could be foregone if we simply resorted to poly-graph results for critical evidence of innocence or guilt. For example, in April 2001, Stephen Jones, defense attorney for Timothy McVeigh, revealed that a lie-detector test had been administered to his client in August 1995. Years before jurors were called upon to make their own determination, the test results confirmed McVeigh's involvement in the Oklahoma City bombing.

Similarly, polygraph tests could be used to "clear" innocent suspects and free police to pursue other lines of investigation. Several years into the continuing investigation of the murder of their daughter, the parents of Jon Benet Ramsey arranged to take polygraph tests in order to remove themselves from the list of suspects. (The polygraph results indicated that the Ramseys were not lying when they said they didn't know who killed their daughter.) So the question that begs to be answered is why haven't polygraph tests replaced the need for formal trials and investigations? Why aren't lie-detector tests standard, even mandatory, legal tools for determining innocence or guilt? In general, it is because the courts do not recognize the *validity* of the polygraph as a measure of honesty or decep-tion. The courts agree with critics who argue that the polygraph really doesn't measure whether or not someone is telling the truth. Because it lacks measurement validity, the polygraph remains inadmissible as evi-dence in a court of law.[3]

On another front, consider the controversy surrounding a common measure of intelligence: the IQ score. IQ scores are derived from tests that are thought to measure a person's innate capacity to deal effectively with his/her environment. In the 1970s an educational psychologist at Berkeley, Arthur Jensen, advanced a rather controversial view regarding IQ. He argued that IQ differences between Blacks and Whites were genetically based (1973). Jensen's work reinvigorated a central debate in the social sciences: the nature/nurture debate. Those on the nature side of this debate posit that inherent, biological, or genetic factors are the most important determinants of social behavior. Those taking the nurture side of the debate credit culture and socialization experiences as the most important determinants of behavioral outcomes. Clearly Jensen's work was seen as offering support for the nature side of explaining observed differences in average IQs of Blacks and Whites. Jensen's work also held

---

3 In 1998, the Supreme Court held 8 to 1 that polygraph tests diminish the jury's role and duty to assess innocence and guilt. More recently, in fall 2002 the National Research Council concluded after 19 months of study that polygraphs should not be trusted in matters of national security.

implications for education policy. If intelligence is an inherited mental ability (the nature argument), then efforts to improve intelligence via improving the social environment (the nurture argument) would be in vain.

The nature/nurture debate surrounding IQ has yet to be fully resolved. Most recently the controversy reemerged in Herrnstein and Murray's work *The Bell Curve: Intelligence and Class Structure in American Life* (1994). Their argument echoed Jensen's: the IQ gap between Blacks and Whites is genetically based.

The issue of measurement validity is central to the IQ controversy. The argument supporting genetically based differences in intelligence presumes that IQ tests used to measure intelligence possess measurement validity. Many critics of IQ tests fault them on just this point – i.e., they argue that while these tests measure something, they do *not* measure innate intelligence. Instead IQ tests measure the quality of education and the quality of our social experiences (Fischer et al. 1996). Again, this view has found support in the courts. In the early 1970s, a federal court ruled that IQ tests being used in grades K–12 in California were biased against people of color and should not be used to place children into special education classes. An appeals court later upheld the lower court ruling that essentially questioned the measurement validity of IQ tests. (Larry P. v. Riles, U.S. Courts of Appeals, 1984, 793 F 2d 969.)

Lastly, consider a topic that is a long-standing concern of Americans: fear of crime. Politicians frequently make fear of crime a central feature of their campaign platforms. They do so for good reason. General social surveys tell us that many Americans are worried about crime encroaching on their lives. If you visit the General Social Survey homepage (http://www.icpsr.umich.edu/GSS/) you'll be able to see for yourself how the GSS has been tracking Americans' fear of crime since the early 1970s. By clicking the "trends" link, you'll see that from 1973–98, roughly 40 percent of Americans reported being afraid of crime. Before leaving the GSS homepage, however, you should pay particular attention to the question on the survey that is used to measure "fear of crime." If you click on "fear of crime" in the GSS subject index, you will be shown the exact survey question: "Is there any area right around here – that is, within a mile – where you would be afraid to walk alone at night?" Answering "yes" to this question, puts you in the "afraid of crime" camp. You be the judge: Does the question posed really measure what it claims to measure? Does asking about respondents' fear of walking alone at night really measure their "fear of crime"? If you have your

Figure 3.1 Post-Enron and WorldCom: Do financial *statements* really indicate (measure) the financial health of corporations? It's a question of measurement validity.

doubts, you are questioning the measurement validity of the item (and you are putting yourself in the company of some criminologists who think the measure is faulty).

Lest you think the concern over measurement validity is simply academic, think again about how faulty measures can directly impact our lives. Poor measures of love, health, or home safety are not without serious consequences. Indeed, in the realm of physical safety, the issue of measurement validity can be a life and death issue. Homeowners are advised to routinely test their smoke alarms and carbon monoxide detectors to make sure the devices are doing the job they claim to be doing. Fire marshals are charged with routine inspection of fire alarms and sprinkler systems to assure their working order. To be sure, when we ignore the issue of measurement validity, we risk tragic consequences. In January 2000, three Seton Hall University freshmen died and nearly 60 other students were injured in a dorm fire. Students reportedly ignored the blaring fire alarms because they didn't *believe* them – i.e., they didn't believe the alarms were documenting the presence of a real fire. (In the previous semester, 18 false alarms were sounded thus prompting the students' skepticism in the early morning hours of January 2000.) The measurement validity issue proved to be a life and death one in this unfortunate instance (CNN.com.2000).

Hopefully, I've convinced you that the measurement validity issue is most important. It shouldn't surprise you then to learn that researchers devote much attention to establishing the validity of their measures. Chapter 5 will take a detailed look at the various steps we can go through in order to convince others that our measures really do measure what we

Does the research design allow us to determine if:

Figure 3.2   Internal validity

claim. Measurement validity should remain a constant backdrop for you when you are reviewing each of the chapters on specific data collection techniques.

Internal Validity

Perhaps it is our nature, but humans have a keen interest in causal analysis. Many of us are eager to share our views as to the cause of school violence or divorce or the cause of children having children. Often our motives on this front are quite admirable. If we can put our finger on the cause, we believe we will be that much closer to a plan of action that will cure social ills or promote social health. But our search for causes can present us with a double-edged sword. If we are wrong in identifying the "causes" of some social phenomenon, any of the policies built around our causal model will likely be misguided. These kinds of mistakes have the potential of being quite costly. It is most reassuring, then, to realize that science is once again on the case when it comes to the matter of verifying the accuracy of causal assertions. Science will assess or evaluate causal assertions in light of the standard of **internal validity**. In posing the question of internal validity (aka causal validity) we are asking if the overall research plan or research design is really capable of detecting causal relationships when they exist. Achieving internal validity means that we can demonstrate that changes in one entity are due to changes in another.

Technically speaking, when we are engaged in causal analysis we must distinguish between two kinds of variables: independent (aka predictor) and dependent (aka outcome) variables. **Dependent variables** refer to the outcomes, effects, or results we are trying to explain – e.g., school violence, divorce, teenage pregnancy. **Independent variables** are those factors that we believe are responsible for or able to "predict" the outcomes. For instance, some see easy access to guns as a cause of school violence. Some blame divorce and teenage pregnancy on an erosion of family values. In trying to establish a causal connection between two phenomena, the logic of science requires that three criteria be met (Hirschi & Selvin 1973; Popper 1959). We must show that our independent variable precedes the dependent variable in time (test of temporal ordering). We must show that the independent and dependent variables are "connected" – i.e., that they move together in some patterned way (the test of association). And we must be able to show that any and all rival explanations of the dependent variable have been ruled out (the test for spuriousness). If we can't show that we've satisfied all three conditions, we can't make the case for causality.

Consider some of the causal connections we have been concerned with in recent years. Does increased Internet usage lead to social isolation (Nie & Erbring 2000)? Are coffee breaks (and caffeine intake) more dangerous for people with high blood pressure (McManis 2002)? Can positive thinking help patients fight cancer (Ross 2002; Rudebeck 2003)? Does chocolate help us overcome the blues (*Daily Telegraph* 2002)? What's the causal connection between popular diet supplements and health benefits? Does gingko really improve our memories (Osgood 2002)? And while we're at it, can we finally figure out if wine is good or bad for our health (Norris & Hesser 2003)? Is there any truth to the claim that cell phones cause brain cancer (Grandell 2002; Ranade 2002) or that the measles vaccine causes autism (Allen 2002; Community Pharmacy 2003)? Are hairdressers more likely to give birth to underweight babies (Wilson 2002)? Are kids who watch a lot of television increasing their risk of becoming violent adults (Ritter 2003)? Has our love affair with a low-fat, high carbohydrate diet produced America's epidemic of obesity (Taubes 2002)? And what about hormone replacement therapy? Is this a case where the cure is worse than the disease (National Public Radio 2002)? Surely we all have a very clear vested interest in knowing if any of these causal claims (as well as countless others) is accurate.

In trying to evaluate any causal assertion, the issue of internal validity directs our attention to **research designs**. The key to achieving internal validity is a good solid research plan or strategy. A good design is one that allows us to effectively satisfy the three conditions of causality mentioned earlier (temporal order, association, nonspuriousness). If we don't set up a study so that it is capable of satisfying these criteria, we really can't hope to achieve internal validity. In other words, maximizing internal validity takes some careful planning.

The good news is that science has a good as gold standard for achieving internal validity: the **experiment**. The experiment is a very contrived, specific research plan that strives to maximize control in the interest of isolating and thereby making explicit any connection between the independent and dependent variables. Because the researcher has so much control over the conditions of the experiment, the design has the edge when it comes to satisfying the criteria for establishing causality: the time test, the association test, and the test for spuriousness. Both the experimental design and the criteria for establishing causality will be the focus of another chapter. Here I simply want to acknowledge that anyone who is trying to uncover causal connections must be cognizant of the experimental design. The more our research design emulates a true experiment, the more confidence we can have in the causal conclusions of our research. It's really that simple and that difficult. Simple because the criteria for establishing causality are rather clear and widely acknowledged. Difficult because it isn't always easy to establish that two variables are related or that one clearly precedes the other in time. And the job of eliminating any and all rival explanations is a most arduous one.

To illustrate just how challenging causal analysis can be, let me cite one recent causal controversy: the alleged causal link between the measles, mumps, and rubella (MMR) vaccine and autism. In 1991 and again in 1994, the Institute of Medicine (IOM) convened a committee to assess the causal relationship between specific vaccines and adverse health consequences. In both instances, the committee concluded that the evidence was inadequate to accept or reject a causal connection. The IOM's equivocal finding was followed in 1998 by the Wakefield Study, research done in England that appeared to offer empirical evidence confirming the link between the MMR vaccine and autism. But did the Wakefield Study satisfy the criteria for establishing causal connections? The Center for Disease Control in Atlanta concluded that the Wakefield Study failed to make the case for any causal link between the MMR vaccine and autism (Institute of Medicine 2001). The CDC grounds for refuting a causal link speak directly to the "simple" criteria for causality we've outlined above. Most pointedly, the CDC maintains that in several of the cases of autism documented in the Wakefield study, the symptoms of autism *preceded* the vaccine (with this observation, the CDC is arguing that the temporal order test of causality was not met in the Wakefield Study). Finally, in April 2001, the Institute of Medicine weighed in once again on the subject and this time concluded that there was *no* evidence of a relationship between the MMR vaccine and autism (IOM 2001; CNN 2001).

In all likelihood, we haven't heard the last about the causal link between the MMR vaccine and autism. If only to dispel parents' fears about the safety of vaccinations, more research will surely be conducted on this topic. (Indeed, current research efforts are addressing the role that thimerosal, a mercury-containing vaccine preservative, might play in any link between vaccines and autism.) In each new piece of research, however, the standards will remain the same: Does the evidence "pass" the causal criteria?

Hopefully, you now feel somewhat conversant with the internal validity issue. Chapter 6 will provide a detailed review of various research designs and their strengths (and weaknesses) in terms of causal validity. Once you've mastered the material in Chapter 6 you should be better equipped to weigh in on the internal validity of any piece of causal research.

External Validity

The last trust issue that falls within the validity domain concerns the breadth of our findings. Even if we are satisfied with our study's measures and with our study's overall design, we still must ask if the findings obtained in any one study can be safely generalized to other settings or groups?

Taking one's new found knowledge and "spreading it around" can be most problematic with experimental research. As indicated in the last section, the experiment is a rather special data collection tool. It is a contrived design that exercises much control over the conditions of the research process. It is precisely because the experiment is so contrived that it suffers problems of external validity. Can a contrived, manipulated research endeavor really yield information that we can safely generalize to non-experimental conditions or settings? Under experimental conditions, I may find that a diet regime is very effective in producing weight loss. The question, however, is whether or not the diet will work as well if used in a non-experimental setting? Just imagine the differences: In the experimental setting, participants will be motivated volunteers who are diligently monitored with regard to their daily food intake, daily exercise, mood swings, etc. In the real-world setting, dieters are more likely to "be

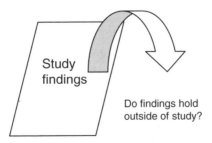

Study findings

Do findings hold outside of study?

Figure 3.3   External validity

on their own." Without the special attention of the experimental setting, they may feel more defeated than motivated in their weight loss efforts. Who will know if one is consuming appropriate serving sizes or sneaking an extra helping at lunch or dinner? In short, findings that are produced under the "ideal" conditions of an experiment may be hard to reproduce in the less than ideal conditions of the real world.

For a concrete example of the problem of generalizing findings, we can once again turn to the world of medical research. Experiments are often conducted to assess the effectiveness of new drugs or treatment modalities. Without such research, medical breakthroughs and advances would not be possible. Yet the medical community must always be cautious when discussing promising research results. In part this is due to the difficulty of establishing causal connections. But the caution is also due to the fact that so often medical research is conducted on lab animals. Pharmaceutical companies, for instance, *must* initiate the testing of new drugs on animals. For example, some of the newly proposed treatments for spinal cord injuries are based on research with paralyzed dogs (see http://www.vet.purdue.edu/cpr/). The external validity question looms large: Will the promising results found with lab animals be as promising when humans are brought into the picture?

Of course it isn't just experimental research on lab animals that gives us pause when trying to generalize our findings. To be sure, there is always a critical moment in medical research when the decision is made to move on to "clinical trials" – i.e., studies involving humans. Even experiments that involve humans may not be the best for generalizations. Clinical trials involve the use of **research protocols** – an explicit set of rules for carrying out the study. Protocols dictate which individuals are selected for clinical trials. Inevitably, fewer individuals are involved in the study than initially volunteer. For instance, patients who don't fit a certain profile or who aren't able to make the time commitment to the study are not selected for clinical trials. (For an interesting discussion of research protocols for clinical trials on new treatments for paralysis visit http://www.miamiproject.miami.edu/and follow the "Research," "Clinical Science," and "Clinical Trials" links.) Knowledge of research protocols forces us to think twice about generalizing from small studies of volunteers. We have to ask what kinds of people are willing to volunteer for experiments, what kinds of people are actually selected and are they like the rest of us? Do the dynamics of the experiment influence how these "hand-selected" people will react under experimental conditions? Do these restrictive conditions limit our ability to generalize beyond the experimental setting?

External validity and survey data

Our concerns with accurate generalizing don't evaporate simply by moving away from the experiment. Data collected via surveys or polls must also be assessed for their generalizability. Indeed, since survey analysis is a mainstay of much social research, we must always be prepared to critically assess the "reach" of survey findings. Data from a small sample of Vermont consumers might indicate preference for fuel-efficient vehicles. But can we safely generalize these findings to a larger group of Vermont consumers or to consumers in other states? This concern with the ability to generalize from small to larger groups of similar elements is referred to as **sample generalizability**. Similarly, you may have survey data that indicate emergency room doctors support a patient's bill of rights. But can you generalize these findings to other emergency room personnel – to nurses or technicians – or to hospital administrators? This second concern raises the issue of **cross-population generalizability** – do the findings from one group or population also hold true for a totally different group or population?

Selecting research participants and external validity

In grappling with how far the data can take us, we must pay careful attention to how study participants are selected for various research projects. As we saw earlier, the special circumstances that surround the experiment can weaken the experiment's external validity. In particular, one of the special circumstances – its reliance on volunteers and selection protocols – make it extremely difficult to argue that experimental findings will hold true for other groups or settings. Similarly, generalizing from survey data can be problematic if the researcher doesn't employ sound sampling strategies. **Sampling** refers to the process whereby we study a "few" in order to learn about the "many." The success we have with this plan depends on how good a job we do at selecting a sample that accurately represents the larger group. Sampling is an extremely important task in survey research and will be the focus of Chapter 8. As we will see in Chapter 8, any probability sampling technique should allow the researcher to confidently make generalizations from samples back to larger populations. When probability sampling techniques haven't been employed, however, the ability to generalize findings is seriously compromised.

Repeat after me: external validity and replication

So how does a researcher address the question of whether experimental findings are true for other groups or settings? Or in survey research, what must the researcher do to achieve cross-population generalizability – i.e., to convince others that findings from one group or population are also true for a *different group or population*? The researcher must rely on **replication** – i.e., a research "do over."

We saw in Chapter 1 that replication is an extremely important characteristic of science. In the final analysis, science demands redundancy. Studies need to be repeated and findings need to be reproduced in order for science to increase its confidence in scientific knowledge. This is not to say that science doesn't value new studies and new discoveries. It *is* to say that discoveries or breakthroughs are met with a healthy skepticism until they are subjected to some verification efforts – until they are subjected to replication. Once we are familiar with the idea of external validity, we can see the value of replication in a slightly different light. In obtaining the same results each time an experiment is repeated with different subjects or in different settings, the researcher improves his/her claim for the external validity of the findings.

Consider two recent examples of research findings that clearly raise the question of external validity. In 2002, the *American Journal of Epidemiology* published a study that found an inverse relationship between water consumption and the likelihood of dying from a heart attack (Chan et al. 2002). This study was conducted over a number of years on a group of Seventh-day Adventists in California. The question that begs to be answered is whether these findings are unique to this group? Will the health advantage of water consumption in staving off heart attacks be found in other religious groups or for non-Californians? The only way to know the answer to this question is through replication. Repeat the study using different religious groups and/or different locations and see if the findings "hold."

Similarly, in the fall of 2002, French researchers reported some intriguing findings on the potential health benefits of wine. The researchers found that middle-aged French men who had one heart attack and who consumed two or more glasses of wine regularly were far less likely than non-drinkers to have a repeat heart attack (de Lorgeril et al. 2002). Before toasting these findings, however, more work needs to be done. Will the findings hold for other nationalities or cultures? Will the health benefits be found among female patients? Only replication will tell.

Conclusions

We have devoted a great deal of attention in this chapter to the essential validity issues of research: measurement validity, internal validity, and external validity. We pursued this course of action because these issues go to the heart of the matter of science as a superior source of knowledge. They also help to reveal an underlying structure of the rest of the book: the chapters that follow (i.e., on measurement, on research designs, on data collection strategies, on sampling, on statistical analysis) are "dictated" by these three dimensions of validity. There's also a practical reason for presenting this overview of validity. Whether assessing someone else's research or planning a project of your own, you are well advised to use the validity issues as "north stars" of trustworthy data. Research that doesn't attend to these issues is likely to lead us down the misguided path to erroneous information.

Expanding the Essentials

Bill Trochim's web page offers a good review of the validity issues facing the researcher: http://trochim.human.cornell.edu/.

The following web sites offer more information about safe vaccines and immunization: Center for Disease Control: http://www.cdc.gov/nip; Vaccine Education Center: http://www.vaccine.chop.edu.

For a discussion of the nature of intelligence and our attempts to measure it, see Fischer et al.'s *Inequality by Design: Cracking the Bell Curve Myth* (1996).

After reading this chapter, you may be convinced that the validity issues would make science converts of us all. For an interesting review on why some people resist science and are instead attracted to extra-scientific explanations of reality, see Erich Goode's *Paranormal Beliefs* (2000).

Exercises

1   Think again about *Consumer Reports*' assessment of the Mitsubishi Montero as unsafe (note 1 on p. 32). Find the "measure" *Consumer*

Reports uses to determine the safety of SUVs. Do you think the measure is a valid one?

2 Let's stay with *Consumer Reports* for another minute or so. Look through a recent issue and get a sense of the range of products they evaluate and the kinds of measures they use to rate the various products. Which measures do you think are the most valid? Which the least valid?

3 Monitor several issues of a news magazine or a newspaper and locate stories that report on some "research." Are questions of measurement validity or internal validity or external validity adequately addressed?

4 Measure by Measure: Making the Abstract Concrete

Picture adults interacting with infants and you will have immediate insight into our conceptual nature. The adult–child interaction is largely an exercise in concepts. The adult points to the neighborhood dog while saying the words "bow-wow" or "dog" over and over again, all in hopes that the child will make the connection between the pooch and the word "dog." Or parents will repeatedly point to themselves or their spouses while repeating the word "mommy" or "daddy," again hoping the child will make the connection between the persons and the words. In these earliest exchanges, the child is learning about the world of concepts.

As the above examples illustrate, **concepts** are mental images, abstractions, or terms that symbolize ideas, persons, things, or events. In the natural sciences, concepts are often expressed in symbolic notation. In high school algebra, we learn about pi (the ratio of the circumference of a circle to its diameter) and denote it with the following symbol: π. Math classes also teach us to associate the $=$ symbol with equivalence and to recognize % as a symbol for percentage. In physics we learn that the symbolic notation of $s = d/t$ stands for the concepts of speed being equal to distance divided by time. In statistics we learn to recognize Chi Square as χ^2 and $\sum$ as a summation sign.

In the social sciences, concepts are most often expressed in words. So, if the "idea" we want to express concerns a legally recognized social and economic relationship between a man and a woman, we would invoke the concept (or the word) *marriage*. To describe the constant bickering and fighting between brothers and/or sisters, we invoke the concept *sibling rivalry*. *Blended family* is the concept used to describe the merger via a second marriage of previously existing families. Criminologists, in describing a lethal exchange between loved ones, invoke the concept *friendly murder*.

From the early days of childhood learning through our adult years, we strive to know and master useful, relevant concepts. There is a good reason for this – concepts are essential tools for communicating. Concepts enable us to give and receive information efficiently. Reconsider the examples offered in the previous paragraph and you should immediately appreciate how difficult communication would be if we couldn't express ourselves via the mental shorthand of concepts. (If you've ever played the game TABOO, you know this challenge first hand. Players are forbidden to use the most obvious concepts when trying to get their partners to guess the targeted word.) Imagine the difficulty of communicating the weather on the nightly news if we couldn't use such concepts as *rain, cold fronts, heat index*, or *hurricanes*. Imagine how lost we would be every four years if we couldn't use the concepts of presidential campaigns: *front runner, grandstanding, dark horse, lame duck president*. Concepts are essential to our thinking; they are essential to our communicating with others. And as you might well imagine, concepts are also central to the business of social research.

Concepts and the Research Process

At first glance, the connection between concepts and research is not all that apparent. After all, in Chapter 1 we saw that research is concerned with the concrete and the empirical. Concepts are not part of the empirical world. Concepts are *mental abstractions* and as such they are the antithesis of concrete empiricism. How then do they come to occupy a central role in research? Concepts work their way into research via **theory**. At some point in your college education, you've no doubt been introduced to social theory. Theories are sets of logically related or linked ideas (abstractions) about how the world or some process works. The fundamental building blocks of theory are concepts. In other words, theories consist of a series of statements (propositions) about relationships between concepts.

Different theories invoke different concepts. Structural-functionalist theory tries to explain the world around us in light of such concepts as social stability, integration, consensus, etc. Conflict theory offers explanations of social reality that invoke such concepts as dissensus, coercion, power, and social control. Symbolic interactionist theory explains the social by invoking such concepts as social interaction, social meaning, and the social negotiation of reality. Emile Durkheim's theory of suicide (1951) relates the concept of suicide to the concept of social integration. Donald Black's theory of formal social control (1976) relates the concept of law to the concepts of social organization, culture, social morphology, and social stratification.

Bringing Theory Down to Earth

If theory offers **ideas** (concepts) about how the world works, research is about empirically documenting (showing) whether or not those ideas are correct. Consequently, research can be seen as either an effort to (a) test established theory or (b) generate new theory. (Research conducted to test established theory is called **deductive research**; research that starts in the empirical realm and tries to generate theory is called **inductive research**.) In either scenario, research must encounter concepts. Good research either begins with or ends in the realm of concepts and theory.

To conduct research, we must be able to work with concepts. Yet concepts are abstract, mental ideas. They don't lend themselves to the "show me" empirical realm of research. What's the researcher to do? We must engage in a translation process – one that makes concepts understandable to the empiricist. In this translation process, we transform abstract concepts into their concrete, empirical counterparts. In performing this translation process, the researcher engages in the **measurement process**. Measurement, then, refers to the process of transforming the abstract into the concrete; it refers to the process of restating concepts as variables. **Variables** are empirical representations of concepts. Following this logic, the concept of education might find its empirical counterpart in counting the number of years one has spent in school. The concept of patriotism might find its empirical counterpart in our counting the number of flags flown in a local community. Civic involvement might be empirically translated into the number of hours a month one spends doing volunteer work.

Translating the abstract into the concrete is not the exclusive work of researchers. Examples of such translations abound in popular culture. For instance, consider the work of advertisement agencies. The process of translating abstract concepts into concrete empirical representations is really at the heart of advertising. Ad people work hard to get us to associate success with a variety of costly consumer items: the latest luxury sedan or a De Beers keepsake diamond. Advertisers urge us to equate "cool" with the latest clothing line, popularity with the right beverage (or fast food), and a static-free existence with the correct mobile phone service.

Any one concept, of course, can give rise to any number of empirical counterparts or variables. Consider the concept of happiness, an abstraction that can mean many different things to many different people. Back in the sixties, a popular cigarette commercial equated happiness with smoking Kent cigarettes. A Peanuts comic strip equated happiness with a warm puppy. A standard kids song instructs that if we're happy and we know it, we should clap our hands and stamp our feet. Today we're encouraged to equate happiness with certain automobiles or shampoos or gourmet ice creams. All of these examples illustrate the essential process of transforming something abstract (happiness) into something concrete. All examples suggest that happiness might best be "seen" or documented in the concrete empirical world via our actions or our possessions. Happiness is the abstract concept, a warm puppy is offered as its concrete embodiment.

Now, consider how the *researcher* might handle the translation of happiness into its empirical counterpart. While it is in the advertiser's vested interest to have us associate happiness with the services or products of the ad agency's clients, the researcher must be sure his/her concept–variable translations live up to the standards or rules of science. The researcher must be concerned about **measurement validity** – i.e., being sure that the variables used in research really do capture the true meaning of the concepts being measured. Owning a warm puppy is not a good measure of happiness for someone who is afraid of dogs. Stamping one's feet *might* show happiness but it might also be a sign of anger or frustration. And for more and more Americans, happiness is certainly not a Kent (or any other cigarette). As indicated in Chapter 1, researchers embracing scientific methods must take extra steps to ensure an error-free translation process. When a researcher equates a concept with a concrete empirical variable, she or he should provide some evidence of the adequacy of the measure.

Conceptualization

The first step toward good measurement is good conceptualization. Since concepts can mean different things to different people, the researcher must be sure to clarify the meaning of the concepts as the researcher sees it. Two different researchers may conceive of "violence" in two different ways. One may view violence as physical action (hitting another), while another may see violence in verbal as well as physical attacks ("slamming" another with a verbal putdown). One researcher might define alienation as a loss of involvement in the activity of working. Another may equate alienation with a sense of separation from our own human nature. One researcher may define civic involvement in terms of long-standing social memberships while another sees it as short-term involvement with special interest groups. Before we can devise adequate empirical measures of abstract concepts, we must work on conceptual clarity.

The researcher strives to achieve conceptual clarity by offering **theoretical or nominal definitions** of concepts. Theoretical definitions are those that clarify a concept by offering synonyms for that concept. You have encountered such definitions any time you have used a standard dictionary or a sociology dictionary. Dictionaries, both standard and sociological ones, offer a collection of reasonable synonyms for the word/concepts we want to define. After consulting a sociology dictionary, a researcher might define alienation as a "feeling of noninvolvement in and estrangement from one's society and culture." Anxiety might be defined as an "emotional state characterized by extreme apprehension... and lacking a clear focus on a specific object." Conservatism can be defined as "an ideological orientation that opposes social change" (definitions from Theodorson & Theodorson 1969).

Theoretical definitions can also be found in the abstracts or opening paragraphs of research articles – their inclusion simply underscores the importance of achieving conceptual clarity in the research process. Consequently, whenever we are embarking on a research project, it is always a good idea to consult and review the relevant literature on our topic. At the very least, we will discover what others can contribute to the conceptualization process. Regardless of our strategies for developing theoretical definitions – e.g., using dictionaries, reviewing the relevant literature – it is likely that we will find multiple definitions for any one concept and informed choices will have to be made. For instance, after reviewing the domestic violence literature, the researcher might encounter two or three different definitions of "spouse abuse" and will need to choose the one that is most in line with the research agenda at hand.

Operationalization

Once the researcher has achieved conceptual clarity, she or he can then get on with the task of finding the best empirical counterpart for the concept. This process is referred to as **operationalization**. Clearly, the researcher is interested in finding the best possible fit between theoretical definitions and empirical embodiments of concepts. Devising good measures is not easy work. (Indeed, the entire next chapter is devoted to reviewing some of the key standards used by researchers to assess the adequacy of their measures.) In working our way through the operationalization process, we may be satisfied that some measurement ideas offer a good empirical fit with the abstract concept. For example, you might be satisfied that conservatism (as defined above) is best measured by a respondent's agreement/disagreement with a series of statements about proposed social innovations – e.g., voting for a female president, supporting gays in the military, approving of women in combat units, etc. We might also conclude that some measurement ideas will have to be abandoned (e.g., we may conclude that happiness is best measured by asking people to self-report their levels of happiness and *not* by observing their smoking habits, their pet ownership, or their clapping or foot stamping behaviors).

In struggling with the operationalization process, we often find that we need to reconsider or revisit our theoretical definitions. Frequently, our measurement difficulties are due to the fact that we really haven't achieved conceptual clarity. We might discover, for instance, that we haven't sufficiently specified the various dimensions of our concepts. In reviewing the literature on alienation (an essential strategy for achieving conceptual clarity) we see that alienation is really a multidimensional or multifaceted concept. Erikson's review of Marx's writing on alienation identifies four separate forms of alienation: (1) a separation from the product of our own labor; (2) a loss of involvement in the activity of working; (3) an estrangement from fellow creatures; (4) a separation from our human nature (Erikson 1986). In measuring alienation, then, we might decide to zero in on just one of the concept's various dimensions – perhaps concentrating on the dimension that focuses on one's estrangement from one's fellow workers. Such give and take is appropriate, indeed it is to be expected, as we strive to produce a good fit between the abstract and the empirical.

Levels of Measurement

One of the most basic yet important operationalization decisions we must make concerns the "level" at which we will measure our variables. There are four levels to consider: nominal, ordinal, interval, and ratio. To understand the differences between these levels of measurement, we need to consider the connection between numbers and the measurement process.

Earlier we defined measurement as the process by which we translate abstract concepts into concrete variables. To understand levels of measurement, we must further specify this definition. That is, measurement entails a numerical translation: it is the process by which we attach numbers to the values of variables. (All variables, by definition, have more than one value. If an entity has only one value it is called a constant.) To illustrate how measurement entails attaching numbers to the values of a variable, consider the variable "yearly salary." The values of the salary variable can range from no salary at all (if one is unemployed) to a million dollars (or more) of yearly salary (if one is a CEO of a major corporation). Attaching numbers to the values of the salary variable works quite well. We can report the values as the actual number of dollars earned: zero dollars for the unemployed, or $10,712.00 for a minimum-wage US worker, or $400,000.00 for the President of the US, or $950,000.00 for the CEO of American Express.[1] Or consider the variable height. The values of the height variable can easily be expressed as numbers: NBA star Michael Jordan is 6' 6" tall; Gheorghe Muresan is 7' 7".

Unfortunately the fit between numbers and the values of variables isn't always as logical or clear-cut as with the examples of yearly salary or height. Consider the variable gender. There are only two values that make up the gender variable: male and female. At first glance, attaching numbers to the values of the gender variable doesn't make any intuitive sense. It is not obviously meaningful to express a person's gender as "1" (whereas it is meaningful to express salary as the number $45,500). Still, attach numbers we must if we want to live up to our definition of measurement. So, in the name of measuring gender, researchers might use the number 1 to denote male and the number 2 to denote the value female. In this case, the numbers (1 and 2) act as labels for the values (male and female). We face a similar "numerical awkwardness" when measuring variables like religious or political affiliations, race, ethnicity,

1   These figures come from 2002 "Executive Paywatch" data: http://www.aflcio.org/corporateamerica/paywatch/ceou/. Also note that the $950,000.00 salary for the CEO of American Express is just a small fraction of the total compensation package for this chief executive. The concept *total compensation* includes salary as well as bonuses, long-term incentive payoffs, and stock awards. In 2002, the total compensation for American Express' CEO was $20,870,154.00. Clearly, then, yearly salary is not the same as total compensation. This example helps illustrate just how important it is to achieve conceptual clarity before developing our concrete measures.

marital status, etc. Attaching numbers to the values of any of these variables doesn't make any obvious sense; the numbers simply function as numerical labels for values.

To indicate the fit (or lack thereof) between numbers and the values of the variables being measured, researchers distinguish various levels of measurement. As we move from nominal to ordinal to interval and lastly to ratio levels of measurement, the "fit" between numbers and the values of variables improves.

Nominal level of measurement

When the numbers we attach to the values of a variable are merely means for identifying *qualitative* differences between values, we are measuring the variable at the nominal level.[2] Here the numbers used are simply names (ergo the term "nominal") or labels for the various values. This is the case, for instance, with the variable gender. The numbers attached to the values male and female are nothing more than labels for these two values. Similarly, the variables "religious affiliation," "political affiliation," "race," etc. are typically measured at the nominal level – i.e., the numbers attached to the values of each of these variables are merely used to label the differences between the values on each variable.

Ordinal level of measurement

The numbers attached to the values of a variable can do more than merely label or identify values. The numbers attached to values might also indicate a ranking or ordering of the values – the values attached to the number 1 might be less than the values attached to the number 2 which in turn might be less than the values attached to the number 3. When this is the case, we are measuring the variable at the ordinal level. For instance, in measuring the variable formal education, we might use the following values: (1) less than high school graduate, (2) high school graduate, (3) some college, (4) college graduate, (5) more than college degree. If you look at the numbers attached to each of these values they indicate an increasing magnitude of the values – i.e., an increasing amount of formal education. Similarly, "interest in politics" could be

---

2   For this reason, nominal level measures are also referred to as qualitative variables.

measured at the ordinal level with the following numbers and values: (1) none, (2) low, (3) moderate, (4) high.

Interval level of measurement

Sometimes the numbers attached to the values of variables can do more than merely label or indicate the "order" of the values. Sometimes the numbers actually indicate an exact and equal distance between values. When this is the case, the variable is measured at the interval level. For example, consider the variable temperature. When temperature is measured using a Fahrenheit thermometer, the numbers on the thermometer indicate various values (ordered from low to high) that are *an equal distance* from each other. A temperature of 34° is *exactly* two intervals above freezing (in Fahrenheit, water freezes at 32°). A temperature of 30° is *exactly* two intervals below freezing. IQ scores also illustrate the interval level of measurement. We recognize equal distances between scores: an IQ of 150 is five intervals more than an IQ score of 145. There is a two-interval difference between a score of 100 and 98.

Ratio level of measurement

When the numbers attached to the values of a variable indicate real quantities or amounts of the variable, we have reached the ratio level of measurement. If we measure income as the total number of dollars earned last year, we have a ratio level measure. If we measure commuting distance as the total number of miles traveled between work and home, we have a ratio level measure. If we measure health status as the number of self-reported symptoms, we have a ratio level measure. The ratio level of measurement is regarded as the highest level of measurement because there is a perfect fit between the use of numbers and the values of the variable being measured. The variables are truly *quantitative* measures. Ratio level measures are also regarded as the highest level of measurement because quantitative measures permit the most sophisticated data analysis – i.e., analysis that entails mathematical manipulation of *real* numbers.

At first glance, many find it difficult to see the difference between interval level measures and ratio level measures. The two can be easily distinguished in terms of one characteristic. Ratio level measures have true and meaningful zeros; interval level measures do not. If I report zero income for last year, my zero means the *absence* of income. If I report zero symptoms on a health measure, the zero indicates the true *absence* of any symptoms. But if I report the outside temperature to be zero, I don't mean there is no outside temperature. Instead, a temperature of zero means it is very, very, very cold outside. A zero in an interval level measure does not mean the absence of the entity being measured.

One additional point about levels of measurement needs to be considered. The researcher must make decisions about levels of measurement – they are not necessarily dictated by the variables themselves. Very often, any one variable can be measured at several different levels of measurement. Again consider the yearly salary variable. We might measure this variable at the nominal level by asking the following:

➤ Did you earn a salary in 2002?

   1. Yes.
   2. No.

We might also measure this variable at the ordinal level:

➤ What was your salary for 2002?

   1. No salary for 2002.
   2. $15,000 or less.
   3. $15,001–$30,000.
   4. $30,001–$60,000.
   5. $60,001–$90,000.
   6. More than $90,000.

And we might also measure the variable at the ratio level by asking respondents to tell us their exact salary for 2002:

➤ What was your personal salary for 2002? (please specify an exact dollar figure)

The decision regarding which level to use is one of the most important decisions a researcher makes. While there is a general agreement that higher levels of measurement are better than lower levels, there is also the possibility that higher levels of measurement require a degree of specificity that may undercut the measurement process. For instance, respondents may not be able to or want to reveal their exact yearly salary (the information required for the ratio level of measurement). But they may be able and willing to supply information about their *salary range* (the information required for an ordinal measure of income). Such considerations are most relevant when making level of measurement decisions.

Operational Definitions

When we have satisfactorily transformed concepts into variables (the abstract into the concrete) and grappled with the level of measurement we want to achieve, we are ready to complete the measurement process by stipulating operational definitions. **Operational definitions** specify the exact steps or procedures employed when carrying out the measurement procedure. It is perhaps most useful to think of operational definitions as "recipes" for measurement. Just as recipes tell us the exact ingredients and steps that go into producing an entrée or a dessert, the operational definition tells us the ingredients and steps required to successfully measure a concept.

Once again, consider our alienation example. In our research we may decide to focus on just two of the four separate dimensions of alienation: loss of involvement in the activity of working, and one's sense of estrangement from fellow workers. An operational definition of the loss of involvement in work dimension might specify that we ask the following concrete questions by way of measuring the abstraction:

➤ In the past month, how many times did you call in sick to work?
➤ In the past year, how many times did you skip department meetings?
➤ In the past year, how many times did you file a grievance at work?
➤ In your working career, how many times have you quit a job?

An operational definition for the dimension that focuses on our estrangement from fellow workers might require that we ask the following questions:

➤ In the past month, how many times did you have lunch with co-workers?
➤ In the past month, how many times did you socialize with co-workers outside of the job?

➤   In the past week, how many times did you discuss personal matters with a co-worker?[3]

In listing these questions, have we completed the operationalization process? Not quite. Typically, operational definitions aren't fully specified by simply listing questions or indicators. Complete operational definitions require more detail than this. (Think about the analogy to recipes. It is not sufficient to merely list ingredients. We typically need some guidance about mixing, combining, baking time, etc.) A thorough operational definition should really "instruct" us on how we might conduct the measurement process ourselves. The researcher, for instance, should also indicate whether questions will be followed by a list of close-ended responses or if the respondent will be invited to supply his/her own answers. If multiple questions will be used to measure a concept, the research should indicate how the specific items will be combined to yield specific values on the variable. For example, if four separate ordinal level questions are used to measure the concept of alienation, the researcher should specify the acceptable range of values that results from combining the questions into a summary measure. If the measurement process depends on the researcher making observations rather than asking questions, the operational definition must instruct us on how to carry out the observation process.

Consider the following example of an operational definition used to measure the concept of pedestrian cautiousness. In this example, the researcher observes (rather than questions) individuals as they are about to cross an intersection. As you read through the example, think about whether or not the researcher has provided enough detail to allow us to execute this measure on our own:

> Pieces of tape were placed unobtrusively on the sidewalk leading into the intersections at intervals of 1 foot or less from the curb, 2 feet from the curb, and 3 feet or beyond. Pairs of observers noted the distance from the roadway at which pedestrians stood while waiting to cross; they also noted whether pedestrians checked for oncoming traffic by recording when the pedestrians explicitly moved their head to the left or right to look for traffic. Those who first stepped into the intersection and then moved their heads were not counted as checking, nor were those who may have used peripheral vision rather than moving their heads. Pedestrians were retained for observation only if they were fully stopped at a crosswalk

---

3   Can you identify the level of measurement achieved in each of these questions?

before the light changed and if they were in the front row (i.e., the group closest to the curb). The measure of caution was constructed by adding together a subject's score on curb position and traffic checking. A person standing 1 foot or less from the curb was assigned a value of 1; a person 2 feet away, a value of 2; and a person 3 feet or more away, a value of 3. A person who did not check for traffic was assigned a value of 0, a person who looked in only one direction was given a value of 1, and a person looking both ways received a value of 2. (Harrell 1991)

Specifying operational definitions in this way helps support a defining characteristic of science: replication. If we report the exact steps and procedures we use in the measurement process, we then give other researchers the tools and information they need to reproduce our research efforts. Recall from Chapters 1 and 3 that replication is an important feature of science – only findings that are replicated are considered trustworthy and reliable information. If we fail to specify our operational definitions, we block the all-important work of replication.

Conclusion

From our earliest years, we learn how to see the world and communicate with each other via concepts. We are conceptual beings. Research, however, with its feet firmly planted in the empirical world, puts a slightly different spin on our conceptual nature. Our earliest training teaches us how to move from the concrete (seeing a creature with four legs and a tail) to the abstract (invoking the word "dog" as a name or label for the four-legged, tail-wagging creature). Our training in research methods asks us to reverse this traditional flow from the concrete to the abstract. Concepts and theories present us with abstract explanations of the world around us. If we hope to test these theories, we must be able to locate clear empirical representations of the ideas/concepts presented in theoretical explanations. This step requires us to reverse our usual practice of moving from the concrete to the abstract. Research requires us to translate concepts into variables; it requires us to move from the abstract to the empirical. Seeing the world in the language of variables requires some practice – after all we are "wired" to be conceptual. Making this "down to earth" adjustment, however allows us to get on with the business of research.

Expanding the Essentials

 A quick way to see the connection between concepts and variables is by visiting the General Social Survey web site. This web site lists the various concepts addressed by survey questions. Visitors can select concepts and "click" on them to activate a link to the exact questions used on the GSS as measures of the concept. Use the following steps to the see the concept/ variable connection for yourself: (1) Access the GSS homepage (http:// www.icpsr.umich.edu/GSS/), (2) click on the Site Map, (3) click on the Subject Index, (4) find a concept of interest to you, and (5) click on it to see its corresponding GSS questions.

An extremely interesting introduction to measurement is offered by the web site for the PBS program *The First Measured Century*: http:// www.pbs.org/fmc/. Once at the site, follow the PBS program link to "The Other Way of Looking at American History." The program takes a look at what has happened in the past century by looking through the "lens of data and measurement." Since numbers tell much of the story, it is also a good way to become acquainted with a *quantitative* approach to studying social reality.

 Good discussions of both theory and the conceptualization process are offered by Earl Babbie in his book *Observing Ourselves: Essays in Social Research* (1998). In particular, see the chapters entitled "Paradigms" and "Making Distinctions."

Exercises

1   Review the four dimensions of alienation offered by Erikson (see page 52 above). Go to the GSS homepage (see the first entry in the above section) and find the questions used to measure alienation. Assess the adequacy of the GSS questions as operationalizations for each of the four dimensions of alienation.

2   For each of the following concepts: (1) offer a clear conceptual definition, and (2) suggest two questions or observations you think would be good ways of empirically documenting the concepts.

The little luxuries generation

Binge drinking

Hackers

Infantilization

(Hint: you may find it useful when working on your conceptual definitions to use a web search engine to learn more about a term's current usage.)

5   If It Glitters Is It Gold? Assessing Measures

Anyone who has studied a foreign language knows all too well that some translations don't faithfully restate the original text. As indicated in Chapter 4, whenever we translate mental abstractions into external indicators we must confront similar problems about the accuracy of our translations. Does the number of toys given to a child accurately measure parental love? Does the size of an engagement ring measure a fiancé's affection? Was the grade you received in your last math class an accurate measure of your knowledge of the course material? Is our "fear of crime" accurately measured by a question that asks if we are afraid to walk alone at night (see Chapter 3)? In this chapter we will review the various techniques available to us in order to establish whether or not our measures are trustworthy ones.

Facing Off Our Measures

The least we can ask of any concrete indicator of a mental abstraction is that it satisfies the condition of **face validity**. Assessing a measure for its face validity merely requires that we ask if the measure "looks good" on surface (face) inspection. If the "empirical translation" doesn't look right (or sound right) then it lacks face validity. For instance, some researchers maintain that the GSS measure of fear of crime lacks face validity. Critics complain that a question that asks about being afraid of walking alone at night lacks any clear or apparent connection to the concept "fear of crime." Or consider measuring the concept of "technological savvy" by asking if one knows how to use a phone. On the face of it, this measure isn't very convincing. Similarly, measuring "college level math ability" with a series of simple multiplication problems doesn't measure up on face validity.

As each of the preceding examples shows, face validity is a very *subjective* test of validity. It is possible that two different individuals might have two very different assessments of the face validity of a measure. What looks good to one might strike another as totally inadequate. Because of this equivocation, face validity is not considered a very demanding or convincing test of validity. While all measures should at minimum possess face validity, many researchers aren't willing to settle for this most basic form of measurement validity.

Content Validity

Content validity assesses how good a fit is obtained between nominal and operational definitions – i.e., do the nominal and operational definitions coincide or overlap? Recall from Chapter 4 that nominal definitions offer theoretical clarifications of concepts. Operational definitions specify the steps or procedures involved in empirically documenting a concept. In determining content validity one is really assessing if the full *content* of the nominal definition is realized in the operational definition. This, of course, is just another way of asking the essential question of measurement validity: Is the measure really measuring what it claims to measure? A few examples should help make the point.

Imagine a researcher who is interested in studying problem drinking. She uses the following nominal definition of problem drinking that she found while doing a literature search: Drinking that is used to escape personal problems or that results in some kind of trouble (Thompson 1989). She measures problem drinking with the following question: Do you ever drink to escape life pressures? If this were the only question asked, the measure would be judged as lacking content validity. The full content of the nominal definition is not represented in the question used to measure problem drinking. In order to achieve content validity, the researcher would need to ask at least one more question, one that inquired about the negative consequences of drinking or consequences that "result in some kind of trouble."

Content validity is an important consideration whenever a researcher is working with complex, multidimensional concepts. If concepts are defined as having more than one dimension (as with the problem drinking example above), then multiple items must be used to document the concept. As is true for face validity, content validity is a subjective validity test. Essentially judgments are made (often by experts in a field) as to whether or not the selected empirical indicators really do represent the full content of a concept's nominal definition.

Criterion Validity

Given that empirical evidence plays a central role in scientific inquiry, you may already be suspecting that some tests of validity demand more than subjective assessments. And indeed this is the case. **Criterion validity** (aka empirical validity) uses some kind of objective, empirical evidence in order to explicitly demonstrate the validity of measures. There are two common strategies for establishing criterion validity: demonstrating predictive validity and demonstrating concurrent validity.

Predictive validity

With **predictive validity**, the researcher demonstrates a measure's validity by showing that the measure is able to accurately predict some other logically related outcome. The accurate prediction is taken as objective evidence that the measure must be tapping what it claims to measure. For example, imagine that someone has developed a ten-item measure (an index) of leadership ability. You examine the index items and while they look good (i.e., they have face validity) you really can't be sure if they measure leadership ability. You want some "proof." Predictive validity for the measure could be demonstrated by the researcher predicting that individuals who score high on the index will go on to occupy leadership roles in an organization. (Leadership *performance* would be an outcome that is logically related to leadership *ability*.) So, if the index were administered to 100 new hires in an organization, predictive validity could be claimed if after 12 months on the job, those with the highest leadership ability scores were actually advancing in leadership positions. Now imagine a twenty-item measure that alleges to document productive study skills in students. You could claim predictive validity for this measure if you could show that those students with the highest scores on the measure were also the students with the highest grades at the end of a course. (High grades would be an outcome that is logically related to having productive study skills.)

Let me review one more example from the research literature. Researchers were interested in assessing the validity of a six-item index for measuring adolescent risk-taking propensity (Alexander et al. 1990).

To establish the validity of their index, the researchers predicted that there would be an association between high scores on the risk-taking index for eighth graders and their subsequent initiation of some risky behaviors as ninth graders. This is exactly what the researchers found – eighth-grade scores were associated with certain activities among ninth graders: namely the initiation of sexual activity among virgins and substance use among nonusers. Consequently, the researchers were able to claim predictive validity for their risk-taking measure.

Concurrent validity

Concurrent validity puts a slightly different spin on demonstrating validity. While predictive validity tests provide concrete evidence of measurement validity by making forecasts about future outcomes, concurrent validity tests offer more *timely* proof. I can demonstrate the concurrent validity of a measure by showing that the results I obtain with the measure are essentially the same as the results I obtain from *another measure of the same concept administered at the same time* (i.e., concurrently). As objective proof of the measure's validity, I want to be able to point to a high correlation between the scores of the two measures. With concurrent validity, the evidence of my measure's validity is its ability to produce results that correlate highly with another valid measure of the same concept. Again some examples.

Imagine that you are a medical researcher and you are working on a new procedure to measure whether or not someone has a rare medical disorder. As it turns out, a test for the disorder already exists. The "old" test, however, is expensive and invasive and patients don't like to go through the procedure. Your goal is to develop a new test that is inexpensive and noninvasive. How could you prove the validity of your new test? You could administer both the old and the new procedures to the same patients in clinical trials. You can claim concurrent validity for your new procedure if it yields results that are essentially identical to the results obtained via the old procedure. The similar results would produce the high correlation evidence that you're looking for as proof of validity.

Or imagine that you are a smart entrepreneur looking for a way to cash in on the huge educational testing market. You know that students dread having to sit through the very long college and graduate school entrance exams (i.e., SATs and GREs). You decide to develop a new, shorter, more student-friendly version of these measures of academic potential. How will you prove your new short test is as good as the old ones? If you can show that the scores obtained on the short test are highly correlated with those obtained on the old test, you will be able to claim concurrent validity for your new test (and smile all the way to the bank).

Construct Validity

There is one other validity assessment to consider – construct validity. Establishing the construct validity of a measure may well be the most demanding and involved validity test. To establish **construct validity** we use a combination of theory and hypothesis testing to demonstrate that our measures are valid ones. A **hypothesis** is a testable statement that predicts a specific relationship between two or more variables. For instance, we might predict that as population density increases, crime rates increase as well. To demonstrate construct validity, we use theory to generate a series of hypotheses. These hypotheses will predict the relationships we expect to find between the measure(s) we are trying to validate and a series of other variables. If we find support for the hypotheses, we can claim construct validity for the measure we are evaluating. For instance, imagine that we are trying to assess the validity of a measure of legal social control. To test the measure we could work with Donald Black's theory of law (1976). According to Black's theory, the amount of law in society increases with culture, stratification, social integration, and social organization (as well as several other variables). If we find that our law measure behaves as hypothesized (i.e., we find an association between it and the other measures of culture, stratification, integration, etc.), we have demonstrated the construct validity of our legal social control measure.

Or imagine that you are trying to assess the validity of a new measure of social capital. Social capital refers to individuals' participation in community networks and activities. Social capital can vary greatly from individual to individual. Some of us have a lot of social capital, others have very little. A review of the literature on social capital indicates that it affects many other areas of life. For instance, social capital is hypothesized to be associated with lower stress levels, with higher feelings of self-fulfillment, with higher rates of trust, with greater accumulation of wealth and with higher levels of education (Bourdieu 1986; Kraut et al. 2002). To establish the construct validity of our measure of social capital, we would need to produce data that supported our social capital hypotheses – i.e., data that showed an inverse relationship between social capital and stress levels, a positive relationship between social capital and feelings of self-fulfillment, etc.

As you can see from the previous discussion, demonstrating criterion and construct validity requires much more work from the researcher than face or content validity. Indeed, demonstrating either criterion or construct validity would be small research projects in themselves. Consequently, if researchers have gone to the trouble of establishing these forms of validity, they are likely to discuss their findings in their research reports.

Reliability Checks

In addition to asking if a measure is valid, we should also ask if it is reliable. In a court of law, reliable witnesses are witnesses who can be counted on to stand by their testimony – i.e., to tell the same story time after time (even under a heated cross-examination). So it is with reliable measures. A measure is considered **reliable** if it yields the same results each time it is used, assuming, of course, that there's been no real change in the variable being measured. In other words, reliable measures do not fluctuate – they yield consistent results.

Think about the standard device we use to measure our weight: a bathroom scale. If we were to step on and off a scale five times in a row, a reliable scale would give us the same reading each and every time. This exercise would demonstrate the consistency of the scale. Now think about a notoriously unreliable measurement device: the standard air pressure gauge for our car tires. If you've had any experience with a simple, mechanical air pressure gauge (the kind that resembles a writing pen in shape), you know first hand that consistency is not often a characteristic of this tool! You attach the gauge to a tire valve and get a reading of 32 pounds. You aren't sure you had a snug fit so you repeat the procedure. The second time around the gauge reads 29 pounds. Which reading is right? You try it a third time and find the same tire now has 33 pounds of air in it! What's going on? You are caught in the unreliable zone.

Testing, Testing, Testing for Reliability

Both the scale and tire pressure gauge examples illustrate the simplest test we have for determining the reliability of a measure: the **test-retest** strategy. As the name implies, we simply engage in the same measurement procedure two times and check to see if we get the same results both times. (As empirical evidence of reliability, we look for a high correlation coefficient between the two results.) This all sounds simple enough, and for the most part it is simple. There is one point, however, deserving further consideration. How long should we wait between the "test" and "retest"?

With the scale and tire gauge examples, the retesting could be done immediately. Take one measure, and then take it again. There's no complication with any immediate follow-up. (The measurement devices can't *remember* anything about each test.) But now think about what might happen when we engage in some measurement involving human respondents (as opposed to scales or tire gauges). What if I were to give you a ten-item anxiety index and then immediately repeat the index so I can assess its reliability. What might happen? Chances are good that my repeating the measure will strike you as funny (or anxiety-provoking). You may work very hard at remembering exactly how you responded the first time around and complete the second measure on the basis of memory. I'll wind up with responses that "look" consistent, but the consistency is "artificial," a byproduct of your good memory. So, can I avoid this problem just by waiting longer? Well, it depends on how long I decide to wait before doing the retest. Say I decide to wait a month – long enough so you couldn't remember your first set of responses. Now I find that your responses from the first test are very different from your responses to the second test. Does this mean my measure is unreliable? Not necessarily. By waiting the extended time, I must now consider the possibility that your anxiety level has *really changed*. The low correlation between time one and time two results could reflect an unreliable index *or* it could reflect a real change in your anxiety level over time. Clearly the time delay is an important consideration in the test-retest procedure.

Multiple-Forms

If a researcher will have only one-time access to respondents (a likely condition in most survey research), she or he should consider using a **multiple-forms** (aka **alternate-forms**) method for checking reliability. With this technique, two alternate versions of a measure are developed. The reliability of these measures can then be established by comparing the results obtained from each form. For good reliability, the results should be nearly identical.

The alternate-form technique is a fairly common strategy in survey research. For instance, experience has taught survey researchers that measures of age can be very unreliable. Indeed demographers have long noted an amusing (but frustrating) tendency for people reporting age data: they find an age they like and then stick with it for several years! Consequently, survey researchers will often try to document the reliability of age measures via a multiple forms method. At one point in the survey, respondents may be asked to report their age in years. At another point in the survey, they may be asked to list their year of birth. Reliability is demonstrated if the results obtained from both questions are consistent.

The multiple-form technique is rather easy to execute when we are assessing single-item measures. As in the age example above, we devise a question and then devise another question that essentially asks for the same information. The alternate-form technique is much more challenging when trying to establish the reliability of a multiple-item index. The challenge here is to develop two different yet functionally equivalent **composite measures** (measures that use two or more items to document a variable). If I first develop a ten-item anxiety measure, the multiple-form technique requires that I develop a *second* ten-item anxiety measure that appears to be "different" but is really the same as the original. This task can be quite tricky – for example, in changing the wording of the items in the two indexes, we may actually change what it is we are measuring. Given this complication, reliability checks of multiple-item measures often go a different route.

Split-Half Technique

A popular strategy for assessing the reliability of a composite measure is the **split-half technique**. In essence, the split-half strategy is a way of checking to see if all of the items that make up a composite measure are equivalent and consistently measuring the same phenomenon. Consider again the previous ten-item anxiety index. The split-half reliability check would entail us splitting the ten items into two sets of five items each (i.e., consider all even numbered items as a set and all odd numbered items as a separate set). Scores would be generated for each mini-group of five items. If the two sets of scores were highly correlated with each other, we would take this as evidence of the index's reliability. The coefficient that is frequently used to report the reliability of items in an index is Cronbach's alpha. The values of Cronbach's alpha range from 0 to 1.0. Typically an alpha value of 0.80 or higher is taken as a good indication of reliability.[1]

Consider a concrete example of a reliability check offered by Johnson (1991) in her work on job strain among police officers. In measuring the variable "external burnout," Johnson asked respondents their level of agreement/disagreement with the following statements:

- I treat some civilians as if they were impersonal objects.
- Working with people all day is really a strain for me.
- I have become more callous toward people since I took this job.
- I worry that this job is hardening me emotionally.
- I don't really care what happens to some citizens.
- Working directly with people puts too much stress on me.

The split-half technique tells us how consistent these items are with each other. Johnson reports a Cronbach's alpha of 0.87 for these six items. Such a high value is a good sign that the measure of job "burnout" is a reliable one.

By now you may be thinking that devising valid and reliable measures requires a lot of time and effort. You're right! But then good things come to those who wait and work. Good things also come to those who "look." When it comes to measurement, it is not always necessary to start from scratch. There are actually collections of measures available in libraries and online that contain a variety of "ready-made" indicators for a wide range of concepts. Furthermore, these "off the shelf" measures have typically already been put through their paces and been assessed for their validity and/or reliability. A good literature review is also key to locating existing measures. If the measures have been subjected to validity and reliability testing this will surely be noted in any methods discussion (as it was, for instance, in Johnson's discussion of her job burnout measure). Before "reinventing the wheel" in your own research efforts, you should check and see if adequate "tested" measures already exist.

Noise and Bias

While the first part of this chapter is meant to convince you of the importance of striving to produce good valid and reliable measures, it

---

1   Technically, Cronbach's alpha reports an average of all possible split-half combinations of all the items in an index.

is nonetheless the case that measurement should never be thought of as a perfect process. Instead, measurement is better thought of as a process that yields *estimates* of true values. You may step on a scale and see a reading of 142 pounds. Is this *exactly* what you weigh? Probably not. If you have your shoes on or if the scale is old (and has weak springs) or if you're leaning back on your heels, your true weight is probably not accurately reflected in the 142 reading. It is the case that most attempts at measurement contain some degree of measurement error.

One prevalent form of measurement error is known as **noise**. Noise refers to non-patterned error in the measurement process. Non-patterned error simply means that there is no set direction to the error involved in the measurement process. Sometimes the error occurs because measurement overshoots the true value; sometimes error occurs because our measurement process undershoots the true value. If you happen to be a fan of TV cooking shows, you may have noticed that cooks are often guilty of noisy measurement. For instance, when I measure out three cups of flour, I do it in a very noisy way. One cup may be slightly overfilled, one underfilled and one might be perfectly level. I have a somewhat lax attitude about measurement in baking because I am aware of a "forgiving" characteristic of noise: In the end, noise cancels itself out. In my baking example, I probably wind up with three cups of flour because the overfills and underfills cancel each other out.

Not all measurement error is so forgiving. Sometimes error can be patterned – i.e., the mistakes in the measurement process are consistently in one direction or the other and the error may be consistently overestimating or consistently underestimating a true value. Patterned error is known as **bias**. Early in my baking career, I consistently misread the teaspoon abbreviation for a tablespoon. Consequently, the error I introduced into my baking was always in the same direction: I always added too much (a tablespoon instead of a teaspoon) salt or baking powder! Given the patterned nature of bias, there is no chance of bias canceling itself out in the long run (as is true with noise). For this reason, bias is usually the more troublesome measurement error. (And for this reason, my baked goods were never in demand!)

We can live with a little noise in the measurement process in large part because we assume it will work itself out as we continue the measurement process. Nonetheless, noise in a measure decreases the measure's reliability. The consequences of bias can be more severe. Indeed, undetected bias has the capacity to render a measure invalid. Critics of IQ tests, for instance, have long argued that these tests are biased against minorities – i.e., the questions that make up the tests are not equally meaningful to all and thereby systematically under-document the innate intelligence of some groups. Similarly, survey researchers must always consider how the selection of words can bias measures. Asking respondents about their attitudes toward *welfare* will produce lower levels of support than asking about their attitudes toward *assistance to the poor*. While we must expect some degree of measurement error (either noise or bias), we must nonetheless try to keep both types of errors to a minimum.

Sources of noise and bias

Noise in the measurement process can stem from a number of sources. Our research subjects themselves might introduce noise. Tired respondents or inattentive respondents or young respondents can all be responsible for some amount of error in the measurement process. Noise can also be introduced by poorly constructed measures. Excessively complicated measures, poorly designed measures, or measures with vague directions can contribute to noisy measurement. Noise can also be due to the researcher. Imagine 20 undergraduates working the phone banks for an instant feedback survey of a local community campaign. It is certainly possible that each student will put his or her own spin on the survey questions and thereby add some noise to the measurement process. Given the great array of sources of noise, the researcher is well advised to anticipate the most likely sources of noise in the study and do what is feasible to keep the noise level down to a minimum.

A major source of bias in the measurement process can be the expectations of the researcher. You are probably familiar with the old adage that we humans "see" what we want to see. Researchers aren't exempt from this tendency. The researcher may be inclined to interpret ambiguous responses in ways that confirm the researcher's expectations. Or the researcher might inadvertently communicate expectations (via head nods or voice inflections) to research subjects who might then supply the desired answer. To counteract this source of bias, some research will be conducted under "blind" conditions, where those executing the research are intentionally kept in the dark about much of the research.

Bias can also be built into our measurement instrument. As we will see in Chapter 9, questions can be phrased in such a way as to "lead" respondents to one response over another. But bias also can work its way into the measurement process via deliberate choices by the *research subject*. When research topics are threatening or sensitive, there is a tendency for research subjects to answer questions not honestly but rather in accordance with what *they think* the researcher wants to hear. This phenomenon is known as the **social desirability bias** and can systematically distort findings in the direction of social expectations.

Since the presence of undetected bias has the potential to render our measures invalid, some researchers make a compromise with regard to bias and noise. They will intentionally introduce noise into the measurement process in an effort to keep bias at bay. Why this compromise? It has to do with the appealing feature of noise mentioned earlier: Noise will cancel itself out in repeated measurement. So, in the interest of eliminating bias in an interview situation, the researcher might intentionally use multiple interviewers who are randomly assigned to interviewees. This will make for a noisy measurement process, but it will preclude any systematic distortion being introduced by any one interviewer.

Measuring Up and Out

As the above discussion indicates, measurement is a tricky business. On the one hand, we strive to design measures that are valid and reliable. We work to construct as perfect a measure as possible. On the other hand, we must also acknowledge that we conduct our research in an imperfect world. We are well advised, then, to acknowledge that the measurement process really represents (at best) an effort to *estimate* the "true" value of some variable. This mindset encourages us to anticipate noise and bias in the measurement process and do what we can to keep both at an acceptable level. Assuming some measurement error is inevitable is also fully consistent with the skeptical attitude that is a defining feature of the scientific way of knowing. In doubting that measurement is perfect, we are better prepared to catch errors. Such skepticism ultimately serves us well in our pursuit of error-free knowing.

Expanding the Essentials

Visit the Educational Testing Service "Test Link" to learn more about the numerous options for educational measures: http://testcollection.ets.org/cgi/swebmnu.exe?act=3&ini=TestColl.

The Buros Institute offers online reviews of close to 4000 commercially available tests: http://buros.unl.edu/buros/jsp/search.jsp.

 While I have confined this review of validity and reliability to just one chapter, E. G. Carmines and R. A. Zeller have devoted an entire book to measurement assessment: *Reliability and Validity Assessment* (1979).

Here is a list of measurement reference books you might want to consult:

Gordon Bruner and P. J. Hensel, *Marketing Scales Handbook: A Compilation of Multi-Item Measures* (1992).

J. C. Conoley and J. C. Impara (eds.), *Mental Measurements Yearbook* (1995).

Delbert Miller and Neil Salkind, *Handbook of Research Design and Social Measurement* (2002).

Exercises

1 Access the GSS (http://www.icpsr.umich.edu/GSS/) and review the topics index. Select one topic of interest to you that uses a multiple-item index to measure the concept. Answer the following questions:

- Does the measure have face validity?
- What would you need to do in order to judge the measure's content validity?
- Explain what you would do to demonstrate the measure's predictive validity.

2 Use the same index you selected for exercise 1 and offer a detailed explanation of how you would demonstrate the reliability of the measure by either the test-retest or the split-half technique.

3 Reconsider Johnson's measure of external burnout (p. 70). She defines this concept as "feelings of being emotionally hardened by the job and lacking compassion for citizens." Given this definition, how would you rate the content validity of her measure? Next try your hand at developing a "different" but equivalent set of burnout items. Explain how you would go about establishing the reliability of the two forms.

6 One Thing Leads to Another: Causal Analysis

Advertisers have known it for a long time (and freeinternet.com put it to good use in a wildly successful campaign): Babies make good ad copy. (Perhaps you remember freenet.com's talking Baby Bob? He even had his own sitcom for a while.) That babies work in advertising makes perfect sense. Who can resist a cute, inquisitive baby or toddler? Newborns delight us with their engaging curiosity about the world around them. "Why?" is a question that can keep two-year-olds going and going and going. Children remind us that curiosity about how things work may be an inescapable human trait. Indeed, social and evolutionary psychologists maintain that our interest in causal analysis is "hard-wired" (Shermer 1997).[1] Michael Shermer, in embracing an evolutionary theory of our cognitive development, argues that we have evolved into "pattern-seeking, causal-finding creatures" (1997: xxiv). Interestingly enough, Shermer also argues that it is our causal-seeking nature that leaves us so vulnerable to misinformation. We are hard-wired, he says, to *seek* patterns. We are not, however, hard-wired to detect truth or avoid errors. For that, we need to learn and use scientific methods of knowing.

In Chapters 1 and 3 we saw that science is committed to a causal model of the universe. Part of the scientific mindset is the assumption that every event has an antecedent event. Things don't just happen – they are caused. To reflect this commitment to causal analysis, science employs a distinctive vocabulary of **independent** (aka predictor) and

---

1 For a good discussion of cognitive scientists' views on this matter, as well as a discussion of sociologists' objections to this position, see Cerulo (2002).

dependent (aka outcome) variables. A dependent variable is the entity or phenomenon we want to explain. For instance, we might be interested in explaining why people engage in crime or family violence, or why some students get higher grade point averages than others. The independent variable is the "causal agent" – i.e., the factor we think is responsible for bringing about the dependent variable. You might also think of the independent variable as a "predictor" variable. Causal analysis is essentially an attempt to identify the independent variables that predict or account for select dependent variables.

Causal Models: Nomothetic and Idiographic

When pursuing causal analysis, we have two paths we might follow: the nomothetic path and the idiographic path. The **nomothetic** path adopts a generalist or a "macro" approach to causal analysis – it is interested in finding general causal patterns that exist over and above any one individual, case, or event. With this orientation, we are interested in finding the *common influences* that explain a general class of actions or events: e.g., war, crime, divorce, autism, school violence. This search for common, transcendent causal agents is a search for an *efficient* model of causal analysis – i.e., the nomothetic model tries to identify a few key factors that explain the most about our dependent variable. Given that the nomothetic approach is seeking common factors that hold true across a class of actions, it offers a *probabilistic* explanation of outcomes. That is, nomothetic causal research allows us to identify those variables that increase the *likelihood* of certain outcomes. In other words, the nomothetic model may not be able to accurately predict if *you* will wind up divorced, but it will be able to say what variables are common across the greatest number of divorces. The following kinds of statements are indicative of nomothetic causal research:

> Students reporting use of one or more packs of cigarettes per day were three times *more likely* to use alcohol, seven times *more likely* to use smokeless tobacco and 10–30 times *more likely* to use illicit drugs than were students who never smoked. (Torabi et al. 1993, my emphasis)

> …people with alcohol abuse problems or those who have received treatment for the problem were no *more likely* to be chronically homeless than were other homeless people. People with a history of hospitalization for mental health problems were *more likely* to be chronically homeless than were people without a record of institutionalization. (James 1992, my emphasis)

While the nomothetic approach is interested in "general" causal explanations, the idiographic approach is dedicated to specifics. An **idiographic** approach has a micro focus and is much more limited in scope than the nomothetic approach. The idiographic model is interested in thoroughly explaining the sequence of events that lead to *one particular outcome*. With the idiographic approach, we might be interested in explaining our best friend's divorce (as opposed to divorce in general). Or we might be interested in explaining a fistfight that broke out today in the cafeteria (as opposed to school violence in general). Or we might be interested in explaining a neighbor's suicide (instead of suicide in general). Since the idiographic approach is case specific, it strives to provide an *exhaustive* causal explanation of some event. In this sense, then, it is said to offer a *deterministic* explanation of events: it details how one event led to another which led to another which ultimately led to the outcome (the dependent variable) we are analyzing. The following kinds of statements are indicative of idiographic research efforts:

> The research problem was to understand why NASA managers had launched the Challenger in January 1986, despite a recommendation by contractor engineers that the mission be delayed because of unprecedented cold temperature predicted for launch time ... The analysis showed a decision making pattern that was fundamentally like the demise of intimate relationships. The demise of the Challenger was preceded by a long incubation period filled with warning signs that something was seriously wrong with the technology. (Vaughan 2001)

> In accounting for an individual's use of marihuana ... we must deal with a sequence of steps, of changes in the individual's behavior and perspectives, in order to understand the phenomenon. Each step requires explanation, and what may operate as a cause at one step on the sequence may be of negligible importance at another step ... In a sense, each explanation constitutes a necessary cause of the behavior. That is, no one could become a confirmed marihuana user without going through each step ... The explanation of each step is thus part of the explanation of the resulting behavior. (Becker 1963)

While you may not have realized it before, the idiographic approach is the one that motivates much of our day-to-day causal curiosity. We are hooked on getting the "skinny" on specific people and events. Entertainment programs and magazines thrive on satisfying the public's curiosity about what caused Tom and Nicole's breakup or about the sequence of events that led to Chandra Levy's disappearance. Shortly after 9/11, a *NOVA* special provided a detailed (minute by minute) analysis of the structural collapse of the World Trade Towers. The idiographic model is also the dominant model of social workers, clinical psychologists, and historians – professional researchers who are committed to unraveling causal forces in the lives of specific clients or specific historical figures and events. There is no doubt that the idiographic approach to causal analysis can be quite interesting because of its personal, case-specific focus. If, however, our goal is to advance our understanding of *social* phenomena, we would be well advised to become familiar with the nomothetic model. Not surprisingly, the nomothetic model is the dominant model of sociology, a discipline committed to the study of broad social patterns. For the next several pages, we will focus primarily on issues that are most relevant for the nomothetic model. We will return to the idiographic model at the end of the chapter.

Causal Requirements

To contend that one variable *causes* another variable, three conditions must be satisfied: (1) The independent variable must be shown to precede the dependent variable in time; (2) The independent variable and the dependent variable must be shown to be associated with each other; (3) The relationship between the independent and dependent variables must survive any and all attempts to prove it spurious (Hirschi & Selvin 1973; Hyman 1955). These three conditions are **requirements**; all three conditions *must* be met – anything less and we can't claim a causal relationship.

Temporal ordering

The time test of causality is really an exercise in logic. For any factor or event to "cause" another, it *must* precede the other in time. Reason dictates this condition. We can't say a piece of bad news caused us to blow up at our kids if we got the bad news *after* we lost our temper. We can't claim that certain vaccines cause autoimmune disorders if those disorders exist before administering any vaccine.

At first glance the time test for establishing a causal relationship would seem to be an easy one to satisfy. In many instances, it is very easy to establish which variable precedes another in time. Sociologists, for instance, are frequently interested in studying the effects of certain fixed variables. **Fixed** variables are variables that can't be manipulated by the researcher. They are most easily understood as our ascribed statuses – i.e., statuses imposed on us at birth. Sex, age, ethnicity, race, birth order are all examples of fixed variables that might be of interest to a sociologist wanting to explain such things as income, political affiliation, charitable donations, etc. Since fixed variables are imposed on us at birth, we can easily argue that they precede other variables in time. As we move away from such fixed variables, however, figuring out the time order of independent and dependent variables becomes more challenging. Not all variables enjoy clear or obvious temporal orderings vis-à-vis each other. This, of course, is the classic chicken and egg question.

Consider the temporal ordering of depression and drinking. Which of these two variables precedes the other in time? Does one's drinking or one's excessive drinking cause depression? Or does depression cause one to seek some solace in the bottle? How about the relationship between parent–child communication levels and delinquency? Does non-communication precede delinquency? Or does trouble with authority figures or the law give adolescents a good reason not to pursue conversations with their parents? When the temporal ordering of variables is not apparent, the researcher must be prepared to make a case for the ordering they endorse. Very often, this case is most persuasively made via the relevant research literature. What do other researchers maintain is the temporal ordering? What evidence exists in the literature to support this ordering?

Associations

The association requirement merely asserts that if two variables are causally connected, they must co-vary. Are women more likely than men to engage in volunteer activities? (Yes, see Independent Sector 2001.) Do more hours spent on the Internet mean fewer hours spent with friends? (No, see Cole 2001.) Again, logic dictates the association requirement. If two variables do not move together in some patterned way, it would be foolish to try and argue that one is the cause of the other. If we can't document an association, we can't even think about a causal relationship. On the other hand, merely finding an association between two variables does not automatically indicate that a causal connection exists. Perhaps the most common lay mistake in causal analysis is to assume that if two variables are connected, they are causally related. Correlations do not "make" causal relationships. Not all associations or correlations bespeak causal connections. Before we can be optimistic that we have found a causal connection between two variables that are sequentially related, we must satisfy the third requirement for causality: we must establish that the observed relationship is *not* a spurious relationship.

Spuriousness

To fully appreciate why correlation is not synonymous with a causal connection, you must understand what's known as a **spurious relationship**. A spurious relationship exists when there is an *apparent* but not a genuine causal connection between two variables (e.g., variables A and B). With a spurious relationship, the *appearance* of a causal connection between variables A and B is due to the fact that both A and B are causally linked to a third variable C (see Figure 6.1a). If we are unaware of the presence and influence of the C variable, we can mistakenly conclude that A is the driving force behind B. In truth, C is really running the show: C causes A *and* C causes B (see Figure 6.1b).

Several years ago, studies found an association between breast-fed children and higher IQ scores. At first glance, one might be tempted to assume a causal relationship: i.e., that breast-feeding makes babies smarter. (Supporters of this contention claim that the DHA (an essential fatty acid) found in mothers' milk is what positively affects IQ.) The third requirement for establishing a causal connection, however, *forces* us to ask if there might be a third variable that is responsible for the connection between breast-feeding and IQ scores. In suspecting a spurious relationship, we might consider that a "behind the scenes" C variable is at work. Skeptics of the observed correlation between breast-feeding and IQ scores argue that the association is due to an antecedent *social* condition. Perhaps a certain mothering style influences both the decision to breast-feed and the intellectual development of children (Lucas et al. 1992; Horwood & Fergusson 1998).

In testing for spurious relationships, the researcher must be prepared to consider *any and all* rival explanations (i.e., C variables) that might account for the apparent causal connection between A and B. In essence, testing for spuriousness means that the researcher tries to remove the influence of the C variable on the original A–B relationship. When we remove the influence of a variable, we are said to "control" that variable – i.e., we block its ability to impact another variable. If, when controlling the C variable, the original relationship between A and B disappears, we have evidence of a spurious relationship. (That is, if we "block" the influence of C and the *original* relationship between A and B changes,

A and B appear to be "connected to" each other because of their mutual connection to C.

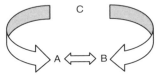

Figure 6.1a Spurious relationship

When we block the influence of C, the connection between A and B disappears.

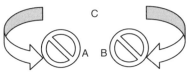

Figure 6.1b Spurious relationship when C is "controlled"

this is good evidence that C had something to do with causing that original relationship.) On the other hand, if, when controlling the C variable, the original relationship between A and B maintains itself, we say that it has survived this test for spuriousness. It is essential to repeat this testing until we have controlled the influence of all likely rival explanations – i.e., all likely C variables. Let's review a specific example.

Imagine that we have found a positive relationship between hair length and Grade Point Average (GPA). If we took this as a causal connection, all college students would be well advised to grow their hair as long as possible! But before assuming a causal relationship exists, we must consider rival explanations of the apparent causal connection. Is there a C variable that might influence hair length and also influence GPA? Gender seems a good place to start. If we control on gender (analyze all male data separately from all female data), we would see that gender influences both A and B variables: females tend to have longer hair and higher GPAs.

In the study of domestic violence, there is a clearly documented association between alcohol use and violent behavior towards spouses. Many researchers, however, are hesitant to argue a causal connection. Instead, some theorize that there is a C variable that leads to alcohol use and that also leads to violent behavior. Perhaps issues of self-esteem or power influence both the use of alcohol and the use of physical force. Finally, consider again the before-mentioned relationship between breast-feeding and IQ scores. To date, this relationship has survived all tests for spuriousness – i.e., the relationship does not disappear when such factors as prenatal care or social status are used as control variables.

Causal Analysis and Research Design

If our research goal is causal analysis, there is one research design or strategy that is superior to all others: the experiment. The **experiment** is a controlled plan of action in which the independent variable is intentionally manipulated in order to assess its impact on the dependent variable. The control that characterizes the experiment allows the researcher to explicitly address the three previously stated requirements of causality. The experimenter controls the introduction and the manipulation of the independent variable, thereby assuring that it precedes the dependent variable in time. The control inherent in the experiment also enables the researcher to clearly document any association or correlation between the independent and dependent variables. The control of the experimental condition also enables the researcher to neutralize the influence of alternate C variables and thereby effectively eliminate rival explanations of changes in the dependent variable. In short, there is no better strategy for examining causal relationships than the experimental design.

Consider the classic experimental design and how it would allow us to investigate the causal connection between using the nicotine patch and changes in smoking behaviors. The classic experiment starts with the experimenter setting up two groups: the **experimental group** and the **control group**.[2] Ideally, these two groups will be created via random assignment. **Random assignment** means that chance and chance alone will determine the placement of study volunteers into the experimental and control groups. The hope is that random assignment will produce two equivalent groups, since *only* chance will determine who is placed in each group. (In the classic experiment, both groups will be checked (pretested) in order to assess their actual equivalence.) Once we have pretested our randomly assigned groups, we can then impose the experimental condition: the experimental group will receive or be exposed to the independent variable; the control group will *not* receive or be exposed to the independent variable. So in our present example, the experimental group will receive the nicotine patch, the control group will not. After the

---

2   The classic design is one of several experimental designs. It is considered "classic" since other experimental designs (e.g., the Solomon Four Group, the Posttest-Only Control Group, Factorial) are essentially variations on this basic strategy.

introduction of the independent variable (the nicotine patch) in the experimental group, we will then measure the smoking activity of *both* the experimental and control groups. If we find that smoking is reduced in the experimental group, we are in a position to attribute the decrease to the nicotine patch.

How can we be so sure of our conclusion? It's all in the design. The experimental design allows us to isolate the connection (if any) between the independent and dependent variables. We control the temporal ordering of the variables (*first* the patch, *then later* a measure of smoking practices). We can clearly see any association between the patch and smoking by comparing the outcomes (number of cigarettes smoked) in the two groups. And since we start with two equivalent groups, we can dismiss any rival explanations of any observed changes in smoking outcomes. For example, we can refute the argument that the experimental group reduced their smoking because they were more motivated since the control group presumably exhibits the same level of motivation. (Random assignment allows us to make this assumption.)

Experimental design and internal validity

Another way to understand the superiority of the experimental design for examining causal connections is through the concept of **internal validity**. A research strategy has internal validity if it is able to eliminate alternate or rival explanations of an outcome – i.e., the dependent variable. These rival explanations are known as **threats to internal validity**. The experimental design is strong on internal validity because it is able to eliminate many standing rival explanations of outcomes. Let's consider a few common threats: history, maturation, and selection bias.

History This threat occurs when some event external to a study occurs at the same time as the study. When "history" happens we can no longer be sure that any observed change in the dependent variable is due to the independent variable; history may be responsible for the change. For instance, imagine that during our nicotine patch study (which is scheduled to last a few months) a famous celebrity dies of lung cancer. This event (rather than the patch) might be responsible for any observed changes in the study participants' smoking behaviors.

Maturation This threat occurs when participants in a study undergo developmental changes or growth, changes that could influence the dependent variable under investigation. With this validity threat, the researcher can no longer be sure whether changes in the dependent variable are due to the independent variable or due to maturation of subjects. Imagine again that our nicotine patch study is aimed at late adolescent smokers and is running for an academic year. At the end of the study period, any changes observed in participants' smoking behaviors might be due to the patch but they might also be due to the fact that the adolescent smokers "outgrew" this phase of risky, rebellious activity.

Selection bias   This threat occurs when participants in a study are not randomly assigned to study groups. Changes in the dependent variable *might* be due to the independent variable, but they may also be attributed to the peculiar characteristics of the people selected for the study. Return again to our nicotine patch study. Imagine that the researchers allowed volunteers for the study to self-select into the group receiving the nicotine patch. Any observed changes in smoking behaviors might be due to the patch but they might also be due to the fact that the extremely motivated (i.e., those desperate to quit) volunteered to be in the group getting the patch.

Now consider how the basic experimental design with randomly assigned experimental and control groups can handle these common validity threats. The presence of an experimental and control groups nicely counters the threats of history and maturation. If history happens, it happens to *both* groups and therefore drops out of consideration as a rival explanation. The same thing can be said for maturation, since any growth or development will happen to *both* the experimental and control groups. If maturation is common to both groups, it can be eliminated as a rival explanation for changes in the dependent variable. The threat of selection bias is eliminated in the experimental design since both the experimental and control groups are *randomly assigned*. Random assignment assures that the same kind of people are found in both groups and the experimental group won't wind up with more motivated (desperate to quit) participants than the control group. In short, the experimental design is one very powerful design for controlling these and other threats to a study's internal validity.[3]

---

3   Other common threats are testing, instrumentation, mortality, regression, contamination, and compensation. See "Expanding the Essentials" for links to learn more about these threats.

Limits of the experimental design

The experiment – it's a powerful, efficient, and internally valid strategy for examining causal connections. Given this, it may surprise you to learn that the experiment is not the inevitable design choice in causal research. This is so for several reasons. First, the experiment requires an independent variable that can be *imposed or manipulated* by the researcher. There are many, many variables of interest to social researchers that simply do not meet this condition: sex, race, ethnicity, age, etc. In general, any variable that refers to a trait or a property of a person is not one that is amenable to experimental research. Yet such variables are frequently the main variables of interest to social researchers. Second, the faithful execution of an experiment may create ethical and/or political dilemmas for researchers. For instance, the random assignment of research subjects to experimental and control groups may strike some as an arbitrary and unfair condition of the experiment. This is especially the case when exposure to the independent variable offers the possibility of some positive outcome – ostensibly those assigned to the control group are denied the opportunity of any positive outcomes that might be linked to the independent variable. Conversely, the intentional manipulation of the independent variable may also pose harm to members of the experimental group. Consider for instance an experiment conducted in the late 1930s with Iowa orphanage children. The study sought to determine if stuttering is a learned behavior. Children in one experimental group were told that they had speech problems (when in fact they had none) and should refrain from talking. The experimental condition had a clear behavioral impact on these children. More than 60 years later, survivors of the experimental group are suing the state of Iowa for emotional distress and fraudulent misrepresentation (Reynolds 2003).

The experiment is also weak on external validity (see pages 41–3 in Chapter 3). The controlled and contrived conditions of the experiment may yield results that do not hold true under non-experimental conditions. In returning to our nicotine patch example, we may find that the patch is effective under experimental conditions but *not* very effective when used by everyday smokers under real-world conditions. The following quote about the limits of experimental research when studying certain health problems illustrates several of the limits of experimental design:

> Scientists are still arguing about fat, despite a century of research, because the regulation of appetite and weight in the human body happens to be

almost inconceivably complex, and the experimental tools we have to study it are still remarkably inadequate...To study the entire physiological system involves feeding real food to real human subjects for months or years on end, which is prohibitively expensive, ethically questionable (if you're trying to measure the effects of foods that might cause heart disease) and virtually impossible to do in any kind of rigorously controlled scientific manner. But if researchers seek to study something less costly and more controllable, they end up studying experimental situations so oversimplified that their results may have nothing to do with reality. (Taubes 2002)

Some experimental designs do try to move beyond the over simplification referred to in the preceding quote and strive for **mundane realism** – i.e., a resemblance of real-world conditions. Such designs, however, can be quite complex and expensive. Consider, for instance, that the classic experimental design examines the causal influence of the presence or absence of *one* variable on another. But what if we want to examine the causal impact of two or more independent variables at the same time? Or what if we are interested in working with several independent variables that have three or more values (e.g., low, medium, or high doses of two or more drugs)? To accommodate such research scenarios, we would need to utilize a **factorial experimental design**. With factorial designs, each independent variable and combination thereof requires its own experimental group. If we were interested in examining two variables with just two values, we would need to work with four groups. But if we were interested in seeing the impact of, say, three independent variables measured at three levels (low, medium, high), we would need to work with 27 different groups! Clearly the more we try to emulate the conditions found in the everyday world, the more challenging it is to go the experimental route.

If experiments are "problematic" for much of our social research, why devote a chapter to this design? The simple fact is that the experiment is still the design that serves as the "gold standard" for assessing any piece of research pursuing causal analysis. The closer a design comes to emulating the experimental design, the more faith we can have in any causal conclusions. With this in mind, we should now review the single most popular research strategy and see how it fares in light of experimental standards.

Causal Analysis and Survey Research

The single most popular and efficient strategy for social research is the **survey**. The survey is a research tool that gathers critical research information via questions. (Guidelines for conducting good surveys are discussed in detail in Chapters 9 and 10.) Surveys are incredibly versatile research instruments: there are relatively few areas of social life that can't be studied by having subjects respond to questions and/or statements about selected topics.

Rather than employing experimental design, the survey utilizes a **correlational design**. A correlation design is one that searches for associations or correlations between various variables of interest to the researcher. On a survey I might ask about respondents' age and their charitable donations in order to see if there is an association between these variables. Or I might ask about respondents' income level and their political affiliation to see if these two variables are related. Indeed, with the use of a statistical package like SPSS, surveys allow the researcher to readily see if there are associations or connections (i.e., correlations) between any of the variables measured by the various survey questions.

While the correlational design significantly departs from the experimental design discussed above, it is clearly well equipped to meet one of the conditions of causality: the association requirement. Surveys have a harder time satisfying the time order requirement of causality. This is because most surveys use a **cross-sectional** time frame. With a cross-sectional study, the researcher obtains all relevant information from respondents at a single point in time, no future follow-up contacts are made. (Cross-sectional designs are discussed in greater detail in Chapter 7.) The cross-sectional time frame of surveys presents a challenge to the temporal order requirement of causality. Since all survey data is collected at one moment in time, the survey researcher doesn't have the option of imposing the independent variable and then measuring subsequent changes in the dependent variable. Consequently, the survey researcher must pursue alternate ways of establishing that the independent variable precedes the dependent variable in time.

Perhaps the most utilized resolution of this time dilemma in cross-sectional research is the use of **retrospective questions** – the researcher can ask a series of questions about the respondent's past. With retrospective questioning the time order of variables is made clear: events that occurred at an earlier point in time (e.g., high school experiences) clearly precede subsequent events (e.g., occupational achievements). Retrospective questions about your childhood experiences with physical discipline can be used to investigate a causal connection with your later disciplinary practices as a parent. Retrospective questions about peoples' experiences of the last 12 months can be used to investigate a causal link with their present attitudes toward national security.

Another strategy for unraveling the time order of variables is the use of fixed variables (see pages 78–9). Since fixed variables frequently reflect statuses or conditions "fixed" at birth, they logically precede all other subsequent outcomes or variables. My age (fixed by my birth year) precedes my income, my political affiliation, my attitude toward abortion, etc., and therefore is logically cast in the role of independent variable in a causal investigation. (Another way of making this point is to ask if any of the previously mentioned variables – income, political affiliation, attitude toward abortion – could *cause* my age? Whenever you find yourself answering no to such a question, you've probably identified a fixed variable.)

Perhaps the most problematic causal criterion for survey research is the test for spuriousness. Ideally, surveys are administered to representative samples of research populations (see Chapter 8). Since surveys don't entail the creation of randomly assigned experimental and control groups, it is difficult for surveys to conclusively address the issue of rival explanations of dependent variables. The survey researcher must engage in some heads-up thinking in order to effectively test for spurious relationships. In essence, the researcher must *anticipate* likely C variables and include measures of them on surveys. These C variables can then be introduced as control variables in the analysis of our survey data – we can control their influence on the observed relationship between variables A and B. (If the observed relationship between A and B maintains itself, we can eliminate the C variable as a rival explanation of the dependent variable.) Consequently, the researcher's ability to eliminate rival explanations will ultimately depend on how thoughtful and diligent the researcher is about including survey questions about pertinent C variables. If questions about relevant C variables are omitted from the survey, the chance to test for spuriousness will be lost.

Causality and Field Research

Before leaving this discussion of causal analysis, we should consider another popular research strategy – **field research** – and see how it sizes up on the causal analysis front. With field research, the social investigator directly observes people/events in their natural settings. The goal of field research is to document the natural flow or sequence of events. (Field research is discussed in detail in Chapter 11.) While we have spent the bulk of this chapter discussing the dominant causal model in the field of sociology – the nomothetic model – it is now time to return to the idiographic model.

Field research is most readily and naturally aligned with the idiographic style of causal analysis. The field research commitment to directly observing events and people *over time* facilitates the detailed examination of causal sequencing that is the heart of the idiographic approach. And while the idiographic model is only interested in an exhaustive causal analysis of *one* specific event, it will still utilize the basic causal standards we reviewed above: time order, association, and nonspuriousness. Additionally, however, the idiographic model will also pay attention to two more standards of causality: specifying a causal mechanism and contextualizing the event under analysis.

In its causal explanation of an event, the idiographic model offers a **narrative** – an account of the connections between sequential events. In this narrative, particular attention is paid to specifying the causal connections between the sequential events. This kind of speculation helps to strengthen the causal argument. Attention is also paid to the *context* of the causal connection. Contextual analysis seeks to identify those factors that might prove relevant for fully understanding the causal sequence. If the narrative fails to offer a convincing analysis on these fronts, the causal conclusions will be compromised. Consider, for instance, the narrative offered by Rubinstein and see how it helps to illuminate the causal sequencing of events that led to a patrolman hitting an elderly black man:

A young white officer noticed a man standing near a street corner turn away as the patrol car approached. He stopped his car and rolled down the window to look at the elderly Negro man. Instead of getting out of the car, he yelled across the deserted street to him. "Take you hand out of your coat." The man had turned back toward the car when it stopped, and he had his right hand jammed inside. He did not react to the command. They were frozen for several seconds; then the patrolman repeated his demand. When the man remained silent, the officer drew his pistol, continuing to remain seated in his car. He placed his gun in plain view and again ordered the man to show his hand. The man was very agitated but he remained silent. Slowly he began to extract his hand, but he gave the appearance of concealing some intention which threatened the patrolman, who cocked his gun and pointed it directly at the man. Suddenly the old man drew out his hand and threw a pistol to the ground. He stood trembling. The patrolman uncocked his gun with a shaking hand and approached. He was on the verge of tears, and in a moment of confusion, fear, and anxiety, he struck the man with the butt of his pistol. "Why didn't you take your hand out when I told you? I almost shot you, you dumb bastard." (Rubinstein 1973: 304–5)

If you call to mind any recent criminal trial, you will discover a fundamental weakness of the idiographic narrative. It is totally possible for different individuals to observe the same events and yet construct different narratives. Consider the strikingly different narratives that are likely to emerge in a typical criminal murder trial. As part of the trial, the two opposing attorneys will each present a case that they contend best describes the events that led to the murderous outcome. The defense will construct a causal narrative that exonerates the accused, while the prosecutor will construct one that alleges a very different story of the defendant's guilt. Constructing a narrative does not guarantee that the causal argument is a correct one. Once again we would be well advised to invoke the skeptic mindset of science and assess the narrative's temporal argument and its elaboration of causal mechanisms.

Conclusions

Trying to establish causal connections is a fundamental human and research activity. Uncovering the causes of family violence, drug addiction, eating disorders, mental illness, autism, recidivism, etc. on either an individual or social level could mean life-changing consequences for countless individuals who are directly and/or indirectly affected by these problems. Similarly, *misstating* the causes of these problems could also spell life-altering *negative* consequences for countless individuals. Errors in causal analysis can be quite costly; our standards for establishing causal connections must be high.

In striving to produce high quality causal research, we are well advised to utilize the experiment. This research design offers us the best chance of correctly identifying the causal connections between independent and dependent variables. The experiment sets the standard for assessing all causal analysis. Still, there are times when the experiment is not a practical or feasible design choice. Limitations imposed by the nature of variables being investigated, by ethical or political implications, or by the issue of external validity can force the researcher to employ non-experimental research strategies. Ultimately, however, we will judge the adequacy of these non-experimental designs by the standards set by the experiment.

Expanding the Essentials

 A thorough discussion of causality and an extensive review of internal validity threats can also be found at Bill Trochim's web page. Once at the page, follow the links for "Establishing Cause & Effect," "Single Group Threats," Multiple-Group Threats," and "Social Interaction Threats": http://trochim. human.cornell.edu/kb/.

 You will find a very down to earth discussion of causal relationships and validity threats in Jeffrey Katzer, Kenneth Cook, and Wayne Crouch's *Evaluating Information* (1998). In particular, you should consult chapters 11 and 12.

Exercises

1 Consider a recent major motion picture that tells a causal story (e.g., *Road to Perdition, The Divine Secrets of the Ya-Ya Sisterhood, The Green Mile*). Which model of causality is most clearly illustrated in the work?

2 Recently efforts have been made to bring lawsuits against fast food chains on behalf of clients who say that fast foods have caused them serious health problems. Which criteria of causality will be the most challenging one(s) for plaintiff lawyers to satisfy?

3 You have been asked to develop a questionnaire that will investigate the causal connection between drinking and family violence – i.e., is alcohol use/abuse a major cause of the use of violence against loved ones? Itemize the kinds of questions you would want to ask. Which of the questions will allow you to address the issue of a spurious relationship between alcohol use and violence?

7   Designing Ideas: Research Strategies

The best laid schemes o' mice an' men
Gang aft a-gley.

Robert Burns

Robert Burns (and later John Steinbeck) warned us that the best laid plans of mice and men can often go awry. This is certainly true – planning doesn't guarantee good results. Still, it is also probably safe to say that some planning is better than none. Jumping into our research without giving sufficient thought to key design issues is inviting disaster. In this chapter we will review two important design issues: a study's time dimension and its units of analysis.

It's All in the Timing

Ever since life as we know it began, humans have been fascinated and preoccupied with time. Einstein observed that "space and time are modes by which we think ... " The 60-second minute and the 60-minute hour have been with us since Babylonian days. We structure our days, weeks, even our lives with an eye to time. Ignore time and we run the risk of losing jobs, money, our health, and even our friends and loved ones. Many would argue that success in life is all about time management – learning how in some instances to seize the moment and in other instances to take things in stride. (There is even a science of timekeeping – horology.) The story of time, however, is also the story of *change*. To move through time is to experience change. Time and change are inevitably linked. Indeed change *requires* time. For change to occur, *time* must pass. Time, then, is of the essence in any study of change.

Not surprisingly, we are also a culture that likes to *document* both time and change in our everyday lives. When we want to capture a moment in time, we pull out our cameras. The pictures we take in effect "freeze" a moment in time forever: a child's first step, a high school graduation, a wedding day. And as most of us have all learned, if we take enough of these pictures throughout our lives, we can arrange them in a sequence that will tell a story of change. Picture collages allow us to see babies turn into toddlers who turn into adolescents and young adults who turn into middle-aged and senior citizens. (Collages also allow us to see adults grimace at the hair loss and weight gain of the last 20 years!)

This interest in time and change is not lost on social researchers. Research, like art, mimics life. Researchers often find themselves occupied with projects interested in documenting select moments in time as well as with projects interested in studying change over time. Where do Americans stand on the issue of gun control? Has their support changed in light of school shootings or the DC sniper shootings? What percent of families today are "blended"? How have these numbers changed in the last decade? Are we becoming more or less tolerant of politicians' indiscretions? Are today's youth more or less enamored with the concept of marriage than their parents? How has September 11th changed Americans' sense of national security? To answer these various questions, the researcher must employ research strategies that accommodate time and change. To pursue such projects, researchers will choose from a selection of various cross-sectional and longitudinal research designs.

Cross-Sectional Research Designs

Cross-sectional research addresses our need to document facts at a single moment in time – it is the research equivalent of the "Polaroid moment." Just as a snapshot freezes a moment in time, cross-sectional research "captures" information at one moment in time. A cross-sectional design, then, obtains information from a single group of respondents at a single point in time without any attempt to follow-up over time. In executing a cross-sectional study, the researcher might ask a series of questions (e.g., via a survey) of a broad *cross-section* of people in order to address the topic of interest. Several of the topics raised earlier could be addressed via a cross-sectional design: Where do Americans currently stand on gun control? What percent of families today are "blended?" How do Americans feel about homeland security (especially in light of 9/11)?

Cross-sectional designs are quite common in social research. Obtaining information from a cross-section of a population at a single point in time is a reasonable strategy for pursuing many descriptive and exploratory research projects. Indeed, the cross-sectional design is the heart of the National Opinion Research Center's General Social Survey (GSS), a major research effort that documents a large array of Americans' attitudes and behaviors. Every few years, the GSS interviews a cross-section of Americans in order to learn their views on a variety of topics. (While it takes the GSS approximately two months to complete their study, it still is considered a single point in time study design – i.e., each respondent is only contacted once.) This slice into time and across the population provides an extremely valuable and timely look at what Americans are currently thinking and doing.

As useful and popular as cross-sectional research is, however, it has its limitations. Anytime we are pursuing an analysis of *change*, we must be prepared to go beyond the simple cross-sectional design. One-moment in time data collection is perfectly adequate for assessing or describing current situations (e.g., present tolerance levels for politicians' indiscretions or current attitudes on homeland security). If, however, we want to know if situations or conditions have changed *over time*, we must use data collected at multiple points in time. This "time-extension" is the defining feature of longitudinal designs.

Longitudinal Research Designs

Longitudinal research collects data at two or more points in time. In so doing, longitudinal research is better equipped than cross-sectional research to address the question of change. So if we want to know if attitudes about gun control have changed in light of the Columbine school shooting or the DC sniper case, we would ideally want data from two time periods (pre-Columbine and post-Columbine; pre-October 2002 and post-October 2002). If we want to know how September 11th affected Americans' views on national security, we would need to compare data from pre-September 11th with data from post-September 11th. If we want to know how the profile of American families has changed in the past decade, we would want data from at least two time periods: current family information and information from ten years ago. It is the presence of multiple data points that allows the researcher to confidently address the issue of change. In selecting a longitudinal design the researcher has several options to consider: the fixed-sample panel design, repeated cross-sectional design (aka trend analysis), and an event-based design.

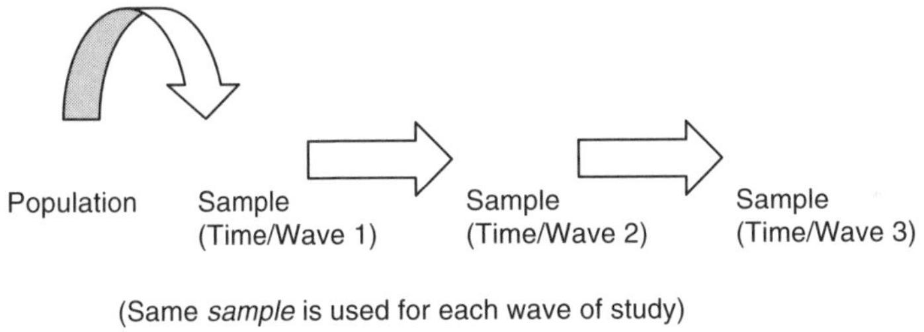

Figure 7.1   Fixed-sample design

Fixed-sample panel design

Perhaps the "purest" form of longitudinal design is the **fixed-sample panel design** (aka panel study). As the name "fixed-sample" suggests, data is collected from the *same* sample of respondents at multiple points in time. In longitudinal designs, each data collection point is referred to as a wave of the study. Since the panel study follows the exact same people through time, it is a superior way to analyze the process of change as it occurs in specific individuals. The panel design, for instance, would allow us to document changes (if any) in an individual's attitude toward abortion as they age or to document changes in how individuals cope with personal tragedy over time. (See Figure 7.1.)

Despite its recognized strength for studying individual change, the panel design can be a difficult one to execute. There is, of course, the problem of tracking people and data over time. Keeping such records is challenging, expensive, and frequently frustrated by the mobility of respondents. While respondents may let friends and the motor vehicle agency know when they move, notifying the local researcher is probably not such a high priority. Consequently, panel studies always face a very real problem of **panel mortality** – i.e., the loss of research subjects over time. Subjects may drop out of panel studies because they die, move away, or simply lose interest. Whatever the reason, attrition is a serious issue. If our respondents aren't available for subsequent waves of our study, we have lost the defining feature – the *raison d'être* – of the design.

Repeated cross-sectional design

A frequent alternative to the fixed-sample panel design is the **repeated cross-sectional design**. Again, as the name implies, this design essentially

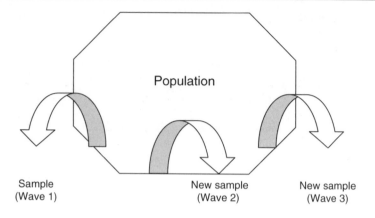

Sample   New sample   New sample
(Wave 1)   (Wave 2)   (Wave 3)

(Same *population* is used for each wave of study)

Figure 7.2   Repeated cross-sectional design

"repeats" two or more cross-sectional studies in an effort to address time and change. More specifically, the trend design calls for data collection at two or more times from *different* samples of respondents who all come *from the same population*. So a trend analysis investigating whether or not urban Americans' views on gun control are changing might gather such information from a sample of urban Americans in 2002 and then gather the same information from *another* sample of urban Americans drawn in 2005. If the researcher has done a good job drawing the samples for each wave of the study (i.e., if she or he has selected a representative sample each time), then a simple comparison of the data from each wave will reveal whether or not the *population* has changed its attitudes toward gun control.

Sample selection, then, is the critical difference between the trend and the panel design. While the panel study must repeatedly contact the exact same respondents in each wave of the study, the trend study selects a different sample of respondents from the same population at each point of data collection. This feature of the trend study frees trend analysis of the major drawbacks of the panel design. Since the trend design allows us to work with a new sample at each wave of our study, the researcher is not encumbered by excessive record keeping or by the threat of panel mortality.

This change in sampling strategy carries an important implication for the conclusions we can draw from trend analysis. Given the fact that only populations remain constant in the trend analysis (i.e., different samples are used in each wave of the study), the *trend researcher can only document change at the population level*. That is, by comparing data from 2002 with data drawn from 2005, we can say if the *population* has changed its views on gun control. We can't say if the individuals we interviewed in 2002 have changed their views since we did not reinterview these same people again in 2005.

At first glance, this point may seem impossible. If populations change with regard to some variable don't individuals who make up those populations change as well? Not necessarily. Consider the following scenario. Imagine that we want to know how current college students at Whatsamatter U feel about environmental issues. We draw a representative sample in 2002 and learn there is a moderate concern about environmental issues. Now imagine we repeat our study in 2007. This time around we learn that the students at Whatsamatter U are quite passionate about environmental issues. Have those individuals from the 2002 sample changed their views? We don't know. All we know is that the *population at large* is more concerned. How might this happen if we can't assume that the 2002 students have changed? Well, in the five years between the two waves of the study, new environmentally astute students may have entered Whatsamatter U (and consequently show up in the 2007 sample), while "old" environmentally neutral students may have graduated from Whatsamatter U (and are missing from the 2007 sample). The end result is that the *population* can very well change over time without any necessary change in the exact individuals who participated in earlier waves of a study. To be able to answer this kind of question – the question of individual change – we would, of course, need to conduct a panel study.

One final point should be made about trend designs. Our ability to use such designs to document population change is dependent on two conditions. First, for successful trend analysis, we must make sure that each wave of the study employs a representative sample of the same population. A trend study of Whatsamatter U students should not use graduate students at wave one and undergraduates at wave two. A trend study of American voters should not use registered Republicans at wave one and registered Democrats at wave two. Successful trend analysis is also dependent on consistency in the measurement process. In other words, to accurately document change, we must be certain that the exact same measures of variables being investigated are used in each wave of data collection. If these conditions are not met, then any "change" we observe from one wave to the next *may* be due to population differences but it may also be due to measurement differences and not be reflective of true population change. Box 7.1 illustrates the complications that can ensue from even rather subtle changes in the measures used over the course of a trend study.

We have devoted quite a bit of space to trend analysis for the simple reason that it is a popular design, especially in the realm of political

Box 7.1   Those Troublesome Wording Effects

Richard Morin

Pollsters know words matter. And here's more evidence, taken from Gallup overnight surveys for *USA Today* and CNN conducted the night of President Clinton's speech admitting an improper relationship with Monica Lewinsky and the following night.

The speech night poll analysis reported a stunning 20 percentage point drop in Clinton's favorable rating, from 60 percent to 40 percent, in just one week.

One problem: In the heat of battle ... Gallup used a slightly different question in the two surveys.

Gallup's standard question, asked in a survey conducted Aug. 10–12, read: "I'd like to get your overall opinion of some people in the news. As I read each name, please say if you have a favorable or unfavorable opinion of this person – or if you have never heard of him or her." I'll call this the standard version.

When Bill Clinton was named, 60 percent said they had a favorable impression of him.

But the following Monday night, after the president's mea culpa speech, they asked this slightly different question: "Now thinking about Bill Clinton as a person, do you have a favorable or unfavorable opinion of him?" Let's call this the enhanced version. Anyway 40 percent said they had a favorable impression of him when asked this question.

Of course, both questions are perfectly good. Gallup's problem came when the pollster ... treated the questions as identical and trended the two results to report a 20 percentage point drop in Clinton's favorability rating.

Why do these two questions produce such different results? My guess is it's the words "as a person" in the enhanced version ... Those missing words make the standard wording more general and undoubtedly capture people's favorable impressions of the way Clinton is doing his job as president, as opposed to the way Clinton is handling his personal life.

Thus the standard version may be a surrogate for job approval, which stood above 60 percent in the two Gallup polls, while the enhanced version forces people to focus on Clinton's decidedly unenviable personal character.

"What Americans Think," *The Washington Post* National Weekly Edition, Monday August 24, 1998 analysis. Every four years, for instance, Americans are fed a rather constant diet of preference polls that track how presidential candidates are faring with the public. Throughout the course of any presidential term, The Gallup Poll will document the trend of a president's favorability ratings. And while earlier we identified the GSS as an example of cross-sectional research, it is also the case that it is set up for trend analysis. That is, since the GSS repeats its survey of a representative sample of Americans every two years, and since it makes concerted efforts to use the exact same questions over and over again, the GSS is capable of pursuing trend analysis. You can find a discussion of the GSS design and its commitment to trend analysis by following relevant links on the GSS homepage: http://www.icpsr.umich.edu/GSS/.

Event-based designs

Researchers considering longitudinal designs also have the option of employing an **event-based design** (aka a cohort design). With the event-based design, data are collected at multiple points in time from a specific segment of a population – i.e., a **cohort**. A cohort consists of people who are defined by a common event – they experience a common life circumstance within a specified period of time. Some typical events used to define cohorts are common birth periods (e.g., Baby Boomers), same year of graduation (class of 2000), same period of military service (Vietnam Vets), etc. Cohort analysis should be considered whenever the researcher suspects that change in specific subpopulations (cohorts) may be different than change in the general population. Cohort analysis allows the researcher to consider how certain life events (e.g., coming of age during the depression, serving in the Gulf War, being born at the start of the new millennium) may impact on life change and development. For instance, cohort analysis would enable a researcher to see if retirement experiences of World War II vets are significantly different than those of Vietnam veterans.

Units of Analysis

My focus could be the...

Individual
Group
Formal Organization
Geographical Area
Social Artifact
Etc.

A discussion of research design decisions would not be complete without consideration of units of analysis. The **unit of analysis** refers to the level of social life that is the planned focus of a study. It is the entity about which data will be collected. In planning a study, researchers can select from several different units or levels of analysis: the individual, the group, the organization, the geographical location, and the social artifact (i.e., the cultural byproducts of human interaction). In most social research, the unit of analysis is the individual. That is, we frequently collect data by asking respondents to answer questions about themselves: their background traits, attitudes, and behaviors. We then use this information to examine relationships between such variables as age and political affiliation, or gender and attitudes toward abortion, or personal income and charitable donations.

While the individual is the typical unit of analysis in social research, it is also the case that research efforts can be focused on any level of social life. If budgeting strategies of families is our research topic, we would be utilizing the group (family) as the unit of analysis. If we were interested in studying the glass ceilings of major corporations, we would be utilizing the formal organization (corporations) as the unit of analysis. Or if we were interested in analyzing the content of automobile ads over the last decade, we would be using the social artifact (auto ads) as our unit of analysis.

Often students find the topic of units of analysis to be quite confusing. After all, groups, organizations, even geographical locations are all "made up of" individuals. How can we tell for sure the proper unit of analysis in a study? Ideally, if specific research hypotheses are stated for a study, these hypotheses should clearly specify the study's unit of analysis. That is, hypotheses should explicitly state which entity is expected to display the predicted relationships:

- There is a positive relationship between the number of memberships reported by individuals and self-reported feelings of powerlessness. (unit of analysis = individual)
- As organizational complexity increases, rates of horizontal task communication increase. (unit of analysis = organization)
- There is a positive relationship between a region's per capita kilowatt consumption and property crime rates. (unit of analysis = geographical area)

Such hypotheses clearly identify the appropriate unit of analysis for the planned research. Unfortunately, not all research involves hypothesis testing. Further, when hypotheses are presented, they do not always carefully or explicitly state the relevant analysis unit. Another technique, then, for identifying units is to determine the characteristics, properties, or traits that are of interest and being measured in the study. Certain characteristics "belong" to certain units of analysis. Only individuals, for instance, have attitudes, IQs, or behaviors. Only social aggregates (e.g., groups or formal organizations) have "size" or "social structure." Only geographical locations have "area" or population density. Gaining a clear understanding of the primary research questions behind a study should help you correctly identify the corresponding unit of analysis.

Ecological fallacy

Interest in correctly identifying a study's unit of analysis is driven by our concern with minimizing errors when drawing conclusions based on our research. The unit of analysis restricts the conclusions we can draw from our research efforts. If our unit of analysis is the individual, we can only draw conclusions about individuals. If we collect data about groups, we can only draw conclusions about groups. Gathering data about one unit of analysis and drawing conclusions about another unit leaves the researcher vulnerable to error. One common error linked to confusion over our units of analysis is the **ecological fallacy**.

Researchers risk the ecological fallacy whenever they obtain aggregate level data (i.e., data about the *supra*-individual level: groups, organizations, geographical areas) but draw and state conclusions about individuals. These conclusions are inappropriate since the data collected were not about individuals. Imagine, for instance, that you have the following information about several East-coast cities: those cities with the highest percentage of senior citizen populations also have the highest property crime rates. These two "traits" are about the cities and therefore any research conclusion should be limited to statements about cities. You would commit an ecological fallacy if you were to conclude that senior citizens are behind the property crime wave. In reaching this conclusion, you would be making the mistake of obtaining information about aggregates and drawing conclusions about individuals in those aggregates. Correlations can exist at the group level without being present at the individual level. Indeed, the group level correlation between a large senior citizen population and a high property crime rate may be the result of senior citizens being the *victims* of property crimes rather than being the *perpetrators* of these crimes. The only way for us to know for sure would be for us to use the individual as our unit of analysis and obtain our data about individuals.

A classic example of group level correlations being different from those found at the individual level of analysis is provided by Robinson's work on literacy. When using geographical regions as his unit of analysis, Robinson found that *areas* with higher percentages of foreign-born immigrants also had higher literacy *rates*. When he switched his unit of analysis to individuals, he found that within geographical regions, foreign-born individuals were less literate than native-born individuals (Robinson 1950). As the units of analysis changed, so did the patterns of association.[1]

Let's consider one more example. Imagine that a study of churches finds a positive correlation between the average income level of a congregation and average weekly church offerings. This group level correlation might tempt us to conclude that the wealthiest parishioners give the most money each week at collection time. In fact, we don't know if the wealthiest are the most generous or if other less affluent parishioners are "giving until it hurts." To know something about the giving patterns of individuals, we would have to use individuals as our unit of analysis – i.e., we would have to collect data about how much money each individual puts in the basket each week.

Conclusions

A successful study requires some forethought, some careful planning. Indeed, if you think that a particular piece of research isn't worth planning, it probably isn't worth doing either! This chapter addressed two of the most important issues in research design: a study's time dimension and its unit(s) of analysis. The time dimension helps us anticipate the number of data collection points needed to address the questions raised in our research. Can we learn what we need to find out, for instance, by just talking to respondents once or do we need to re-contact respondents for follow-up information? If our interest is in change, some sort of longitudinal design is in order. Paying attention to units of analysis should also help us in our search for answers to our research questions. If we want to generalize about individuals, we must make individuals the focus of our data collection efforts. If, on the other hand, we are content with generalizing about aggregates, we are safe collecting and working with group-level data.

There are, of course, many more issues to be considered in order to successfully execute a research project. Decisions must still be made with regard to sampling, specific data collection strategies, analysis, etc. We will pursue these issues in the remaining chapters of the book.

---

1   How is it that areas with higher percentages of foreign-born people could have higher literacy rates? One possible explanation is that immigrants sought out and settled in literate regions – i.e., regions with high quality public education systems.

Expanding the Essentials

If you would like to spend some more time on the topic of time visit the University of Amsterdam's SocioSite. Click on the "Subject area" and then click the time link to find an array of interesting articles/sites: http://www.pscw.uva.nl/sociosite/.

Anyone interested in seeing some trend analysis in action should visit the Gallup web page. Gallup's latest news releases frequently present results from repeated cross-sectional surveys: http://www.gallup.com/.

For an example of how the selection of units of analysis can have important implications for research findings as well as social policy, see Jennifer Van Hook, Jennifer Glick, and Frank Bean's article "Public Assistance Receipt Among Immigrants and Natives: How the Unit of Analysis Affects Research Findings" (2004).

Exercises

1 Visit Gallup's Web page (http://www.gallup.com/) and find their latest featured report. Did the survey employ a cross-sectional or longitudinal design? What was the unit of analysis for the survey?

2 Locate three recent issues of three journals serving different fields of interest (e.g., nursing, police work, education, sociology, etc.). Note (a) the time dimension (cross-sectional or longitudinal) and (b) the unit of analysis used in each of the featured articles for each journal. Is there any pattern you can detect as you move from one field to another regarding these two design issues?

3 Formulate two or three research questions that could be answered with a simple cross-sectional research design. Now revise the questions so that they would require a longitudinal design. Specify the exact type of longitudinal design that would be required (e.g., trend, panel, cohort).

4 If you want to document any changes in senior citizen support for a universal prescription health plan, what kind of time design should you employ?

8   An Informative Few: Sampling

Most of us have some first-hand experience with the world of sampling. In our everyday experiences, we use samples to give us a glimpse or a "taste" of some larger entity. Indeed, samples work their way into our lives on a fairly regular and far-reaching basis. For instance, many colleges now require various majors to assemble portfolios containing samples of the students' work over their college careers. Likewise, job applicants might be asked to submit samples of their professional wares as part of the application process. In reaching into our mailboxes on any given day, the chances are good that we'll pull out a trial pack of the newest super-strength painkiller. We can't watch a feature film without first being "treated" to short snippets of coming attractions. And as the recent months have so clearly demonstrated, Americans closely monitor the movement of key samples of stocks – the *Dow Jones Industrial Average*, the *S&P 500*, and the *Nasdaq* – for their daily dose of insight into the entire stock market. While each of these examples is quite different, they all help establish a simple point: Samples play a central role in our obtaining and processing information.

The everyday uses of samples take their cue from the world of formal research. Researchers are often interested in learning something about large groups of peoples or things. These larger aggregates are known as our **research populations**. We might be interested in studying the elderly, elementary school kids, millennium babies, Supreme Court rulings from the turn of the century. As these examples suggest, many research populations are simply too large to be studied in their entirety. In fact, the study of entire populations is so unusual that we have a special term for it: a census. Studying an entire population is such an arduous undertaking that even the US government with all of its resources only attempts a census of the US population once every ten years!

If we are not willing or able to study a research population in its entirety, what can we do? We can elect to study smaller subsets of our research population – i.e., we can study **samples**. Researchers may want to know something about the changing aspirations of college students in the US. To get this information, however, the researcher need not survey all but just a small group – a sample – of college students. Similarly, researchers might be interested in the violent content of videogames. In carrying out this study, it is most likely that those involved will analyze the content of a select group – a sample – of the various videogames on the market. Drug companies test new drugs not on all targeted patients, but rather on a much smaller group – a sample – of willing volunteers.

Samples, then, offer a practical solution to the daunting task of studying entire populations. We can use samples to "stand in" for a larger population. In this sense, samples can be very efficient devices – they allow us to look at the "few" in order to know about the many. Working with samples saves time and money. When doctors need to check our blood, they don't have to "drain" our entire circulatory system – a few ounces will do it. Wine tasters don't have to consume the whole bottle to assess a wine. Ideally, then, samples should "mimic" or accurately depict the larger whole or population from which they come.

Samples that do a good job at conveying accurate information about the whole are referred to as **representative samples**. Representative samples allow the researcher to take the information obtained from the small sample and generalize it back to the entire population. So, if the average age of individuals in your sample is 32, and your sample is a representative one, the researcher can safely conclude that the average age in the population is also 32. This ability to generalize sample findings or information to the larger population is known as **sample generalizability** (or as **external validity** in some circles).

Using samples to make accurate generalizations about populations is a central concern of good sampling. This point alerts us to one important caveat about samples. Only representative samples are trustworthy in providing information about entire populations. Can we assume that most samples are good, representative ones? Well, let's go once again to some of our common sampling experiences.

Reconsider for a moment those movie trailers that precede the feature film. Coming attractions clearly illustrate just how misleading samples can be. As you well know, movie attractions typically cram the less than two-minute "sample" of the coming attraction with the funniest or most dramatic or the most action-packed moments of the new release. All too often, however, the trailer wildly misrepresents what the viewer will find in the rest of the film. Technically speaking, these small samples of feature films contain **sampling error**. Sampling error refers to the inaccuracies of samples vis-à-vis their populations.

Sampling error is attributable to the fact that samples are typically imperfect. That is, samples don't always accurately reflect the whole population. Let's return for a moment to the previous age example. While the average age in the *sample* is 32, the average age in the *population* is likely to be slightly different – say 31 or 33. This difference between a **sample statistic** (a value based on sample data) and a **population parameter** (the true value for the entire population) constitutes sampling error and it is something to be expected in the sampling process. Our goal in obtaining samples, then, is to try to select samples that minimize sampling error (*totally* eliminating it is really too much to expect). Why is it that some samples do a better job than others at representing their populations and minimizing sampling error? We consider this question next.

Obstacles to Representative Samples

As noted above, the quality of samples can vary widely. The sample of blood drawn in the doctor's office is safely taken to be representative of all the blood in our body. On the other hand, we would be foolish to be so trusting of the typical movie trailer sample of movie highlights. Why the difference? Sampling with regard to the blood running through our veins is nonproblematic because the blood in our body illustrates a **homogeneous population**. Homogeneous populations are those that consist of identical elements. (The entities that make up a population are known as **elements**.) The blood running through our feet is the same as the blood running through our hands, through our hearts, etc. Sampling from homogeneous populations is easy. If all the members of a research population are identical to each other, then a sample of one would be sufficient to tell us about the entire population! Consequently, physicians are usually satisfied with one sample of blood when doing a blood work-up.

The trouble for social researchers is that homogeneous populations are relatively rare in the social world. The research populations that social scientists study are typically **heterogeneous** ones – i.e., they are typically characterized by great diversity. For an illustration of population heterogeneity, consider once again the typical movie and movie trailer. Feature movies often run over 100 minutes in length. As movie fans know, these 100+ minutes can contain a lot of variation. The average movie will contain slow moments, exciting moments, funny moments, poignant moments, dull moments, etc. This variety in the total collection of a movie's moments or scenes illustrates the concept of **population hetero-geneity**. If you think about it, population heterogeneity is just what we want in a full-length film. These 100+ movie minutes would be painfully boring if we were to see essentially the same scene over and over again.

Population heterogeneity simply acknowledges the fact that many populations contain extremely diverse elements. Think for a moment about your local college population. Despite the fact that college students all have college in common, there is still a great amount of diversity in this population: students vary in social class, gender, race, ethnicity, age, religious background, marital status, etc. In many areas of life, we appre-ciate this diversity. Variety, we say, is the spice of life. Monotony, or the same thing over and over, is a fate worse than death.

The simple fact is that population heterogeneity is one of the realities of life and it is one of the great obstacles to obtaining good representative samples. The more heterogeneous a population, the more difficult it is to obtain a sample of that population that adequately captures *all* the vari-ation therein. If movie trailers were to faithfully represent *all* the moments of the feature film, they would have to show the good and the bad, the exciting and the boring. This, of course, doesn't make for good business if you're trying to sell tickets! This point brings us to yet another obstacle to good samples: the sample selection process.

How is the sample selected?

As suggested by the movie trailer example, the desires, motives, or biases of those selecting samples can certainly undermine the sample's ability to represent the population. Those who select the scenes to include in movie trailers aren't really interested in presenting a representative sample of movie moments. Instead, they are interested in presenting the scenes that have the best chance of convincing people to buy tickets. Individuals who book guests for television talk shows aren't necessarily interested in representative samples either. The shows may advertise that they will feature "mothers who date their daughters' boyfriends." In reality, however, talk shows will likely book those mothers who will do the most for ratings: the outrageous, the outspoken, the flamboyant etc. Similarly, people who conduct mall surveys for marketing researchers can easily stray from selecting representative samples. Surveyors might purposely avoid certain people (the disheveled, the elderly, geeks) and happily pursue others (young, attractive potential dates). While these decisions may make sense for the survey worker, they seriously undermine the selection of a representative sample. Clearly, leaving the selection process open to such influences as personal motives and agendas greatly challenges the goal of achieving a representative sample.

Size matters (to a degree)

Some samples do a poor job representing their populations because they are too small. While small samples can adequately represent homogeneous populations (remember, a sample of one is all that's needed to perfectly represent a totally homogeneous population), diverse populations require larger samples. The reasoning is straightforward, the more heterogeneity in the population, the more elements we need to include in the sample in order to represent all the diversity.

There is a catch-22, however, with the issue of size. Earlier we noted that sampling was an attractive option in research because it is so efficient. Samples allow us to use a few to learn about the many. Large samples, however, can undermine this efficiency. Consequently, researchers recognize a point of diminishing return with the issue of sample size. While in general it is true that larger samples will be more representative than smaller ones, the advantages of larger samples can be outweighed by the increased cost of large samples. Doubling sample sizes will double the cost of sampling, but it will not double the accuracy of sample data. Indeed, probability theory indicates that increasing the size of a carefully selected random sample from 1,000 to 2,000 (a 100 percent increase) will only increase the accuracy of the sample by 1 percent! (Newport et al. 1997). Consequently, larger is not necessarily better when it comes to samples. Instead, researchers will employ sampling ratios that establish acceptable sample sizes for various population sizes. As a general rule, the larger the population size, the smaller the sampling ratio needed to obtain a representative sample. Gallup and other major survey groups are able to obtain accurate information about our national population by using sample sizes of between 1,000 and 1,500 (Newport et al. 1997). Figure 8.1 presents the standard sampling ratios for various population sizes. (This last point about sample size is one that confuses many students of sampling. Reason would seem to dictate that larger populations would require larger samples to represent them. And indeed, if you take another look at Figure 8.1, the largest population sizes do require the largest samples. It is only the sampling *ratio* that is small.)

For very small populations (under 200), do a census.

For a population of:	Use a ratio of:
500	50%
1,000	30%
10,000	10%
150,000	1%
1 million	0.025%

Figure 8.1   Conventional sampling ratios

A Representative Sample: Take a Chance

The best strategy for overcoming these obstacles to obtaining a representative sample entails the use of some kind of **probability sampling**. A probability sampling technique is one where the probability of selecting any element or member of the entire population is known. The key to probability sampling is found in the **random selection** process. A random selection uses chance and chance alone to determine which members or elements of the population are selected for inclusion in the sample.

This random selection process is frequently employed in elementary school classes when it's time to put on a special school event. In the interest of fairness, the selection process is often taken out of the hands of the teacher (who might play favorites in selecting students) and instead put into a hat! To carry out a random selection of students for the event, all the names of members of the class (the population) are placed in a hat. A small set of names (the sample) is then randomly drawn from the hat. In pulling a name from the hat, every element in the population (i.e., every name in the hat) has a known and equal chance of being selected for the sample. The selection of names is repeated until the desired number of students is obtained for the sample. The names selected are determined by chance (and not by teacher bias or student popularity). This is a classic illustration of a random selection process. The more our sample selection process resembles this chance drawing, the more confident we can be that our sample will be a representative sample. Indeed, a major premise of probability sampling is that a sample will be representative of its population if all members of the population have an equal chance of being selected for the sample.

The idea of chance playing a significant role in selecting a good representative sample may strike some as odd. After all, our culture often warns against our leaving important outcomes to chance. We are urged to be prepared, to leave nothing to chance. We buy insurance and obtain wills in order to guard against disasters, diseases, and death – the fickle finger of fate. And such advice is sound when we want outcomes that complement our personal preferences, traits, or lifestyles. As indicated above, if we want samples that reflect our preferences, we should be deliberate in selecting them (e.g., booking the most loquacious guests for a talk show). But if we want samples that truly represent their population, we need to eliminate our personal preferences (biases) and allow chance to guide the selection process. Chance is our best antidote to idiosyncratic preferences and biases.

The sampling frame

In order to employ probability sampling, the researcher must work with a **sampling frame**. A sampling frame refers to an exhaustive listing of all the elements that make up a research population. The sampling frame is an essential ingredient for probability sampling. Indeed, it is the sampling frame that enables the researcher to "know" the probability of elements being selected for a sample. If a researcher knows that a sampling frame contains 1,000 elements, then the researcher also knows that any one element has one chance in 1,000 of being selected for the sample. Without this total listing of all the population elements, probability sampling is impossible.

Obviously, before frames can be constructed, the researcher needs to have a clear definition of the research population. Clear population definitions will help the researcher identify the specific group the sample needs to represent. Vague or ambiguous definitions of research populations will only lead to problematic sampling frames and samples. Rather than defining one's research population as supporters of public television, we would do better to clearly state all the delimiters of the population we want to represent with our sample: i.e., individuals who have pledged financial support to their local PBS stations in the year 2002. Instead of broadly defining our research population as sociologists, we might do better to specify the population as current members of the American Sociological Association. Achieving this level of specificity when defining our research populations greatly enhances our ability to assemble or find a good sampling frame.[1]

Constructing good sampling frames, then, becomes a critical task in probability sampling. Ultimately, the adequacy of our samples really depends on the adequacy of our sampling frames. Good frames (complete, accurate, non-redundant lists of elements) will make for good samples. Bad frames (incomplete, inaccurate, or redundant lists of elements) will make for bad samples. The time spent clarifying the definitions of our research populations and evaluating sampling frames is time well spent.

While the researcher may actually have to construct a sampling frame from the ground up, many research populations have readily available sampling frames. If you want to interview a sample of sociology majors, it is likely that the registrar's office or the sociology department could supply a list containing all the relevant names. A minister who wants to send a questionnaire to a sample of parishioners should have a readily available list to use as a sampling frame. With this list in hand (and once it's checked for any glaring errors like missing names or repeated names), the researcher can then go about selecting a variety of probability samples. Box 8.1 contains a list of all US Supreme Court Justices, past and present. The list was available online from the Oyez Project of Northwestern University (http://oyez.itcs.northwestern.edu/oyez/frontpage) and could easily be used for a sampling frame in a study of Supreme Court Justices.

Simple random sample

The most basic probability sample is the simple random sample. This sampling technique sees the researcher executing the following *simple* steps: numbering all the elements in the sampling frame and randomly selecting some of the numbered elements for inclusion in the sample. (For example, if we numbered all of the Justices listed in Box 8.1, we would be set up to do a simple random sample of the Justices.) Random selection can be done with the assistance of a table of random numbers (a table of random numbers can usually be found in an appendix of a statistics book). In using such a table, the researcher selects a number (by chance)

---

1 Such specificity helps the researcher construct a good sampling frame but it does come at a cost – it can decrease the researcher's ability to generalize. Using the ASA membership list means that the researcher is limited to generalizing about *ASA* sociologists, not *all* sociologists. If there is a big gap between these two populations, the researcher may want to rethink this strategy.

Box 8.1   US Supreme Court Justices–alphabetical by last name

Henry Baldwin
(Associate: 1830–1844)

Philip P. Barbour
(Associate: 1836–1841)

Hugo L. Black
(Associate: 1937–1971)

Harry A. Blackmun
(Associate: 1970–1994)

John Blair
(Associate: 1790–1795)

Samuel Blatchford
(Associate: 1882–1893)

Joseph P. Bradley
(Associate: 1870–1892)

Louis D. Brandeis
(Associate: 1916–1939)

William J. Brennan, Jr
(Associate: 1956–1990)

David J. Brewer
(Associate: 1890–1910)

Stephen G. Breyer
(Associate: 1994–)

Henry B. Brown
(Associate: 1891–1906)

Warren E. Burger
(Chief: 1969–1986)

Harold Burton
(Associate: 1945–1958)

Pierce Butler
(Associate: 1923–1939)

James F. Byrnes
(Associate: 1941–1942)

John A. Campbell
(Associate: 1853–1861)

Benjamin N. Cardozo
(Associate: 1932–1938)

John Catron
(Associate: 1837–1865)

Salmon P. Chase
(Chief: 1864–1873)

Samuel Chase
(Associate: 1796–1811)

Tom C. Clark
(Associate: 1949–1967)

John H. Clarke
(Associate: 1916–1922)

Nathan Clifford
(Associate: 1858–1881)

Benjamin R. Curtis
(Associate: 1851–1857)

William Cushing
(Associate: 1790–1810)

Peter V. Daniel
(Associate: 1842–1860)

David Davis
(Associate: 1862–1877)

William R. Day
(Associate: 1903–1922)

William O. Douglas
(Associate: 1939–1975)

Gabriel Duvall
(Associate: 1811–1835)

Oliver Ellsworth
(Chief: 1796–1800)

Stephen J. Field
(Associate: 1863–1897)

Abe Fortas
(Associate: 1965–1969)

Felix Frankfurter
(Associate: 1939–1962)

Melville W. Fuller
(Chief: 1888–1910)

Ruth Bader Ginsburg
(Associate: 1993–)

Arthur J. Goldberg
(Associate: 1962–1965)

Horace Gray
(Associate: 1882–1902)

Robert C. Grier
(Associate: 1846–1870)

John M. Harlan
(Associate: 1877–1911)

John M. Harlan
(Associate: 1955–1971)

Oliver W. Holmes, Jr.
(Associate: 1902–1932)

Charles E. Hughes
(Associate: 1910–1916,
Chief: 1930–1941)

Ward Hunt
(Associate: 1873–1882)

James Iredell
(Associate: 1790–1799)

Howell E. Jackson
(Associate: 1893–1895)

Robert H. Jackson
(Associate: 1941–1954)

John Jay
(Chief: 1789–1795)

Thomas Johnson
(Associate: 1792–1793)

William Johnson
(Associate: 1804–1834)

Anthony Kennedy
(Associate: 1988–)

Joseph R. Lamar
(Associate: 1911–1916)

Lucius Q.C. Lamar
(Associate: 1888–1893)

Brockholst Livingston
(Associate: 1807–1823)

Horace H. Lurton
(Associate: 1910–1914)

John Marshall
(Chief: 1801–1835)

Thurgood Marshall
(Associate: 1967–1991)

Stanley Matthews
(Associate: 1881–1889)

Joseph McKenna
(Associate: 1898–1925)

John McKinley
(Associate: 1838–1852)

John McLean
(Associate: 1830–1861)

James C. McReynolds
(Associate: 1914–1941)

Samuel F. Miller
(Associate: 1862–1890)

Sherman Minton
(Associate: 1949–1956)

William H. Moody
(Associate: 1906–1910)

Alfred Moore
(Associate: 1800–1804)

Frank Murphy
(Associate: 1940–1949)

Samuel Nelson
(Associate: 1845–1872)

Sandra Day O'Connor
(Associate: 1981–)

William Paterson
(Associate: 1793–1806)

Rufus Peckham
(Associate: 1896–1909)

Mahlon Pitney
(Associate: 1912–1922)

Lewis F. Powell, Jr.
(Associate: 1972–1987)

Stanley Reed
(Associate: 1938–1957)

William H. Rehnquist
(Associate: 1972–1986,
Chief: 1986–)

Owen J. Roberts
(Associate: 1930–1945)

John Rutledge
(Associate: 1790–1791,
Chief: 1795–1795)

Wiley B. Rutledge
(Associate: 1943–1949)

Edward T. Sanford
(Associate: 1923–1930)

Antonin Scalia
(Associate: 1986–)

George Shiras, Jr.
(Associate: 1892–1903)

David H. Souter
(Associate: 1990–)

John Paul Stevens
(Associate: 1975–)

Potter Stewart
(Associate: 1958–1981)

Harlan Fiske Stone
(Associate: 1925–1941,
Chief: 1941–1946)

Joseph Story
(Associate: 1812–1845)

William Strong
(Associate: 1870–1880)

George Sutherland
(Associate: 1922–1938)

Noah Swayne
(Associate: 1862–1881)

William Howard Taft
(Chief: 1921–1930)

Roger B. Taney (Chief:
1836–1864)

Clarence Thomas
(Associate: 1991–)

Smith Thompson
(Associate: 1823–1843)

Thomas Todd
(Associate: 1807–1826)

Robert Trimble
(Associate: 1826–1828)

Willis Van Devanter
(Associate: 1911–1937)

Fred M. Vinson (Chief:
1946–1953)

Morrison R. Waite
(Chief: 1874–1888)

Earl Warren (Chief:
1953–1969)

Bushrod Washington
(Associate: 1799–1829)

James M. Wayne
(Associate: 1835–1867)

Byron R. White
(Associate: 1962–1993)

Edward D. White
(Associate: 1894–1910,
Chief: 1910–1921)

Charles E. Whittaker
(Associate: 1957–1962)

James Wilson
(Associate: 1789–1798)

Levi Woodbury
(Associate: 1845–1851)

William B. Woods
(Associate: 1881–1887)

Oyez Project of Northwestern University, http://oyez.itcs.northwestern.edu.oyez.
frontpage

from the random numbers table. The element in the sampling frame with that number then gets included in the sample. This step is repeated until the desired sample size is achieved.

Systematic random sample

As you might imagine, the simple random sample is simple for small research populations, but it quickly gets tedious for larger populations. A systematic sample is a reasonable alternative. Once again the researcher will start with a sampling frame and will use a table of random numbers to select the *first* element for inclusion in the sample. Once a starting point is determined, the rest of the elements for inclusion in the sample will be systematically selected via a sampling interval. The sampling interval is a systematic skipping pattern that will speed up the selection process. It is calculated by dividing the total population size by the desired sample size. If you have a population of 10,000 and you want a sample of 500, you would work with a sampling interval of 20 (10,000/500 = 20). Using a table of random numbers, you would randomly select a starting point. (The starting point should be a number selected at random that falls *within your sampling interval*: in this case, it would be a randomly selected number between 1 and 20.) If our random starting point were number 8, we would include elements number 8, 28, 48, 68, etc. in our sample. (You would continue selecting every twentieth element until you reached your desired sample size of 500.)

Stratified sampling

Recall from our earlier discussion that representative samples are more easily obtained from homogeneous than from heterogeneous populations. Stratified sampling takes advantage of this insight. With this technique, the researcher organizes the sampling frame into relatively homogeneous groups (strata) before selecting elements for the sample. This step increases the probability that the final sample will be representative in terms of the stratified groups. So, if we are particularly concerned that our sample faithfully represents our population in terms of gender, we would stratify the sampling frame on gender – i.e., we would list/group all males together and then list/group all females together. We would then proceed to draw either a simple or a systematic sample in each group. If a researcher sees a critical need for accurately representing some key variable (e.g., gender, race, ethnicity, political affiliation, age, etc.) then she or he would be well advised to stratify the sampling frame along the values of that variable. Once lists are stratified along the values of a key variable, the researcher might then pursue **proportionate stratified sampling**. This strategy enables the researcher to select sample elements in proportion to their actual numbers in the overall population. For instance, imagine a volunteer organization that is 60 percent female and 40 percent male. The researcher who wants to interview a sample of 100 members could randomly select 60 women and 40 men from a stratified sampling frame, thereby achieving a sample that accurately mimics the gender distribution of the population. (Conversely, the researcher could also engage in **disproportionate stratified sampling**. Here certain small but important subgroups might be "oversampled" in order to ensure sufficient numbers of subjects for any planned statistical analysis.)

There is one hitch to stratified sampling. It often requires the researcher to have quite a bit of information about the research population at his or her fingertips. Consider, for example, the sampling frame for Supreme Court Justices in Box 8.1. On the basis of first names, we could easily stratify the list by gender. (That's right, we have only seen two female justices to date.)[2] But if we wanted to stratify the list on another variable (e.g., religious background, age at appointment, party affiliation of nominating president), we simply could not do it with the list presented in Box 8.1. We would first have to obtain this additional information about each Justice in order to create these subdivisions within the sampling frame. If the additional information required for stratification isn't readily or easily available, stratification may not be a practical endeavor.

Cluster sampling

We have already noted that a sampling frame is an essential ingredient for probability sampling. And we have noted that often sampling frames might be relatively easy to obtain. What, however, happens when an exhaustive listing of all the elements in a research population is an unreasonable proposition? Say you want to sample high school students in your home state. Do you really have to start by compiling a list of every single high schooler in your state? Fortunately, the answer is no. Cluster sampling is a probability technique that can be used when the construction of a sampling frame is theoretically possible but not a very feasible course of action. Cluster sampling sees the researcher attack the sampling process in multiple stages. The idea is to identify naturally occurring, increasingly

2 In this example, we find that stratifying by gender doesn't really give us workable subgroups to sample from since there have only been two female Supreme Court Justices. Here's an instance, then, when the researcher might decide to do disproportionate sampling and include all the elements in the small group so that they are not eliminated from the final sample by chance.

inclusive "clusters" of one's ultimate sampling unit. You want to study graduating seniors. Where do seniors "exist"? They exist in high schools. Where do high schools exist? In cities. Where do cities exist? In states. Finally we are at the "top" cluster for our sampling problem. Now the researcher starts working backwards. Is it reasonable to construct a sampling frame of all the cities in your state? Yes (in fact one probably already exists on your state's homepage or in your state's Automobile Association tour book.) From this sampling frame, one can select a simple, a systematic, or a stratified sample of cities. Is it possible to construct a sampling frame listing all the high schools for the selected cities? Yes. From this list, one can then select a sample of high schools. Is it possible to construct a sampling frame of graduating seniors for the selected schools? Yes (and once again this list probably already exists in the selected schools' registrar's office). As you can see, cluster sampling is not for the faint of heart. It entails much more work and effort than other probability techniques. (And since cluster sampling entails repeated sampling, it presents greater opportunity for sampling error.) Still it offers a practical solution to obtaining a representative sample of very large research populations.

Non-Probability Techniques

As cluster sampling shows us, researchers sometimes have to be extremely creative (and patient) in constructing sampling frames. Nonetheless, we must also acknowledge that not all research scenarios allow for probability sampling. There are times when the essential ingredient for probability sampling – the sampling frame – is impossible for the researcher to construct. Imagine that you want to study the homeless in your state. Is probability sampling possible? Can you assemble (either immediately or eventually) a sampling frame? Here the answer is no. Unlike high school students whose names and addresses are certainly known to administrative offices, the homeless are essentially an anonymous research population. Even groups that befriend the homeless, e.g., soup kitchens or religious organizations, often do so under conditions that safeguard anonymity. As another example, think about the task of sampling heavily tattooed individuals or "collectors" as they are known in the field (Vail 2001). This is a group that is decidedly "marked" as outside mainstream society. How realistic is it to construct an exhaustive list of such people? Some people with full-body tattoos go to great lengths to hide this fact from conventional others. They wear concealing clothing to their jobs and are quite selective in revealing their tattoos

(Sanders 1999). Compiling an exhaustive list of your research population, then, will be an unrealistic (and certainly incomplete) undertaking.

So, what is the sampling alternative when probability sampling is impossible? The researcher who can't construct a sampling frame must consider a non-probability sampling technique. As is the case with probability sampling, the researcher has several non-probability sampling options to consider.

Convenience samples

Probably the oldest sampling strategy is the convenience sample (aka accidental sample). As the name implies, this technique builds a sample on the basis of finding convenient or available individuals. Those who are selected for the sample are those who are close at hand. If you've been asked to fill out a questionnaire in your college student center or as you exited the college library, you've experienced convenience sampling first hand. Clearly there is an obvious shortcoming to this kind of sampling. Individuals who are not "conveniently" located have no chance of being selected for such samples. For instance, students who never frequent the student center (or the library!) would never have a chance of making it into the previously described convenience sample. The omission of all but the most conveniently accessed elements in a population greatly undermines the representativeness of a convenience sample.

Snowball samples

Snowball sampling is essentially a sampling strategy built around referrals. (The technique's name invokes the image of rolling small snowballs into larger and larger snowballs.) The researcher will start the sampling process by contacting a few individuals for inclusion in the sample. These people will then be asked for names of additional people who might be willing to be part of the research project. Snowball sampling might be a good technique to consider for the tattoo project mentioned above. After making contact and winning the trust of a few "collectors," the researcher would then ask these individuals for names of other collectors. The new names would then be contacted and asked for names of still more collectors. This process is repeated until a satisfactory sample size is achieved. There is again a clear shortcoming of snowball samples. Individuals who are "loners," who are not "networked" with others in the research population, will likely be excluded from snowball samples.

Quota samples

It is perhaps useful to think of the quota sample as the non-probability equivalent of the stratified sample. Here the researcher selects sample members on the basis of key traits assumed to characterize the research population. Sampling is done to fill set quotas for these traits. You may have been involved in such a sample if you've ever been approached in a mall by a marketing researcher looking to fill a quota for some predetermined characteristics: e.g., female, contact wearers in their twenties. Once researchers fill a quota on one set of characteristics, they move onto another: e.g., male contact wearers in their thirties. Again this process is repeated until every specified quota is filled.

The most important point to remember with all of these non-probability techniques is that they can't be assumed to produce representative samples. Sampling strategies that are not based on probability theory and techniques leave the researcher in the dark with regard to either estimating sampling error or achieving any degree of confidence in how well the sample truly represents the larger population. For these benefits, the researcher must employ some form of probability sampling.

Estimating Sampling Error

In the end, the researcher wants a sample that does a good job at providing information about the entire research population at hand. In other words, the researcher wants to work with a representative sample. As we've just seen, the best chance one has of obtaining a representative sample is via some kind of probability sampling. In effect, probability sampling increases the *probability* of obtaining a representative sample. But does it *guarantee* a representative sample? Well, look again at the term probability sampling and you'll have your answer. Probability sampling makes representative samples more likely but not a certainty. What's the researcher to do? Doesn't this uncertainty undermine one's ability to generalize sample information back to the entire population? Yes and no. While it is true that probability sampling doesn't offer guarantees, it does allow the researcher to cope with the uncertainty of achieving a representative sample. Probability sampling enables the researcher to *estimate* the amount of sampling error that exists in the sample.

When using information obtained from a sample to infer something about the larger population, the researcher should always acknowledge the possibility of some sampling error. That is, the researcher must be prepared for the possibility that samples never perfectly reflect their respective populations. There is always some lack of "fit" between the sample and its population. To acknowledge this lack of fit the researcher can calculate a correction factor to use in conjunction with any sample data. This factor suggests how the sample data should be amended in order to bring them more closely in line with the true population value.

You use such correction factors whenever you find yourself making "give or take" statements. Someone asks you to estimate the amount of time you spend each day on the Internet. You say three hours *give or take 30 minutes*. Someone asks how much you spend on gas for your car each month. You say $100, *give or take $20*. Your amended "give or take" estimates illustrate the correction term of the researcher. These correction terms are formally known as **confidence intervals** – i.e., we are confident that the true population value actually falls somewhere in this range of numbers. So, in estimating the average age in a research population (say the membership of a national bird-watching organization), the researcher might report an average age of 55 (+/− 2). Fifty-five is the average age in the sample used for the study and the +/− 2 is the correction factor – i.e., the confidence interval or the range of values within which the average age for the entire population of bird watchers is expected to fall.

Confidence intervals are always stated for corresponding **confidence levels** – i.e., the degree of confidence the researcher has that the stated interval really captures a true population value. Most often, social researchers elect to work at the 95 percent or the 99 percent confidence levels. With these levels, the researcher is calculating confidence intervals that have either 95 chances in 100 or 99 chances in 100 of "capturing" the true population value. If you've already had a statistics course, you have probably encountered these terms before. In order to increase one's level of confidence, one must set wider or more inclusive ranges of values within which population values might fall. Increased confidence, then, comes at the cost of decreasing precision.

While all of this may sound unduly complicated or involved, it really is an extremely valuable benefit of probability sampling. We started the chapter noting that samples are often used to give us insight into larger populations. In the final analysis, sample accuracy is an extremely important issue. Ultimately, we want to have some confidence that our sample is trustworthy regarding the information it provides about the population. One recent political event will help make this point. In the final days of the 2000 presidential election, pollsters were claiming that the November election was literally too close to call. For example, a CBS

News poll in early October found 46 percent (+/−3) of likely voters sampled intended to vote for Bush while the percent intending to vote for Gore was 47 (+/−3). If you do the math (i.e., if you add or subtract the correction factor for each percentage) you'll see that the pollsters were admitting that *either* candidate might actually have the edge in voter support in the population at large. As you may remember, the pollsters were indeed correct. The presidential election was extremely close (so close that contested ballots in one state determined the outcome of the election). Without the use of probability sampling, these kinds of accurate insights about populations would be impossible to make.

Just a Sampling of the Issues

Sampling is a common and useful strategy for gathering information. Oddly enough, however, it is still an idea that prompts considerable skepticism. A recent Gallup poll on American's confidence in polls illustrates this point. Gallup discovered that while most of us trust what polls tell us about public opinion, we don't believe that samples of less than 2,000 respondents can accurately tell us about the views of all Americans (Newport et al. 1997).

This skepticism about sampling has worked its way into an important political debate – the use of sampling techniques to supplement the US Census. The Constitution mandates that a census – an enumeration of the US population – be taken every ten years. Census data in turn is used to determine congressional, state, and local voting districts as well as to determine the yearly distribution of billions of federal funding to the states. An undercount of population can have very serious ramifications, costing states seats in Congress and monies for social programs, schools, hospitals, roadways, etc. It is estimated that the 1990 census undercounted 4 million people; the 2000 census "missed" approximately 3 million. Consequently, getting the census count right is a very big deal. As it turns out, however, what is "right" is very much a matter of politics.

In general, Democrats support the use of sampling strategies as a way to adjust census figures for the undercounting of hard to reach groups in the population[3] – those in rural areas and inner cities, minorities, the poor, etc. In contrast, Republicans have opposed the use of sampling "corrections."

3   Many sampling experts agree that the Democratic position is methodologically sound – the use of strategic sampling will produce more accurate population counts. For more information, see relevant links in the *NewsHour* census entry in "Expanding the Essentials."

White House preferences follow these party lines: the Clinton administration advocated sampling strategies while the Bushes (father and son)
have opposed them. (The opposing Democratic and Republican positions
are in line with party interests since the undercounted groups tend to vote
Democratic.) The Supreme Court has even weighed in on the issue. In a
1999 ruling, the Court held that sampling violates federal census law and
consequently could not be used in the 2000 census for the purpose of
reallocating seats in the House of Representatives. The court's 5:4 decision
left open the question of whether sampling *per se* is an unconstitutional
census practice. Given the political implications of the sampling issue (e.g.,
possible reapportionment of Congressional districts and the federal
monies and power attached), there is little doubt that this question will
be revisited as the 2010 census approaches.

Despite the skepticism and the political intrigue that surrounds sampling, it is a firmly established social and research practice. It is also a
trustworthy practice – good probability sampling techniques can give us
remarkably accurate information about entire populations. Good, representative samples, however, require a lot of care and effort. Hopefully
this chapter has offered a reasonable sampling of the issues that must be
considered in order to achieve good results.

Expanding the Essentials

While much of social research utilizes sampling, we shouldn't
look a population gift-horse in the mouth! You can find a
vast array of Census data at your fingertips at the American
FactFinder web page. From the US Census Bureau web
page (http://www.census.gov/) click on the link to American
FactFinder.

There are several sites you can visit to learn more about the census and the
sampling controversy. Interested readers can start with "NewsHour Extra:
Census 2000-February 28, 2001" and follow the embedded links to other relevant topics: http://www.pbs.org/newshour/extra/features/jan-june01/census.
html.

The Gallup Poll is dependent on good sampling, as well as on American's
faith in sampling. Not surprisingly, then, the Gallup site offers a very cogent,
reader-friendly explanation of probability sampling. See the link "How Polls
are Conducted" on the Gallup homepage: http://www.gallup.com/.

Several Internet sites are available for helping researchers calculate the
right sample size for a given study:

Six Sigma's "How to Determine Sample Size": http://www.isixsigma.com/library/content/c000709.asp

University of Florida, Cooperative Extension Services' "Determining Sample Size": http://edis.ifas.ufl.edu/BODY_PD006

Wildman and Freudenthal's STAT 2005 lecture, "Determining Sample Size": http://wind.cc.whecn.edu/~pwildman/statnew/determining_sample_size.htm.

 A brief review of sampling terminology as well as of the "great" moments in the development of sampling can be found in an article by Tommy Wright of the US Census Bureau: "Selected Moments in the Development of Probability Sampling: Theory and Practice," *Survey Research Newsletter*. Issue 13, July 2001.

Exercises

1   Obtain a membership list for a group, organization, or cause with which you are familiar. Following the steps outlined in the chapter, proceed to draw a simple random sample of names from the list. Critique your sample in terms of its representativeness. What steps would you suggest taking to improve your chances of obtaining a truly representative sample?

2   Imagine you've been hired by a college's food service office to help them figure out their menu "hits and misses." (1) You come up with the idea of checking the cafeteria garbage containers in order to figure out what students liked and disliked on the menu. What research population is being targeted by this strategy? What kind of sampling strategy is this? What are the obvious downsides to this strategy? (2) After two weeks of checking out garbage, you decide to change tactics and talk to students while they sit in the cafeteria eating their food. What research population is being targeted now? What kind of sampling strategy is this? What are some of its obvious downsides?

3   Read the article by Frank Newport, Lydia Saad, and David Moore, "How Polls are Conducted" (see "Expanding the Essentials" above). According to the article, what's the one requirement for being included in a Gallup National Poll? Provide a concise definition of Gallup's sampling frame for national polls. Who is not included in Gallup's sampling frame for a national poll? Are you insulted or not?

9 Our Inquisitive Nature: The Questionnaire

Your next trip to the supermarket can provide a good gauge of our dependence on one basic tool for knowing. While waiting in the checkout line, take a look around at the tabloids and you'll find yourself adrift in a sea of questions. Will the latest Hollywood love-match last? Will Madonna reinvent herself yet again? When will Oprah and Stedman finally get hitched? Similarly, a sampling of morning, afternoon, and evening talk shows remind us that "inquiring minds" want to know the answers to many, many questions. Posing and answering questions seems to be at the heart of our popular mass media culture.

Finding out by asking questions is not the exclusive domain of news tabloids and talk shows. It is also the heart of survey research – the primary data collection tool of the social sciences. Simply put, the **survey** is a research instrument that allows us to gather critical information by posing questions. In general, we follow one of two paths in survey research. We ask our questions via an **interview**, or we ask our questions via a **questionnaire**. An interview is the more personal form of survey research – questions are posed in a face-to-face or telephone exchange between the interviewer and the respondent. (The interview technique will be the focus of the next chapter.) A questionnaire is a self-contained, self-administered instrument for asking questions. While the questionnaire lacks the personal touch of the interview, it can nonetheless be an extremely efficient data collection tool. Indeed, the self-sufficiency of questionnaires makes them the most popular survey option. A good questionnaire can "stand on its own" and enable a researcher to collect data without requiring any personal contact with the respondent. This trait means that questionnaires can transcend most barriers of time and space. By utilizing the mail system (snail mail or email), a researcher can execute a national survey of Americans without ever "leaving home."

And as news tabloids and talk shows reveal, there is hardly any limit to what it is we can find out by asking questions. Indeed, the survey is a popular tool for data collection precisely because it is so versatile. Any one of the several goals of research (exploration, description, explanation, or evaluation) can readily be pursued via survey research. Similarly, there is no limit to the *kinds of information* we might obtain via questions. We can ask questions to find out objective facts and conditions (What is your age? Where were you born?). We can ask questions about behaviors (Do you smoke? Do you participate in any team sports?). We can ask questions to learn people's attitudes, beliefs or opinions (Do you support term limits for members of Congress? Do you favor a mandatory waiting period for the purchase of handguns? Is the president doing a good job with the economy?). We can ask about people's future hopes and expectations (What's the highest educational degree you plan on obtaining? How many children do you see in your future?). We can ask questions about knowledge (In your state, is it possible to legally charge husbands with raping their wives? Are there any age restrictions for the office of President of the United States?). Indeed, as long as we pay careful attention to how we phrase our questions, there is virtually no limit to what we might find out via surveys.

For many, survey research is a natural and familiar way of gathering information, as second nature to us as talking and writing. This familiarity causes some to think that survey research is easy. Many adopt an "anyone can do it" attitude. As we will see in this chapter, however, such an attitude is extremely naive. Much thought must be given to the exact wording of our questions, the structure of our questions, and the way we sequence and format our questions. This holistic approach is mandated by the fact that survey research has a terribly vulnerable Achilles heel. The fact is that we can ask great questions and still fail at survey research! How so? Above all else, successful survey research requires that we secure respondents' *cooperation*. We must convince potential respondents that our questionnaire is worth their time and effort and we must convince them that the questions are worthy of honest, accurate answers.

Neither of these tasks is easy. In general questionnaires suffer low **response rates** – i.e., the percentage of potential respondents who actually return the questionnaire. It is not unusual for questionnaires to initially generate very low response rates – less than 30%. Such low response rates are extremely worrisome for the havoc they can cause on our sampling strategies. The fact is a researcher might do *all* the work required for securing a representative sample (i.e., constructing an accurate sampling frame, stratifying on essential variables, using a random selection process) only to see this work defeated by a low response rate. When only a minority of those sampled return a questionnaire, we must consider the possibility that the few who elected to respond are significantly different from the majority of non-respondents. In short, response rates are taken as proxy measures for response *bias* (Hager et al. 2003); low response rates should raise concerns about a "self-selection" bias that undermines the generalizability of survey findings.

In the final analysis, the survey researcher cannot afford to be nonchalant about response rates. Part of good survey design is considering those factors that impact on response rates – i.e., compelling cover letters and/ or introductions, appealing layouts and coherent organization, judicious use of open-ended questions, systematic follow-ups, etc.[1] Indeed, given the right planning and follow-through, it should be possible for the survey researcher to achieve rates that are in line with recommended minimal response levels of 50–60 percent (Babbie 2001) or even 70 percent and higher (Bailey 1987; Dillman 2000).[2]

The issue of respondent honesty is more difficult to assess and control. Perhaps it's just human nature, but many of us like to present ourselves in the most favorable light. (This tendency to answer questions in a "socially appropriate way" is referred to as a social desirability bias.) Surely this explains respondents' tendency to overreport "good things": e.g., the amount they give to charity and the happiness they derive from their marriages. We also tend to underreport our negatives. Americans, for instance, "fudge" a bit when it comes to self-reporting our eating habits:

> Forty pounds of white bread, 32 gallons of soft drinks, 41 pounds of potatoes and a couple of gallons of vegetable oil in which to fry them. No, it's not a roster of provisions for the troops on the Fourth of July. It's a sample of what the average American eats in a year.
>
> Bear in mind, that's only what consumers admit to eating. If there is one thing researchers have learned while surveying the nation's gastronomic habits, it is that, whether from modesty or sheer denial, Americans are prodigious liars about how much they really eat. (Winter 2002)

---

1   These factors will be addressed later in this chapter. For a thorough discussion of still more strategies for improving survey response rates, see Dillman 2000.

2   Even the Census Bureau, an organization rich in resources and know-how, only obtained a 67 percent response rate on the 2000 Census. On the other hand, this rate was a noticeable improvement over earlier census efforts and marked a reversal of declining Census cooperation (http://rates.census.gov/).

In short, survey research in general and questionnaire development in particular are *not* "no brainers." This kind of research requires a lot of attention to many different details.

The Way We Word

In survey research, the exact questions we ask are our operationalizations (see Chapters 3, 4, and 5). That is, the concepts we are interested in studying (e.g., fear of crime) are measured via the questions or statements we pose to respondents (e.g., to measure fear of crime, the GSS asks, "Is there any area right around here where you would be afraid to walk alone at night?" Yes/No). Given that questions are our measures, the assessment of measurement validity and reliability demands that we give careful attention to the exact wording of our questions. We must choose our words wisely. An early experiment on question wording by Donald Rugg found that Americans' support for freedom of speech was drastically altered by different wordings of the following questions:

> Do you think the United States should *forbid* public speeches against democracy?
> Do you think the United States should *allow* public speeches against democracy?

(Schuman 2002, my emphasis)

The "forbid" question generated a much lower agreement rate (54%) than the "allow" question (75%) Similarly, several decades later, Smith (1987) found that respondents to the GSS responded more negatively to the term "welfare" than the term "poor." When asking questions about the public's attitudes toward abortion, might it make a difference if the words "end pregnancy" were substituted for the word "abortion"? Sociologist Howard Schuman (2002) suspected the switch would lead to an increase in support for legalized abortions but was surprised to find no difference between the two wordings. Rugg's "public speech" example clearly shows us that wording *can* matter. And while the "abortion" example runs counter to the researcher's expectations, his findings nonetheless yield some valuable insight into the measurement process. *Both* examples reveal the importance of considering and evaluating the impact of the words we use in our measures.

The rules

Survey data is only as good (i.e., as valid and reliable) as the questions posed and all too often these questions leave much to be desired. Quality survey data require us to follow certain rules for asking questions. The rules that follow might strike you as common sense. Faithful adherence to them, however, is not so common.

The questions we pose should be clear in meaning and free of ambiguity.   This rule sounds simple enough. A moment's reflection, however, will reveal how our everyday speech is laden with ambiguity. Consider the following questions.

➤   Do you exercise on a regular basis?
➤   What is your total financial worth?

At first glance these questions may strike you as perfectly adequate for "finding out" some key information about the respondent. Both questions, however, are plagued by ambiguity. How, for instance, should the respondent interpret the phrase "regular basis" in the exercise question? Does regular mean that someone exercises daily or simply that they exercise several times a week? If respondents faithfully jog every Saturday morning, should they answer this question in the affirmative? In general, frequency terms like "regularly," "often," and "seldom" are inherently vague and contribute imprecision to the measurement process. We should think twice about freely using them in our questions. Similar observations can be made about the financial worth question. Will the respondent know to include *all* income (earned and unearned) as well as assets such as property and stocks? Is the question asking about personal worth or family worth? Should the respondent adjust figures for any outstanding debt? The critical point is this: Ambiguous questions produce ambiguous data. The more ambiguity we leave in our questions, the more ambiguity we will encounter in our findings. The survey researcher is obligated to remove as much guess work from questionnaire items as possible.

Survey questions should use common everyday language; the use of specialized language such as jargon, abbreviations, or acronyms should be avoided.   This rule is especially noteworthy for those of us trained in the social sciences as well as for those doing research on behalf of special interest groups.

The various disciplines of the social sciences are replete with their own special language, a language that helps identify us as members of our respective fields. Sociologists, for instance, speak of families of orientation vs. families of procreation. They speak of our anomic society and the collective conscience. These terms, while meaningful to sociologists, are clear examples of the rather mystifying jargon of a discipline. It would be a serious mistake for a sociologist to use these terms when posing questions to respondents (e.g., What was the size of your family of orientation?). Similarly, it would be a mistake to use terms that assume respondents' knowledge of abbreviations or acronyms associated with special interest groups. Questions about the respondent's support for the NRA may find them focusing on the right to bear arms, but it is also possible that some respondents will simply not know the letters stand for the National Rifle Association and give you their thoughts about protecting redheads (National Redheads Association).

Survey questions should use neutral language; emotional or leading language should be avoided.   All of us know the power of words. Words can cut, sting, placate, or motivate. The power of words doesn't disappear in survey research. Emotional language can produce biased responses by "pushing our buttons" and encouraging respondents to react to the *language used* in a question rather than to the issues raised by a question. Consider the following question found in a recent national survey about marine mammals:

> On December 31, 1992, a United Nations ban on the use of high seas driftnets, the modern monstrosities of plastic filament that trap and kill any living creature that enters their paths: dolphins, seals, marine birds, even whales, went into effect. Presently there is no way to ensure that the ban is working or that driftnets are no longer being used. Would you support an international system to monitor and enforce the UN driftnet ban?

As you read this question, if you found yourself having an emotional reaction to the idea of monstrous nets trapping and killing defenseless marine life, you experienced first hand the influential power of language.

Typically, emotional language is used to lead respondents to the desired response. Leading questions suggest to the respondent that one response is better than or preferred over another. Clearly, the above question on the use of driftnets is not neutral. The question is trying to lead the respondent to a stand that supports the banning of driftnets. To avoid leading questions, the survey researcher must phrase questions in such a way as to make respondents feel that all answers are equally legitimate. Consider how the following questions violate this principle:

> What do you find offensive about flag burning?
> Why do you think hitting children is wrong?

Both of these questions lead the respondent by suggesting a desired response: flag burning is offensive and hitting children is wrong. As presently phrased, the questions are telling the respondent that alternate views of flag burning (i.e., an act of free speech) or of hitting children (i.e., an acceptable disciplinary tactic) are not appropriate *regardless of how the respondent may actually feel.*

Survey questions should be simple and easy for respondents to answer
Again, this rule may strike you as so obvious that it need not be stated. Still, it is a rule that is frequently violated. For instance, surveys often pose "double-barreled" questions – questions that are not easy to answer. Double-barreled questions are those that ask the respondent two (or more) questions under the guise of one question. Consider the following item that appeared on a recent survey on community policing:

> How do you rate police response time to emergency and non-emergency calls?

Respondents were provided with just one set of response alternatives (answers ranging from adequate to inadequate) despite the fact that they were really being asked to assess two different kinds of police activity: emergency and non-emergency calls. Respondents who had different experiences for emergency and non-emergency encounters with the police would find this question impossible to answer as currently phrased.

Questions can also prove difficult to answer when they ask respondents to perform unreasonable calculations. A medical researcher may want to know about respondents' health risks. Asking how many cigarettes the respondent smokes in a year (or even in a month) is not a good way to get this information. Years and months are not the usual timeframes smokers use to quantify their smoking habits. (Smokers usually characterize their habit in terms of daily consumption: e.g., a pack a day.) Similarly, a researcher may be interested in obtaining information about household spending. Asking respondents about their annual expenditures for food, however, would not be a user-friendly question. In fact, the calculations required to answer this question would encourage a high non-response rate – i.e., respondents would be tempted to skip the question altogether. The researcher would be better advised in this situation to ask a question about respondent's average food bill for a typical time period (e.g. a weekly order). Once this basic information is obtained, the researcher can then do the calculations needed to estimate yearly food expenses.

Questions that don't follow rules of good grammar can also prove difficult for respondents. Particularly troublesome are questions that employ a double negative. Double negatives *don't make no good sense in our writing or in surveys*. (See what I mean?) If the respondent is forced to re-read a question in an attempt to figure out what it's really asking, then the question isn't an acceptable one. Consider the following double-negative question that was used in a recent Roper survey of Americans' beliefs about the Holocaust:

> Does it seem possible or does it seem impossible to you that the Nazi extermination of the Jews never happened?

With this wording of the question, 22 percent of respondents indicated that they thought it possible the Holocaust never happened! Jewish leaders were shocked by these findings. Researchers reconsidered the actual phrasing of the question and determined that the use of a double negative (impossible and never) in the original question was the culprit behind the surprising findings. The question was asked again without the confusing double-negative phrasing:

> Do you doubt that the Holocaust actually happened or not?

This time the proportion of respondents who thought the Holocaust probably didn't happen fell to less than 3 percent.

The Structure of Questions: Closed- and Open-Ended Questions

In addition to carefully considering the exact wording or phrasing of our questions, the survey researcher must also decide the amount of freedom she or he wants to give respondents when answering the questions posed. This freedom issue is addressed by the researcher's use of closed- or open-ended questions. With **closed-ended** questions, the researcher provides a set of pre-determined (fixed) response alternatives for the respondent to use when answering the question. With **open-ended** questions, respondents are free to devise their own unique answers to the questions posed. You have probably encountered these two versions of questions in a typical classroom exam. The multiple-choice questions on an exam illustrate closed-ended questions. The essay portion of an exam illustrates the open-ended style of questions.

There are a number of considerations that should influence the use of closed- or open-ended questions. Providing a pre-determined set of responses is advisable when it is possible to anticipate the full range of possible responses and when these responses are relatively few in number. Questions about respondents' marital status, political affiliation, or favorite fast food restaurants would all be good candidates for closed-ended questions. Open-ended questions are advisable when posing a complex question that defies any ready or apparent answer. The open-ended approach is also recommended when we are interested in obtaining the respondent's unique views on an issue or topic. Questions about respondents' hopes for the future or about their views on charging adolescent law offenders as adults would be good candidates for open-ended questions.

In deciding on closed- or open-ended questions, the researcher should also consider the advantages and disadvantages of each style of questioning. As you probably know from experience, closed-ended questions are easier to answer. (When was the last time you intentionally skipped circling an answer on a multiple-choice exam because it was just too much trouble?) Since closed-ended questions are easy to "answer" they tend to cut down on non-responses. They also carry a clear benefit for the researcher: They reduce the time and effort needed to code responses for data entry and analysis. "Coding" decisions are achieved via the pre-determined response alternatives. These advantages, however, can also alert us to some disadvantages of closed-ended questions. Because closed-ended questions are "easy" to answer, they may encourage respondents to circle or check a response even when the responses don't really "ring true" for the respondent. (Again, think about your experiences with multiple-choice exams. Any time you "guess" at an answer you are pretending to know something you don't really know.)

Closed-ended questions can also misrepresent or obscure true differences or similarities in respondents' answers. Consider, for instance, the following question about a person's height:

➤ What is your height?

   1. Above average
   2. Average
   3. Below average

One respondent may be 6'9" tall and select option 1 (above average) to describe him- or herself. Another person may be 5'9" tall and also select option 1. There is a foot difference in these respondents' heights yet both appear the same in their closed-ended responses. Conversely, we can imagine a scenario where respondents of the exact same height (e.g., 6'2") might choose different options with one person reporting average height and the other reporting above average height. Here we have the "same" traits appearing as different responses in our closed-ended question. You can imagine how these obfuscations can confound the researcher's data analysis.

The clearest advantage of open-ended questions is that they don't put words in respondents' mouths. This feature means that open-ended questions may do a better job than closed-ended questions at measuring what respondents actually think or do (and not just measure what the *researcher believes* respondents think or do). Open-ended questions also allow researchers to find out something unanticipated. The freedom offered with open-ended questions means that respondents may report something the researcher would never have thought of including in a closed-ended set of responses. Once again, however, these advantages foreshadow some of the disadvantages of open-ended questions. Giving respondents total freedom to supply their own answers means that the researcher will have to work harder at coding responses. Indeed, it's possible that responses will be widely different from one person to the next. Open-ended questions are also "harder" for respondents to complete. Open-ended questions require respondents to work harder in the sense that they have to "write" something in order to provide an answer. Consequently, open-ended questions suffer a lower response rate than do closed-ended questions. (Again, think about your typical exam. Essay exams are usually more work for students since they actually have to write out answers and not just select a listed option. Consequently, it is not so unusual to find students leaving essay questions blank. Writing an answer to a question you don't know may be more trouble than it's worth.)

Closed- vs. open-ended questions and levels of measurement

Our selection of closed- or open-ended questions carries implications for the level of measurement we achieve in our survey items. As we change the response alternatives we offer in our closed-ended questions, we can change the level of measurement achieved. Consider the following questions:

➤ Do you rent videos?

1. yes
2. no

➤ In a typical month, how often do you rent videos?

1. never
2. 1–3 times a month
3. 4–6 times a month
4. 7 or more times a month

➤ In the last two weeks, how many times did you rent videos? (Please specify an exact number)

The first item reaches the nominal level of measurement. The numbers attached to the various response alternatives merely label two qualitatively different answers: yes and no. The second item with its different set of fixed choices reaches the ordinal level of measurement. The numbers attached to the various response alternatives express a rank ordering – as the numbers increase, so too does the frequency with which one rents videos. A switch from the closed-ended forms to an open-ended question about renting videos enables the researcher to achieve the ratio level of measurement. The "number" attached to the third item above is an actual count of the number of times the respondent rented videos in the last two weeks.

The general rule of thumb is to utilize ratio level measures whenever it is feasible. The ratio level is considered the "highest" level of measurement because of its versatility. With ratio level data, the researcher can always "collapse" data into lower ordinal or nominal level data. The ratio level also offers the most versatility in terms of statistical analysis. For some kinds of information, however, respondents are often reluctant to answer open-ended ratio level questions (e.g., questions asking for exact yearly income or exact ages). In such instances, lower level closed-ended questions can be the better choice.

Putting It Together

As indicated in the opening pages of this chapter, one of the major obstacles that must be overcome when using questionnaires to gather information is the problem of cooperation. Recall the point made earlier that questionnaires must function as "stand-alone" tools – they must contain everything needed to get respondents to answer the questions posed. This means that the questionnaire is required to do all that it can to persuade potential respondents to cooperate and supply the requested information. Certain questionnaire design and formatting issues are critical to securing this cooperation.

First things first: Persuasive cover letters or introductions

It is a mistake to think that a good survey starts with a good question. Before a respondent will ever look at specific questions, she or he must first be convinced that the survey in hand is a worthy one. The very best questions will never do a good job at collecting information if the entire questionnaire winds up in the respondent's wastebasket. To preclude this cruel (and all too common) fate, a questionnaire must first sell itself to the potential respondent. This sales job is best accomplished with a persuasive introductory statement or cover letter (for mailed questionnaires). The introduction should serve to assure the respondent of the survey's importance and legitimacy. It should convince the respondent that the time they spend filling out the questionnaire will be time well spent. To accomplish this, the researcher is well advised to specifically address the saliency of the research topic. Tell the respondents why your project matters and why their cooperation is so critical. Introductions and cover letters should also directly address the issues of confidentiality or anonymity (see Chapter 2). The researcher should tell respondents how their privacy will be protected. When cover letters are used, they should be personalized – i.e., they should address the respondent by name and they should bear the personal signature of the researcher. Cover letters should also contain phone numbers that the respondent may use to obtain additional information about the study. When possible, it's best for cover letters to be printed on letterhead that will lend credibility to the research project.

Sequencing

The order or sequence of our survey items can greatly influence a respondent's decision to supply the requested information. Getting off on the wrong foot may mean the researcher will never see their survey returned to them. Sequencing can also influence the quality of the information we obtain. Which questions should be placed at the start, at the middle, and at the end of the survey? Is it appropriate to group certain questions together? Will the order or flow of the questions influence people's answers?

Primacy effects   After presenting respondents with a persuasive introduction to your project, it is best to open the survey with interesting or pleasant questions that are easy to answer. Remember, you must still be concerned with securing the respondent's cooperation – even a powerful introduction or cover letter will find it hard to overcome a tedious or boring or threatening set of opening questions. For this reason, many experts advise that questionnaires should *not* begin with background or demographic questions. Such questions often strike respondents as either invasive or dull. Similarly, don't go the route of starting with provocative, open-ended questions! While you may think this a good way to grab the attention of your respondents, it is just as likely that they will find this approach presumptuous or offensive. Any questions that might threaten the respondent should really be delayed until *after* you have won the trust of your respondent. Instead, consider starting off the questionnaire with some interesting opinion or attitude questions – such questions will help reinforce the point that the researcher is really interested in hearing what's on the respondent's mind.

Logical flow   It is usually a good idea to try to achieve some logical order to the questions you pose in a survey. You might consider grouping questions by time order (e.g., you might first ask questions about the respondent's adolescent years and then ask questions about their young adulthood). Or you might group questions by topics (i.e., put all questions about family together and all questions about work together, etc.). As you move from one group of questions to another, you should try to assist respondents in making any necessary mental shifts demanded by the new group of questions. Transitional statements can help respondents achieve the right mindset for the new set of questions: "Now I want to shift the focus to your high school years..."

When deciding on the order of questions, the researcher must be cognizant of the fact that earlier questions can influence respondents' answers to later questions. If we first ask respondents if they consider themselves overweight and then ask them about their eating habits, we can expect that their answers to the first question will influence what they say to the second question. Knowing what to do about the effect of question order, however, can be a tricky business. The researcher might follow a number of strategies. The researcher might simply decide to be sensitive to the possibility that question order may influence responses. The "order" effect could then be part of their data analysis. The researcher might pre-test the questionnaire and explore with the "trial" respondents whether or not the order of the questions influenced their responses. A more formal strategy might be to develop two forms of the final questionnaire with different question ordering adopted in each form. This solution would enable the researcher to empirically assess if question order actually influenced responses.

To ask or not to ask

A sure-fire way to discourage respondents' cooperation is to force them to read questions that are not relevant to them or their experiences. Respondents who have no children don't want to be asked a slew of questions about their parenting practices. Respondents who aren't married will not appreciate a series of questions about the division of domestic chores with their nonexistent spouses! We can most effectively spare respondents from questions that are not relevant to them by using filter and contingency questions. A **filter question** is one that determines if it is appropriate or necessary for the respondent to read a subsequent set of questions. **Contingency questions** are a subset of questions that are only answered by those who have been given the "green light" by a preceding "filter" question. For example, if respondents answer "yes" to the filter question of whether or not they have any children, they might then be instructed to go onto a set of questions regarding their interactions with their children. Those who don't have children would be instructed to skip these questions and to move onto the next relevant section of the questionnaire. When setting up filter and contingency questions, it's best to set the contingency questions "apart" from the rest of the questions and use arrows or lines to direct appropriate respondents to these sections of the questionnaire.

➤ Do you currently smoke cigarettes?

   1. yes (if yes, please answer question 3)
   2. no (if no, please skip to question 4)

                           3. In the past year, have any family members or close friends tried to get you to stop smoking?
                             1. yes
                             2. no

The long and the short of it

Not surprisingly, researchers usually prefer long questionnaires (and interviews) to short ones. Long questionnaires are more cost efficient – once we have respondents at hand, we are tempted to get as much information from them as possible. The risk of giving in to the "economy" size questionnaire, however, is great. Generally, as the length of questionnaires increases, the response rate decreases (Smith 1994). Lengthy questionnaires can discourage respondents from starting or completing the survey. While there are no hard and fast rules about questionnaire length, it is generally advised that questionnaires should be designed so that they take no more than 30 minutes to complete (Monette et al. 1998).

Formatting

The way a questionnaire appears on paper (or on a computer screen) is certainly relevant to securing respondents' cooperation. Questionnaires that look unprofessional, sloppy, or cramped will not inspire respondents to put pencil to paper (or finger to mouse). The formatting or presentation of our survey questions is also an important consideration in developing valid and reliable measures. If we don't pay sufficient attention to how our questions appear on paper, we may wind up with some unfortunate surprises. (See Box 9.1.) If you find this hard to believe, just recall the fiasco that developed on Election Day 2000 in Florida! In retrospect, was it really such a good idea to use a "butterfly ballot" –

Box 9.1　Little Things Matter

Tom Smith of the National Opinion Research Center has found that "little things" matter in formatting of surveys. All of the following "simple" mistakes can decrease data quality and undermine replication efforts:

- misalignment of response boxes,
- overly compact (dense) question format,
- faulty placement of filter and contingency questions,
- leaving too little space for answers to open-ended questions.

Smith (1993)

i.e., one that staggered the candidates' names on two separate pages and positioned the selection column down the center? Clearly there were many Florida voters who maintained that the markings on their ballots did not accurately record (measure) their true voting intentions.

Formatting decisions are particularly relevant for closed-ended questions. The most basic question is how many response categories should be listed? For nominal level measures, the number of categories should be exhaustive and they should be mutually exclusive. To offer an exhaustive set of response options, the researcher should include as many options as needed to cover all feasible answers. Mutually exclusive response options are ones that don't overlap. For some variables, these conditions of exhaustivity and mutual exclusivity are easily met. In asking a closed-ended question about the respondent's sex, the researcher only need supply two response options: male and female. These choices are both exhaustive and mutually exclusive. In asking a closed-ended question about the respondent's college major, the challenge of providing an exhaustive list of options is much greater. Some colleges offer hundreds of majors! Here the researcher must figure out an acceptable solution. She or he might list broad categories of majors (e.g., social science major, natural science major, humanities major, etc.) in order to keep the list of options to a manageable size. If the researcher goes this route, it is always wise to include an "other" option (followed by a "please specify" prompt) for the student whose major doesn't fall into any of the conventional categories. (The "other" category allows the researcher to satisfy the condition of exhaustivity.) Rather than trying to provide a full list of options, the researcher might decide the question is better posed as an open-ended one which invites the respondent to write in the name of their major. The researcher would then face the task of reviewing all the responses and imposing an after the fact coding scheme.

Like nominal level measures, ordinal response options must also be mutually exclusive and exhaustive. This rule, however, doesn't tell the whole story. In creating a ranked list of response alternatives, the researcher has considerable latitude. For instance, she or he must decide the number of ranked alternatives to offer. In measuring the level of agreement with certain views the researcher might provide three alternatives: (agree; neutral; disagree), four alternatives (strongly agree; agree; disagree; strongly disagree), five alternatives (strongly agree; agree; neutral; disagree; strongly disagree), or perhaps six alternatives (strongly agree; mostly agree; agree somewhat; disagree somewhat; mostly disagree; strongly disagree). The choice of response alternatives should be guided by our research needs – how fine-tuned or precise do we want the information? The number of response alternatives also influences how much "hedging" respondents are allowed. An even numbered set of ordinal response categories forces respondents to come down on one side of an issue (e.g., strongly agree; agree; disagree; strongly disagree). An odd numbered set of ordinal response categories allows respondents to take a "middle" position and avoid committing themselves to either side of an issue (e.g., strongly agree; agree; neutral; disagree; strongly disagree). Again, the researcher should be aware of these implications and make an informed decision as to whether an odd or even numbered set of choices is preferable.

The "strongly agree to strongly disagree" format presented above illustrates a **bipolar** or **two-directional** response option. Such closed-ended choices present a range of opposite alternatives for the respondent to consider (e.g., strongly agree to strongly disagree; strongly endorse to strongly oppose; strongly like to strongly dislike, etc.). At times, the researcher may want to present **unipolar** or **one-directional** responses – i.e., alternatives that move in one direction only, thereby avoiding negative or neutral responses. To accomplish this the researcher can resort to asking respondents to evaluate statements on a multiple-point scale (e.g., 1–5 or 1–7 or 1–10) where 1 indicates the lowest rating and the highest number the highest rating. For instance, respondents might be asked to rate their interest in reality television shows on a scale of 1 to 5 where 1 represents the lowest and 5 the highest interest.

What's the best layout for the response alternatives? Should they be listed vertically or horizontally? (Typically, vertical listing of response options is thought to lead to fewer errors.) Should we have respondents indicate their answers by filling in circles (●) or checking boxes ☑️? Should we use letter or number prefixes for identifying the various response alternatives? (Numerical prefixes enable us to "pre-code" response alternatives and thereby facilitate data entry.) These decisions are not irrelevant. The survey researcher must give serious thought to which option will produce the least amount of measurement error.

Frequently we will pose a series of items that all employ the same response alternatives. We might present a series of statements and ask respondents the degree to which they agree or disagree with each statement. Similarly, we might ask them to indicate their level of interest (from low to high) in a series of items. This style of questioning invites the use of **matrix formatting** where statements or items are vertically stacked on the left of the page and the response alternatives are vertically stacked on the right side of the page.

➤   For each of the following statements, please indicate whether you strongly agree (SA), agree (A), disagree (D), strongly disagree (SD), or are undecided (U):

	SA	A	U	D	SD
Children should be seen and not heard	[ ]	[ ]	[ ]	[ ]	[ ]
Children are our most precious commodity	[ ]	[ ]	[ ]	[ ]	[ ]

While matrix formatting is an attractive and efficient use of space, it can also invite trouble: a response set. **Response set** refers to a pattern in the respondent's answers that is not attributable to the actual content of the questions. If, for instance, the respondent strongly agrees with the first few items in a matrix set of questions, they may continue to check the strongly agree response to all the remaining items *without ever actually reading them!* Response sets can greatly undermine the validity and reliability of our survey items. The best strategy for combating a response set is to discourage it by intentionally mixing the "direction" or sentiment of your matrix items. Some items should be stated in a "positive" and some in a "negative" direction. Look again at the above example. The first statement about children can be seen as making a negative assertion about children. The second item is essentially a positive statement about children. Individuals who strongly agree with the first item would be expected to disagree with the second. Juxtaposing contradictory statements in a matrix of questions should discourage respondents from falling into a response set. To answer an intentionally mixed set of items consistently, respondents would have to agree to some and disagree with others.

Pre-Testing

After developing a good solid questionnaire, the researcher should always plan on conducting a pre-test. There is no better way to see what others think about the questionnaire than to ask them. To pre-test, we should administer the questionnaire to a small group of people who closely resemble our research population. (Those involved in a pre-test are no longer eligible for inclusion in your final sample.) A particularly effective pre-test technique is the "think aloud" (Patten 2001). Here we ask respondents to talk out their reactions to each of the items on the survey – how did they understand the questions and the response options? This is a most effective strategy for seeing if both the researcher and the respondent are "on the same wavelength" and for detecting bad questionnaire items. To strike a more technical note, the "think aloud" provides critical feedback for assessing a question's validity and reliability. Pre-testing also allows the researcher to assess the impact of word selection, question sequencing, and various formatting and layout issues.

Return to Sender: The Special Challenge of the Mailed Questionnaire

Throughout this chapter we have made repeated reference to the importance of obtaining respondents' cooperation and securing a high response rate in survey research. All that we have said so far is directed at building a good survey instrument as a way of encouraging high response: pay attention to question content and form, pay attention to formatting and question sequencing. Below are a few more tips that are particularly relevant when using the mail system for the delivery and the return of our surveys.

Cover letter

As indicated earlier, the best strategy for increasing the response rate to a mailed questionnaire is a strong, persuasive cover letter.

Convincing respondents that your research project is a worthy one will go a long way toward encouraging them to complete it and return it to you.

Make returning easy and attractive

You need to stay one step ahead of all the reasons why a respondent won't return your questionnaire. Provide a self-addressed stamped envelope. Resist making the questionnaire any longer than it really needs to be. It's easier to convince someone to fill out a short rather than a long questionnaire. Timing of mailed surveys is also relevant to good response rates. You should avoid sending questionnaires out at "busy times" of the year. Don't expect people to pay attention to your questionnaire request at holidays, at tax time, or at the start of school years. You should also think twice about sending out questionnaires during the height of the vacation season. Questionnaires may languish in mailboxes for two or three weeks while the respondent is off on their annual camping trip.

You might also consider some kind of payment for your respondents. Before you dismiss this idea as beyond your budget, remember that it's the gesture not the amount that seems to count. The payment you offer might be a token or a symbolic one. You might include a few pennies for your respondents' thoughts. You might offer coupons or bookmarks or even a list of useful URLs relevant to the survey's topic. Some suggest treating respondents to "first class" postage for use on a mailing of their choice! The idea is simply to let the respondents know that you are not taking their time and input for granted.

Systematic follow-through

In the interest of securing good response rates, you should also plan on conducting systematic follow-ups with your respondents. If respondents haven't returned their questionnaires by the appointed time, you should be prepared to contact them (either by mail or phone) and address once again the importance of both the study and their input. You should also be prepared to send out a second and even a third copy of the questionnaire. Such systematic follow-ups have been credited with significantly increasing final response rates.

Delivering Questions Electronically

The computer age has opened yet another major avenue for delivering questionnaires to respondents: questionnaires can be delivered via email or launched online via web pages. Proponents of electronic surveys contend that such surveys are the wave of the future. And given the increasing number of homes with computers and Internet connections, it is quite likely that the web page questionnaire may well become the telephone interview of tomorrow. While electronic surveys increase dramatically the ultimate reach of surveys, they don't offer any magic fixes for the inherent problems of questionnaires. Electronic surveys must still grapple with the myriad of challenges presented throughout this chapter: question wording, question sequencing, formatting, survey and item non-response, etc. Concerns over issues of anonymity and/or confidentiality will likely loom large given the public's wariness about the Internet's profound potential for privacy abuse (Cole 2001). Furthermore, electronic surveys must confront problems of access. Despite the Internet's rapid growth, electronic surveys systematically "miss" individuals, homes, and businesses without Internet access. Conversely, given the incredible "linking" capacity of the World Wide Web, web page surveys are often accessed by inappropriate respondents who are not part of the intended sample. In short, electronic surveys have a place in survey research and, as issues of restricted access are resolved, that place will likely be a most secure one in the world of market, political, and social research.

Ask and You Shall Receive

In considering the various research options for systematically gathering information, the questionnaire has earned the right to be a perennial favorite. It is the real workhorse of research tools – a frequent choice of researchers because of its versatility, its time and cost efficiency and for its overall ability to get the job done. Still, questionnaires are not foolproof. Indeed, any fool can develop a questionnaire and by now you've probably been subjected to quite a few foolish questionnaires! Hopefully this chapter has convinced you that much care and work must go into questionnaire construction if we're to reach the goal of asking the right questions in the right way in order to obtain valid and reliable information.

Expanding the Essentials

There are a number of good Internet sites devoted to the survey method. The reader will certainly find something useful at any of the following locations:

The American Statistical Association offers a series of "online" brochures about survey research in general and questionnaires in particular: http://www.amstat.org/sections/srms/whatsurvey. html.

The homepage for the General Social Survey offers links to GSS Methodological Reports on various survey issues. Once on the homepage look under the section for GSS Publications and click on the link for Reports and then the link for GSS Methodological Reports: http://www.icpsr. umich.edu/GSS/.

Bill Trochim's web page is (as usual) filled with very useful information on the topic of surveys: http://trochim.human.cornell.edu/kb/survey.htm. The "Decisions about Question Wording" and "Types of Questions" pages are particularly useful.

Anyone interested in exploring how survey instruments change over time should visit the following web site: http://www.bls.census.gov/cps/. The site details the changes and refinements to the Current Population Survey – the premier instrument for measuring unemployment in the US for the last 50+ years. (Follow "History and Concepts," "Basic Monthly Survey," and "History" links.)

For a short but informative chapter on "conceptual fundamentals" in questionnaire construction, see Michael Patton's "Thoughtful Questionnaires" in *Practical Evaluation* (1982).

For a more thorough review of survey issues, see Seymour Sudman, Norman Bradburn, and Norbert Schwarz's *Thinking About Answers: The Application of Cognitive Process to Survey Methodology* (1996).

Gary Langer, director of polling for *ABC News*, offers an informed discussion of response rates in his article "About Response Rates: Some Unresolved Questions" (2003).

Exercises

1   Devise three different questions (and answer choices when appropriate) to measure respondents' (a) commuting routine or (b) family

food budgets. Have one question capture the information at the nominal level, one at the ordinal level, and one at the ratio level of measurement.

2 Critique the following questions. Revise as needed:

Why should evil rulers like Saddam Hussein be removed from office?

Do you think IT should be a required component for every college major?

Are you a regular contributor to non-profits?

How much money do you spend each year on highway tolls?

3 Find either an online or a recent direct mail survey and critique its content and format.

4 Revisit Johnson's index of job "burn-out" presented on page 70. What changes might you now recommend for this index?

10   Talking Heads: The Interview

Every Sunday morning, *Meet the Press* and *Face the Nation* vie for the most compelling one of these. For the past several seasons, CBS's *The Early Show* and Letterman's *Late Show* have been scheduling them with each player as they are voted off *Survivor*. And no self-respecting police show could get through an episode without going at one "in the box." What's the common ingredient that crosses so easily between the world of news and entertainment? The interview. Of all the data collection techniques available in our search for information, the interview strikes many as the single best device for promoting understanding and "getting at the truth."

In popular culture, the interview is the hallmark of a person's claim to fame. You know you've made it when Barbara Walters wants to interview you for her "most fascinating people of the year" special. An interview with Oprah tells us you have arrived. (Not too long ago David Letterman undertook a campaign to get Oprah to interview him!) Indeed, the interview may be the best sign of someone's "fifteen minutes of fame." While no longer hot commodities, interviews with Monica Lewinsky, Gary Condit, and OJ Simpson were highly desirable not too long ago.

The interview also has a prominent place in our everyday lives. The interview is a staple of many academic experiences: admission to programs or graduate schools and selection for scholarships or fellowships. Entry to the work realm often turns on the all-important "first" and hopefully subsequent interviews. (Tips on good interviewing strategies are standard entries in job-hunting advice web sites and manuals.) And if we turn a sociological eye to our dating rituals, we will quickly realize that the interview process is clearly part of the "getting to know you" phase of dating. Indeed, a new time-sensitive industry is emerging around this interview part of dating: speed dating. In these intentionally short (seven minutes!) "dates," participants quickly exchange vital information about themselves. This time- and cost-efficient meeting puts the interview function of the first date "front and center." (See Box 10.1.)

The popularity of the interview isn't limited to the worlds of news and entertainment or work and dating – it is present in the world of research as well. Perhaps the positive reaction to interviews is due to the fact that interviews enjoy a much higher response rate than questionnaires. (A well-executed interview study can achieve response rates of 80–85 percent). Perhaps some researchers feel that interviews make more sense than questionnaires. Questionnaires can too often be dismissed as either superficial or tedious endeavors. (Critics of closed-ended questionnaires complain that they put words in respondents' mouths – they don't permit the researcher to collect in-depth, meaningful information. Critics of open-ended questionnaires complain that respondents aren't likely to invest the time required to write out answers to these probing yet "impersonal" surveys.) Perhaps too it is our social nature that makes interviews an attractive research option. No doubt, the appeal of the interview for many is its focus on the individual and its reliance on just plain talk. Many of us are flattered at the prospect that someone else is really interested in *talking* with us. With the interview, the researcher takes the time to contact the research subject, to build rapport with the research subject, and to listen to, interact with and "get to know" the research subject.

Conversational Exchange

In large part, the **interview** refers to a personal exchange of information between an interviewer and an interviewee. Good interviews strive to make the exchange a comfortable, conversational one. As in everyday conversations, participants should experience the interview as a pleasant social encounter. To a large extent, achieving this standard depends on the researcher's ability to establish "social harmony" or good **rapport** with the interviewee. The interviewer must be able to put respondents at ease, express interest in and be able to listen actively to respondents, and assure respondents that they will be supported throughout the entire process. The rapport issue demands that the interviewer's social skills must be sharp. It also alerts us to the fact that not all social researchers will be good at the interview process – some lack the social skills demanded by the interview process.

Box 10.1   Minute Mates: Speed Dating has flipped the matchmaking industry on its head, but can you really find lasting love in seven minutes?

By Dan Reines

Viewed from the right perspective, seven minutes is a pretty sizable chunk of time. In seven minutes, you can ... run a mile ... or you can cook up a three-minute egg – two of them, actually, with time to spare. In seven minutes you can listen to almost all of "Stairway to Heaven," and if you happen to be holding your breath, seven minutes is an eternity.

But can you meet and identify the love of your life? In seven minutes? Please. Most people can't do that in seven years ...

And yet, all over the country, lovelorn singles are trying to accomplish exactly that feat, every day. They're gathering in coffee shops ... and restaurants and nightclubs ... They're paying 20 bucks a pop to sit across from other lovelorn singles ... Then the sharp ding of a front-desk bell sounds through the hall, and the couples are ordered to Date! ... until someone rings that bell again seven minutes later, at which point they stand up, politely thank one another, and move on to the next "date." They're doing this all night, sometimes 10 or 15 times a night ...

Speed Dating has touched a nerve ... The program has spread to Canada, England and Australia, to Vienna and Tel Aviv and even Kiev. Meanwhile, here in Los Angeles, there are reportedly at least five Speed Dating marriages – and even a Speed Dating baby.

When (Jonathan) Tessler, then 35, discovered Speed Dating back in June 1999, the concept made perfect sense to him. "You get to go out with seven people with very little cash outlay," reasons the Malibu-raised mortgage banker. "You don't have to buy seven dinners. And if you ask the right questions, if you know what you're looking for, you can weed someone out very, very quickly. No matter how attractive they might be, if you ask them the right questions, you'll know if you're on totally different wavelengths, and you don't have to sit down to a four- or five-hour date to figure that out. To me, from a time standpoint, that was awesome."

Tessler definitely knew what he was looking for, and he arrived at Peet's Coffee in Beverly Hills armed with all the right questions. Raised in a wholly unobservant Jewish household, he had in recent years grown more religious, and was itching to settle down with someone who was engaged in the same spiritual journey. He peppered each of his dates with focused queries: What kind of relationship are you looking for? How religious do you want to be? How many kids do you want to have? What qualities do you think are really important in a guy? "I'd dated so many materialistic women that I was trying to screen them out," Tessler says. "I didn't want someone who would say 'I want a big house, I want a BMW, I want ...' And I knew that if they were offended by my questions, that I didn't have to see them ever again."

Remarkably, Tessler's grilling paid dividends. Three women survived the interrogation ... and during the open mingling session, Tessler approached a fourth woman, Traci Newman, whom he'd met once before, though the two had never exchanged contact information. "I'm looking for a mate, not a date," he told the 27-year-old Newman, a sociology researcher at USC. Serendipitously, so was she.

Four nights after their Speed Dating meeting, the pair went to dinner near their Brentwood homes ... and five months later the two were engaged. In April 2000, less than a year after they met, Jonathan and Traci became Mr. and Mrs. Tessler.

While the interview strives to achieve a conversational exchange of information, it would be a mistake to equate interviews with everyday conversations. As you well know, ordinary conversations can be a series of meandering "talking points" that are meant to entertain more than to inform. The interview is a *purposeful* conversation wherein the interviewer has a set research agenda – i.e., key points or questions that must be addressed. To facilitate accomplishing this research goal, interviewers employ either an interview guide or an interview schedule. **Guides** are relatively unstructured tools that list the general topics or issues to be covered in an interview. Interview guides produce unstructured, qualitative interviews. They give respondents considerable latitude in determining the actual content and direction of the interview. Interview **schedules** are more structured than guides, listing the exact questions and, if the questions are closed-ended, the exact answers to be presented to all respondents. Structured schedules produce more standardized interviews and when using a forced-choice format, a more quantitative interview.

One's choice of interview style – unstructured or structured – depends upon the research goal. Unstructured interviewing is a good idea when one is pursuing an exploratory piece of research, when one is trying to paint a detailed descriptive picture of some phenomenon or some process, or when one is trying to understand a respondent's unique experiences or perspective.

Unstructured interviewing can also be an effective strategy for countering memory failure or respondent resistance. Giving the respondent more control over the pace and direction of the interview can allow respondents to get to topics on their own terms, pace, and comfort levels. Following their own pace may also help respondents "stumble" onto memories that would not be so easily retrievable under more direct questioning. In their study of women's ways of knowing, Belenky and her associates (1986) clearly saw the value of unstructured interviewing:

> Each interview began with the question, "Looking back, what stands out for you over the past few years?" and proceeded gradually at the woman's own pace to questions concerning self-image, relationships of importance, education and learning, real-life decision-making and moral dilemmas, accounts of personal changes and growth, perceived catalysts for change and impediments to growth, and visions of the future. We tried to pose questions that were broad but understandable on many levels. (Belenky et al. 1986: 11)

On the other hand, structured interviewing may be more appropriate when the researcher wants to provide an overview of a research population with regard to their behaviors, attitudes, values, etc. Structured interviewing is also appropriate when the researcher is interested in quantifying information about the research population. Unless we ask the same questions of all, we won't be in a position to say what percent favor or oppose a certain social policy or what percent engage in certain behaviors. You may already be familiar with the General Social Survey. It is a prime example of a highly structured interview. Consider the following GSS questions on respondents' attitudes toward abortion:

> ➤ Please tell me whether or not you think it should be possible for a pregnant woman to obtain a legal abortion if ... READ EACH STATEMENT, AND CIRCLE ONE CODE FOR EACH[1]
>
> A. If there is a strong chance of serious defect in the baby?
> B. If she is married and does not want any more children?
> C. If the woman's own health is seriously endangered by the pregnancy?

1   Instructions for interviewer.

D. If the family has a very low income and cannot afford any more children?
E. If she became pregnant as a result of rape?
F. If she is not married and does not want to marry the man?
G. The woman wants it for any reason.

Each interviewee is asked to respond to each statement with the same set of response options: yes, no, don't know, or no answer. By sticking with this regimen, a quantitative profile of respondents can easily be generated. (For a percentage breakdown of answers through the years, you can visit the GSS homepage (http://www.icpsr.unich.edu/GSS/) and look under the subject heading of abortion.)

Developing an Unstructured Guide

While the unstructured guide may seem like an easy tool to develop, it really requires much careful thought and work. Lofland and Lofland (1995) offer a series of suggestions for preparing a guide. The first step is for the researcher to enter what they call the *puzzlement phase*. In this phase, the researcher works at articulating all the things about the research topic that are puzzling. Suppose you want to do a study on personal homepages. In thinking about the topic, the researcher might "puzzle" over the following: What's the function of a homepage? When does someone decide they "need" their own homepage? Are homepages "reality" or "fantasy" documents? etc. During this phase, which may go on for days or weeks, the researcher jots down all of his/her thoughts about the topic. (Lofland and Lofland recommend using a separate note card for each question or issue.) To get a full array of ideas/questions, the researcher should ask others what they find puzzling about the topic and/or consult articles/books on the topic.

Once the puzzlement phase is finished and the researcher has accumulated a stack of cards, the cards can be sorted into several internally consistent piles. A review of the piles should help the researcher assemble a general outline as well as a sequencing of questions for the guide. It is also a good idea to supplement the guide with well-placed probes. **Probes** are questions used to follow up on points mentioned or not mentioned by the respondent. Listing probes on the guide serves to remind the interviewer to pursue important lines of inquiry.

An interviewer's social skills are certainly called into play when conducting a qualitative interview. Since this style of interviewing is very dependent on the respondent's willingness to talk in detail, the researcher must create a warm and supportive "talk" environment. To accomplish this, two strategies are most important: the interviewer must know how to be an "active" listener and the interviewer must know how to handle respondent silences.

Active listening

The idea of an active listener might strike some readers as an oxymoron – listening would seem to suggest a silent, passive role for the interviewer. In fact, good listening calls upon the researcher to actively attend to what the respondent is saying. In effect, the researcher must "hang on" every word out of the respondent's mouth. To let the respondent know that one is actively listening to them, the researcher should periodically supply a verbal mirror of what the respondent is saying. In providing a **verbal mirror**, the researcher paraphrases in a clear, concise, and non-evaluative way exactly what the respondent has communicated. Imagine a college student who has just described her first year at college as a nightmare – a series of failed courses. The interviewer might say "So what I'm hearing you say is that freshman year was an academic disaster." The verbal mirror shows the respondent that the researcher is indeed listening to everything. It also gives the respondent a chance to correct any misunderstandings by the interviewer. Most importantly, though, the verbal mirror provides the respondent with an opening to say more – to continue the dialogue and delve deeper into the topic.

Another essential ingredient of active listening is the previously mentioned probe. A probe is a follow-up technique that encourages the respondent to further elaborate or clarify a point of discussion. To encourage a respondent to say more, the interviewer might simply employ a quizzical look until the respondent starts talking again. The interviewer might also probe with a well placed "uh-huh" or "go on." At times, however, the probe needs to be stated more explicitly. Imagine a college student saying she wants to get her own apartment because home life is so stressful. The interviewer might ask the respondent to discuss in more detail what makes home so stressful and how apartment living would relieve these stresses. Knowing when and how to probe effectively are two critical interview skills. The following two excerpts illustrate these points. The first excerpt from John Kitsuse's research on the imputation of the status homosexual shows how probes can clarify respondent's answers. The second excerpt from Angrosino's research with the mentally challenged shows how probes can help keep respondents focused.

Kitsuse's work (2002: 98):

I: What happened during your conversation?

R: He asked me if I went to college and I said I did. Then he asked me what I was studying. When I told him psychology he appeared very interested.

I: What do you mean "interested"?

R: Well, you know queers really go for this psychology stuff.

I: Then what happened?

R: Ah, let's see. I'm not exactly sure, but somehow we got into an argument about psychology and to prove my point I told him to pick an area of study. Well, he appeared to be very pensive and after a great thought he said, "Okay, let's take homosexuality."

I: What did you make of that?

R: Well, by now I figured the guy was queer so I got the hell outta there.

Angrosino's work (2001: 253):

I: Tell me about what you did at your uncle's café.

R: Yes Uncle John, He's a great guy. I really love him.

I: What did you do there?

R: He cooks all his own food. Even bakes. Bread, cakes.

I: Did you help him?

R: He opens every day for breakfast and then he stays open until really late. He never likes to turn people away.

I: Did you help him in the kitchen?

R: Oh, yeah. I like to help. He's just like my Pop. They always want to help people. That's why he bought the café when he retired. He wanted to help people. People always need good food, he says.

Silences

Active listening is important. However, the technique should never cause the interviewer to interrupt important respondent silences. Rather early in our training as social beings, we learn the value of friendly banter that can keep awkward silences at a minimum. (Think about your own awkwardness when you hear a deafening silence on the other end of a phone conversation – if you're like most people you will rush in to fill the void.) The researcher, however, must put this convention aside during a qualitative interview. Moments of silence in an interview should be appreciated as instances of thoughtful punctuation. Frequently, there is something to be learned from the silence. If the researcher rushes in and prematurely breaks the silence, important data may be lost forever – the respondent may feel embarrassed and never return again to the issue that prompted the silence. A good interviewer will learn to respect silences. In doing so, the researcher is apt to discover how silences can be springboards into important topics of discussion.

The Interview Schedule

When the researcher is interested in standardizing the interview process (i.e., making the experience the same for all respondents), the interview guide of the qualitative interview is replaced by an interview schedule. The points addressed in the previous chapter on questionnaire construction can be applied to the development of the interview schedule: questions should have a singular focus and use neutral language – they should not lead the respondent. Response choices should be mutually exclusive and balanced. Perhaps the biggest challenge to conducting a structured interview is the fact that such interviews can have a rather artificial feel to them. This is especially a dilemma in the most structured of interviews – i.e., an interview where *both* questions and response options are standardized. In these scenarios, the respondent may come to believe that the researcher is less interested in hearing what's on the respondent's mind than in checking off boxes on the schedule. A highly structured schedule can be thought of as a script that is used by the interviewer to ensure that all respondents experience the same interview process. The schedule will typically contain the introductory comments to be made by the interviewer, a list of the exact questions (and response options) to be presented (in order and verbatim) in the interview, a list of the authorized probes and follow-ups for any open-ended questions, and a space for writing in the answers to open-ended questions.

This scripting, of course, can make the standardized interview feel unnatural to the respondent. The burden is on the interviewer to keep the whole process engaging and informative. Once again, then, we see the importance of the interviewer's social skills. The initial rapport established between the interviewer and the respondent will certainly help in keeping the exchange natural. Active listening (even to closed-ended responses) is also an essential strategy.

Covering Sensitive Topics

While the personal touch of the interview is perhaps its greatest strength, it can be a distinct disadvantage under some circumstances. Covering sensitive or threatening topics can be quite challenging in personal interviews. Respondents may resist talking about matters they consider too private or personal: sexual behaviors, family finances, parental disciplinary practices, etc. Respondents might also be tempted to provide **normative responses** – i.e., answering questions in a socially desirable way. The first line of defense against these problems is good rapport. Having trust in the interviewer can help the respondents navigate their way through difficult topics. Discussion of sensitive topics can also be facilitated by carefully matching interviewers and interviewees: e.g., have men interview men, women interview women, age-mates interview age-mates, minorities interview minorities, etc. Matching has been shown to be particularly effective in combating normative responses. Finally, another effective strategy for covering sensitive topics is to change the format of the information exchange. When it comes time to cover threatening topics, the researcher can hand the respondent a self-administered form that contains all sensitive questions. The respondent can then answer the questions privately and return the form in a sealed envelope. This technique has been employed successfully in the GSS for questions on personal sexual behaviors (Smith 1992).

 ## Phone Home

An extremely popular variation on the one-on-one personal interview is the next best thing to "being there" – the telephone interview. This technology dependent technique sees the interviewer questioning respondents by phone and recording their answers (often with the assistance of computers). Reliance on telephone interviewing has increased dramatically in the last few decades, especially in the areas of market, political, and public opinion research (Smith 1990).

There is much to recommend telephone interviews. Telephone interviewing is much more economical than personal interviews, costing anywhere from one-third to one-tenth the cost of an in-person interview.

Telephone interviews are a relatively fast research option. As shown by public opinion polling, telephone interviewing can give us almost instant feedback on the public's reactions to national or world events. Phone interviewing can be set up so that computers randomly generate phone numbers. In this way, respondents are able to provide answers under conditions of total anonymity. Computers can also assist in the verbatim recording of respondents' answers. Lastly, phone interviews can be less intrusive or threatening than in-person interviews. For respondents, letting someone "into" their home via the phone is easier and less risky than opening the front door to a stranger. Similarly, telephone interviewing holds a safety appeal for the *interviewer* as well. Conducting phone interviews in high crime areas is a safer option than going door to door for in-person interviews.

On the other hand, telephone interviewing has some clear weaknesses. While phones may make it easier for us to "reach out and touch" someone, contact is not as easy as it seems. Relying on telephone directories, for instance, will give us a rather biased sampling frame (list of members in our research population). Think about it a minute – what numbers will never make it into our samples? If we use telephone directories to generate samples, residences without phones and those with unlisted numbers will never make it into the sample.[2] Due to the limitations of telephone directories, many researchers will employ some form of computer generated random digit dialing (RDD) to select numbers for telephone interviews. RDD overcomes the problem of unlisted numbers in directories, but it also produces many unacceptable numbers – e.g., out of service and business numbers. For every five or six numbers dialed, the researcher may well find that only one connects with a residential target.

Reaching a working number does not guarantee connecting with the right party. Phone answering machines and busy lifestyles all but assure that interviewers must be prepared to make many call backs (up to 20) before they reach the targeted party. And of course, *reaching* the right party does not in itself guarantee an interview. Especially in these days of

2 A very famous example of the dangers of working with such restricted lists is the 1936 *Literary Digest* poll concerning the Roosevelt vs. Landon presidential election. The *Literary Digest* used telephone directories and automobile ownership lists to generate a sample of voters. The poll predicted that Landon would win the election in a landslide. In fact, Roosevelt had a landslide victory. How did the *Digest* get it so wrong? An upper-class bias was produced in their sampling technique – only the wealthiest Americans in 1936 owned phones and automobiles. Poor Americans were not included in the *Digest* poll and poor Americans were solidly behind Roosevelt and his New Deal.

aggressive telemarketing, people may be less inclined to cooperate with *any* unsolicited phone calls. Not surprisingly then, phone interviews have a lower response rate than in-person interviews.

Because of the limitations imposed by the less personal phone exchange, telephone interviews must be rather short and uncomplicated – getting answers to in-depth, open-ended questions is particularly challenging. It is harder for phone interviewers to maintain control over the interview process. During phone exchanges, other people or activities in the home environment can easily distract respondents. And at any point in a phone interview, the respondent might decide the interview has lasted long enough and simply terminate it by hanging up the phone. Finally, telephone interviews present a certain "coverage problem." While over 90% of American homes have phones, ownership nonetheless varies considerably by a number of factors – e.g., income level: only 75% of the lowest income households own phones while ownership rises to over 97% in the top income households (Smith 1990). Depending on the focus of the interview, these coverage differences could bias the results of phone surveys.

The More the Merrier: Focus Groups

You should now appreciate that there is a significant difference between questionnaires and interviews. The interview is a data collection technique that is dependent on *social interaction* – the give and take between the interviewer and interviewee. There is one special type of interview situation – the focus group – that fully recognizes the value of social interaction *per se* as an important source of data, insight, and understanding. **Focus groups** are guided group discussions of selected topics. With this technique, the researcher will assemble approximately six to twelve people for the specific purpose of discussing a common concern, issue, event, program, or policy. Advocates of focus groups maintain that the social interaction between group members will produce a dynamic and insightful exchange of information that would not be possible in any one-on-one interview situation. The give and take of the focus group exchange gives the researcher a chance to learn more about *what* people think of the topic at hand as well as to learn more about *why* they think as they do. The insight generated by focus groups makes them rather valuable tools for a variety of research purposes: market research, political analysis, and evaluation research.

While focus groups are decidedly different from the traditional one-on-one interview, both techniques are similar in their dependence on talk. Focus groups only work if respondents agree to talk. Indeed, it is the give and take, the point-counterpoint between group members that is critical to providing insight into the process of constructing viewpoints on various issues, attitudes, positions, etc. As is true for traditional interviews, certain social skills are required of the focus group moderator. Since the special contribution of focus groups is attributed to the dynamics of the group, the moderator has a special burden to facilitate group interaction. A particularly tricky dilemma faced by the moderator is to "run" the focus group without imposing his or her own viewpoint on the group. The moderator must guide discussion without overly directing it. In general, lower levels of moderator involvement are usually adopted in more exploratory focus groups. Higher levels of involvement are called for when seeking answers to specific questions or when testing specific research hypotheses.

In guiding focus group discussions, the moderator must be ready to play two roles: an expressive and an instrumental role. In the **expressive** role, the moderator will attend to the socio-emotional expressions of the group and closely attend to the content of the discussion – treating all participants as equals and keeping the tone of the discussion friendly and engaging. In the **instrumental** role, the moderator must make sure that the ground rules for the group are known and honored by all. The moderator, for instance, will inform the group that all opinions are valuable, that no one should dominate the discussion, that cross-talking or verbal put-downs will not be allowed. In fulfilling one's instrumental duties, the moderator will also take care to strategically place focus group members around the discussion table: dominants should be seated immediately next to the moderator while shy individuals should be seated where it is easiest to maintain a direct line of eye-contact with the moderator. (Decisions about dominant or shy group members are made during a period of planned small talk that should precede the start of the focus group session.) As part of the instrumental role, the moderator will also be sure that the research agenda is followed and that the group stays on schedule.

In his work *Talking Politics,* Gamson (1992) employed focus groups to better understand how working-class people come to form their opinions on political issues. His comments on running the groups are quite informative about focus groups in particular and about interviewing in general:

To encourage conversation rather than a facilitator-centered group inter-view, the facilitator was instructed to break off eye contact with the speaker as early as politeness allowed and to look to others ... when someone finished a comment. We relied mainly on two facilitators, both women, matching their race with that of the participants ... If a discussion got off track, the facilitator moved it back on by going to the next question on the list. But we encouraged a conservative approach to what was considered off the track since, in negotiating meaning on any given issue, participants typically brought in other related issues ... Once most people had re-sponded to a question and no one else sought the floor, the facilitator moved to the next question on the list. These follow-up questions also served as a reminder of the issue in the event that a discussion had rambled. (Gamson 1992: 17–18)

Karen Cerulo used focus groups as well in *Deciphering Violence: The Cognitive Structure of Right and Wrong* (1998). Her book examines media portrayals of violence and the varying effects such stories have on the reading and viewing public. Cerulo contends that focus groups are especially well suited to studies addressing culture and cognition.

Focus Groups provide a unique research vehicle. The technique is designed to capture "minds at work" as participants evaluate particular stimulus materials ... focus group interactions encourage subjects to air, reflect, and reason their views aloud. Each session becomes a self-reflexive exercise that is unlikely to emerge from other data-gathering techniques. Further, focus groups are structured such that a study's participants interact *with each other* as opposed to interacting one-on-one with an investigator. In this way, researchers avoid the very real risk of channeling subject responses. The method places the greatest emphasis on the subjects' point of view. (Cerulo 1998: 112–13)

Training Issues

By now it should be clear to the reader that interviewing (one-on-one and group) requires special social skills. Researchers are well advised to select their interviewers carefully. Good interviewers must be motivated indi-viduals who are willing to hit the pavement (or work the phones) in order to secure interviews. They must be flexible people who are willing to work around respondents' schedules. (This often translates to scheduling interviews for evenings or weekends.) Interviewers must come across as nonjudgmental individuals who can inspire the trust of respon-dents. Good interviewers must be able to think on their feet and quickly determine the correct "tone" or style to adopt for any given interview. They must hone their sales skills in order to sell both the project and themselves to potential respondents. On this last point, interviewers must understand the importance of first impressions – good first impressions can be the difference between respondent cooperation and refusal.

Good social skills are essential but successful interviewing also requires specific training. Despite how simple it may look for hosts of late-night talk shows, a good interview does not just happen. Part of the reason that interviewing is the most expensive data collection technique is the fact that training good interviewers is time-consuming and costly. Talk, at least as a data collection tool, is not really cheap.

The interviewer should have a good understanding of the research project – its purpose and how the guide/schedule serves that purpose. For this reason, some might argue that those who are in charge of research projects (PIs – Principal Investigators) would make the best interviewers. In terms of commitment and knowledge of the project, the PI has an advantage. But there is a possible downside to using PIs as interviewers. PIs may lack the social skills that are key to a good interview. Furthermore, their intense involvement with the project could be a source of bias. PIs may be more prone than others with less of a "stake" in the research project to hear what they want or need to hear in the interview process. Even if the PI is up to the job, it is often a practical necessity, especially on large projects, to engage several people as interviewers. Consequently, research projects will frequently resort to working with hired interviewers who are specifically trained for the tasks at hand.

As part of the training process, it is a good idea to provide interviewers with a crash course in methods. They need to understand the basics of sampling and the importance of a random selection process. They need to understand the importance of an operational definition and measurement validity. This insight should help stave off any temptations to change or modify the interview guide. Trainees also need to appreciate how interviewers themselves can introduce bias into the measurement process via their reactions to and recordings of respondents' answers. In qualitative interviewing projects, interviewers must learn how to become active listeners. Trainees must learn when and how to use effective probes. They must learn how to rein in respondents who are wandering off the subject or pursuing irrelevant tangents.

For more standardized projects, interviewers must be trained in how to faithfully execute interview schedules while maintaining enthusiasm. For both interview conditions, the interviewer must also master the social skills that will help them establish the necessary rapport with respondents. Interviewers must also pay attention to how they bring an interview to a close. They need to strike the right balance between abrupt endings and long good-byes. Interviewers should also learn the value of "debriefing" themselves. Once interviewers have left the actual location of the interview, they should write down any interesting thoughts or observations regarding the interview. Such notes can prove quite helpful in the analysis phase.

Training should always involve some practice sessions. Running through several mock interviews is an essential preparation step. These practice interviews will help interviewers get comfortable with the questions, identify potential trouble spots, and prepare acceptable clarifications. It is also a good idea for interviewers to commit to memory the opening portions of interview guides or schedules. With enough practice, the interviewer should be able to conduct a smooth-flowing, natural-sounding interview.

Tools of the Trade

Despite the clear importance of the human touch and social skills in conducting successful interviews, the interviewer is well advised to acknowledge the critical "supporting" role of technology in the interview process. No matter how diligent interviewers believe they can be in recording respondent's answers, they should always consider making audiotapes of interview sessions. This step merely acknowledges the importance of faithfully capturing the data without introducing any errors. Interviewers who rely exclusively on note taking during the interview run the risk of distorting information because of selective or faulty memories and/or poor recording skills. Furthermore, the attention and care the interviewer gives to recording duties may come at the expense of attentive listening. Interviewers who are worried about "getting it all down" may not be so ready to pursue strategic probes and follow-ups. Given these considerations, the best line of advice is to plan on taping interview sessions. That said, the final decision to tape or not to tape must rest with the respondent. If the respondent is not comfortable with taping, it should not be done. Taping under protest is unlikely to yield a productive interview exchange.

Regardless of whether or not interviews are taped, the interviewer should *always* take extensive notes during the session. The best advice is to act as if no recorder is running. With this approach the researcher will always have a written record of the interview session. If an audiotape exists as well, it can be used to amend or supplement the notes taken during the interview. Written verbatim transcripts are particularly important in unstructured interviews since the respondent's exact answers constitute the data that the researcher will analyze. In short, written transcripts are our data sets. There is no justification for skipping this step of data preparation. Indeed, experienced interviewers know all too well that the presence of a transcript greatly facilitates the job of analysis. Transcripts can be read and re-read and compared and scrutinized in the service of thorough analysis.

The Final Word

As the preceding review indicates, talk is an important research tool. It is also a versatile one. With the selection of in-person interviews, phone interviews, and group interviews the researcher has the ability to custom-fit the element of talk to the research job at hand. Whether the research task is exploratory or explanatory, quantitative or qualitative, simple or complex, the interview may well be the right way to talk your self into a good study.

Expanding the Essentials

The Survey Research Center at the University of California at Berkeley offers a series of tips on telephone sampling at the following site: http://srcweb.berkeley.edu/res/tsamp.html.

Useful information on focus groups (i.e., planning, running, analyzing results, etc.) can be found in David Morgan's *Focus Groups as Qualitative Research* (1996) and in Richard Krueger and Mary Anne Casey's *Focus Groups: A Practical Guide for Applied Research* (2000).

No one who is seriously considering an interview project should proceed without reading John and Lyn Lofland's *Analyzing Social Settings* (1995).

Exercises

1   Using the steps outlined in the chapter, devise an unstructured guide for use in a study of (a) long distance commuting marriages or (b) participation in x-treme sports.

2   Tape two to three nights each of two competing late night "talk" shows. Critique the interview styles and skills of each show's host.

3   Conduct an online search for job-hunting interview skills. Would the tips work well in a research setting?

11 Watch and Learn: Field Research

Think for a moment. What's the best way to *really* know what it means to be President of the United States, a New York City firefighter, or a cast member of a Broadway production? If you're thinking you'd like to spend some time with these people and follow them through their daily routines, you're thinking like a field researcher. Those dedicated to field research see much wisdom in pursuing the advice of "walking a mile in someone's shoes" in order to know something about their life. In essence, this "put yourself in my place" way of knowing is the heart of field research. In pursuing this data collection strategy, we take our study to the natural "field" or setting of our research topic and we literally watch (and listen to) what happens.

Of all the data collection techniques available to the social researcher, field studies may have the most intuitive appeal. After all, field research is essentially about people-watching. It entails spending time observing the normal or natural flow of social life in some specific social/cultural setting. To some degree, all of us have engaged in such observations at one time or another. People-watching is a good way to pass the time and/or amuse ourselves during long layovers at airports or long lines at motor vehicle agencies. Few of us, however, have taken our people-watching as seriously as the field researcher. **Field research** involves an extremely systematic and rigorous study of everyday life. Field researchers are committed to long-term observation. To maximize their understanding of some social phenomenon, they will actively seek out interactions with specific people or in specific places and they will intentionally vary the times and days of their field experiences. Their observations will be conducted in the interest of answering specific research questions. Field researchers are also committed to a full documentation of their observations by recording complete field notes.

Location, Location, Location ... and More

To fully appreciate field research, we must view it with an eye to two separate research endeavors. First, field research entails doing our research in a *certain place or setting* – i.e., the natural setting of the phenomenon being studied. Our field studies may take us to the halls of Congress, an urban police precinct, or to a corner of a local neighborhood. Field research also entails a *certain way of knowing* – i.e., knowing that comes from immersing ourselves in the social world of our research setting. It is this feature of field research that sees the researcher trying to understand the meaning of events from the perspective of those being studied. While both of these features are defining ones for field studies, they are also challenging ones.

In *entering* the natural setting of some social phenomenon, the researcher must confront access problems. Not all settings will welcome the researcher with open arms. Successful entry requires the researcher to do some background homework about the setting and its local culture. The researcher might actually need the assistance of a gatekeeper for gaining access. **Gatekeepers** are individuals who can give the researcher legitimate access to the field. In entering the field, the researcher must also take great care not to disrupt its "naturalness." Indeed, if the setting significantly changes by virtue of the researcher's presence, the purpose of our research is seriously undermined. This problem of disrupting the routine is known as **reactive effects** in field research and it demands some careful attention in the planning stages of our research.

In *immersing* oneself in the field, researchers must decide the level of involvement they will assume. To what extent will they participate in the setting? They must also decide whether or not they will disclose their research agenda. Will their research activities be open or covert? The following levels of involvement – complete observer, observer as participant, participant as observer, and complete participant – each take somewhat different stands on the involvement and disclosure issues. All levels have both advantages and disadvantages.

Complete observer   In entering the field as a complete observer, the researcher minimizes his or her immersion in the social phenomenon being investigated. This strategy is really one of *non-participatory* observation. The researcher tries to remain as detached as possible from the situation being observed. Complete observation may be accomplished via some kind of hidden observation (e.g., watching children play through a two-way mirror) or via simple detachment (observing hospital emergency room behaviors by sitting in the waiting area). Ideally, field subjects will be totally unaware of the ongoing research efforts. Consequently, researchers who hope to keep the reactive effects of field research to a minimum frequently adopt the complete observer role. The shortcoming of this strategy, however, is somewhat apparent. Critics argue that the distance and detachment implied in this role limit the amount of insight or understanding that can be achieved by the researcher. Some would also argue that any kind of hidden or disguised observation raises ethical dilemmas since research subjects are denied the chance to give their informed consent to the research project. Sometimes the choice of complete observation is a forced one given the clear boundary between researcher and subjects. Consider for instance, Barbara Myerhoff's (1989) observation study of a senior citizen's group in California or Barrie Thorne's (2001) study of children's playgroups. In both instances, natural age differences precluded the researchers from adopting a decidedly participatory stance.

Observer as participant With this level of involvement, the researcher acknowledges his or her research agenda and participates to a limited degree in the field. By way of example, you might envision a researcher studying a weight watchers group who tells the members about the research project and who attends weekly meetings but doesn't commit to the dieting process. This strategy is more ethically defensible than the complete observer but it has a drawback. In going public about one's research agenda and in limiting one's involvement, field interaction may be strained and once again insight might be limited or superficial. There is also a greater chance that this level of involvement will encounter stronger reactive effects. Still, there are many field projects where the researcher's involvement is necessarily limited. For a good example of such restricted involvement, see Anderson and Calhoun's work on male street prostitutes (2001). The authors readily acknowledge that "learning from doing" was not a legitimate option for them.

Participant as observer The participant as observer becomes fully involved with the group or setting under study and is totally open about his or her research agenda. In entering the field this way, the researcher is trying to maximize participation while maintaining the ethical high ground. Initially, there may be some concern that the known research agenda will encourage a reactive effect. Sincere involvement, however, can effectively offset these effects. Many researchers who have adopted this level of involvement maintain that, with time and effort, they come to enjoy full acceptance in the field. A good illustration of this level of involvement is found in Mitchell Duneier's work (2001) on New York

City street vendors. Duneier devoted considerable time to "clearing" his research interest and project with other key vendors before he ventured into street sales himself. Indeed, Duneier observed street vendors for two years and completed a book manuscript about the everyday life of vendors before deciding to start his project anew. He felt his work needed "more" than observation alone was providing and eventually he ventured into working street sales himself.

Complete participant   In adopting the complete participant role, the researcher *appears* to be a genuine participant in the group or setting being observed. In effect, researchers acting as complete participants are involved in *covert* research – they only let research subjects see them as participants, not as researchers. This level of involvement is often justified as necessary for gaining access to controversial or illicit research settings. Consider Laud Humphreys' (1969) study of tearooms – public rest rooms used for homosexual encounters. Humphreys posed as a "watchqueen" at rest rooms in public parks in order to observe fleeting homosexual acts between strangers. (Watchqueens are lookouts who warn participants of approaching police.) Humphreys defended his covert tactics on the grounds that a "declared" researcher would never have been permitted to observe this activity. Following the same line of reasoning, this level of involvement is also pursued in the interest of lessening reactive effects. While it is true that a covert researcher *should not* destroy the natural dynamics of the field under investigation, it is nonetheless true that the complete participant will inevitably affect the social setting. As apparently genuine group members, complete participants will influence group interactions. Perhaps more than any other level of involvement, the complete participant also runs the risk of "going native" and abandoning their scientific stance. The full immersion necessary to achieve complete participation could very well encourage a loss of objectivity on the part of the researcher. Lastly, since complete participation is a covert activity, critics fault it on ethical grounds.

Fieldwork Tasks

The most basic task of field research is to provide descriptions of the social realm or setting being studied. This description process is not as easy or straightforward as it may sound. Indeed, the biggest challenge is often that of deciding just what the researcher should describe. Description is necessarily a selective and a partial process. In large measure, the process of looking and recording will be guided by the researcher's theoretical and conceptual assumptions. It will also be influenced by the researcher's own history, biography, and training.

The descriptions provided should be **thick descriptions** (Geertz 1973). Thick descriptions are highly detailed accounts of what the researcher has experienced in the field. In providing thick descriptions the researcher is trying to explicate the connection between behaviors or events and their contexts. A concentrated effort is made to identify the *subjective* meanings people attribute to events. The researcher tries to describe social life from an "inside perspective" and to adopt what Matza calls an "appreciative" stance (1969). In so doing, the researcher strives to understand and communicate not only *what* happens but also *how field subjects themselves interpret and understand what happens*. The following quote from Goffman about his year of field work at St Elizabeths Hospital (a federal mental institution) in Washington, DC speaks to this point:

> My immediate object in doing field work at St. Elizabeths was to try to learn about the social world of the hospital inmate, as this world is subjectively experienced by him ... I passed the day with patients ... It was then and still is my belief that any group of persons – prisoners, primitives, pilots, or patients – develop a life of their own that becomes meaningful, reasonable, and normal once you get close to it, and that a good way to learn about any of these worlds is to submit oneself in the company of the members to the daily round of petty contingencies to which they are subject. (Goffman 1961: ix–x)

Description is the *initial* task of field research. The goal of providing thick descriptions of field events and behaviors is to transcend particular events and identify general patterns or regularities of social life. Consequently, field research typically has an inductive quality to it that is different from survey research. In survey research, theoretical ideas are often stated and then "tested" via survey questions. In field research, the researcher starts first by closely examining the social world. These observations are then used to inductively arrive at theoretical propositions that are informed by the field observations. In following this inductive path, field research is most often associated with developing or building "grounded theory." As the name implies, grounded theory is "grounded" or based in the setting being studied (Glaser & Strauss 1967).

Another distinctive feature of field research is its ongoing, dynamic approach to data analysis. In survey research, data collection and analysis are separate stages of work: i.e., first we administer our questionnaires and collect our data and then we enter that data into our computers for analysis. Analysis starts only after the data collection phase is complete. In field research, this separation between data collection and analysis doesn't exist. Analysis occurs at all points of the field study. As theoretical "leads" appear in the field, the field researcher is well advised to follow up on them. Theoretical hunches from yesterday may direct our data collection decisions of tomorrow. Analysis is ongoing and can occur as data are collected, recorded, and reflected upon.

Informal Interviews

Observation work is not restricted to what we see. Much understanding is gained by listening to the noises, sounds, talk, and conversations of the field. An important tool for gaining this level of understanding is the **informal interview.** These interviews are usually less structured than the interviews discussed in Chapter 10. This is largely due to the dynamic nature of field studies. The researcher may make an on the spot decision to ask questions as the need or opportunity arises. In the early phases of field research, the informal interview may simply be a series of broad overview or general information questions. As the research progresses, questions will become more focused and specific (Bailey 1996). As the study progresses, informal interviews are also likely to be supplemented by intensive, in-depth interviews with key members of the field.

Carol Bailey (1996) notes that a key difference between formal and informal interviews is that the latter are really *reciprocal exchanges.* There's a give and take between the researcher and field members – both engage in the sharing of ideas, information, emotions, etc. This reciprocal sharing is particularly important in field studies because it helps establish and maintain rapport. It also helps to eliminate the typical hierarchical nature of relationships between researchers and respondents. Informal interviews are also interested in capturing the context of talk and conversation. In this way, they help to advance the cause of thick description.

Notes

While field research is a rather dynamic undertaking, there is one essential constant in such studies: field notes. In survey research, our data winds up in the form of a data file – i.e., a block of numbers that represent respondents' answers to survey questions. In contrast, the data file of field research consists of recorded **field notes** – i.e., the words or images used to record one's field observations. Our research findings or conclusions will be based on a careful analysis of what it is we have logged in our field notes. Anyone who isn't interested in faithfully recording field notes should *not* be doing field research. No field notes, no data, no go. It's as simple as that.

In the best of all possible worlds, field notes consist of a faithful recording of what we observe while in the field. In effect, then, field notes depend on our ability to "pay attention" – on our ability to watch, listen, smell, feel, and sense what's going on around us. How much of what we observe should be recorded? As much as possible – in field research more is better than less. Given its dynamic nature, it may be weeks or even months before field researchers discover the significance of their observations. Consequently, the more details recorded in one's field notes, the better one's documentation of insights or conclusions.

In light of the importance of logging field notes, you might now be thinking that researchers must enter the field with recording equipment in hand. And in a sense, this is true. Field researchers would never want to be in the field without their powers of observation "activated" or without a trusty notebook and pen. Yet, the actual recording of field information can be a tricky undertaking. Recall the point made earlier: field researchers are loath to do anything that might disrupt the naturalness of the setting being observed. Consequently, making the recording process an obvious or explicit one is not a good idea. It is not unusual, in fact it is rather typical, for the actual recording of full field notes to be delayed until *after* the researcher has left the field. Two of the premier authorities on field research, John and Lyn Lofland (1995), recommend that field researchers master two techniques that will make note-taking as unobtrusive yet as accurate as possible: the taking of mental notes and jotted notes.

With the practice of **mental notes**, the field observer tries to mentally capture or "freeze" a moment or event. The researcher makes a concerted effort to draw as detailed a mental picture as possible for later recording. Taking **jotted notes** is the practice of recording short but evocative words or phrases that will serve as cues to fuller ruminations once one has left the field. To minimize any disruption of the natural flow, jotted notes are best recorded as inconspicuously as possible, A researcher observing the interactions in a neighborhood bar might make jotted notes while appearing to doodle on napkins or beer coasters. The idea behind both mental notes and jotted notes is to develop skills that will support the practice of recording fuller notes once the researcher has left the field.

While the exact content of field notes will inevitably vary from one study to the next, there are essentially five elements that should be included in all notes (Lofland & Lofland 1995):

- a basic record of each observation period,
- afterthoughts and previously forgotten observations,
- ideas for analysis,
- the researcher's personal impressions and/or emotional reactions,
- notes or ideas for future observations.

Basic record The basic record offers a running, chronological account of all research activities. It should include a detailed description of both the setting and the people in those settings. In describing settings, particular attention should be given to the exact physical layout of the setting (providing a diagram or photos is a good idea), as well as to the colors, furnishings, and lighting of the setting. If you have any doubts as to the significance of this kind of information, imagine what understanding would be lost if you weren't able to consider how the physical environment of a nursing home or a hospital influences the interactions that take place there. Descriptions of settings should also detail the smells and the sounds of settings. (Again, think of the hospital and the significance of this kind of data.) In addition to describing the physical environment, the basic record should also include a physical and social description of the main players in the field. How many people are there? How do they occupy the space? What do they look like? What information do they communicate to others via their clothing, hairstyles, accessories, or other "props"? How do they behave? What are the lines of interaction between players? Who are the social isolates and the social butterflies? What kind of verbal and nonverbal communication is taking place? Is there a special language of the setting? Particular care should be taken when recording talk and conversation. Lofland and Lofland (1995) recommend developing a system where it is quite clear whether the notes are recording paraphrases vs. exact quotes of others or whether the notes are recording the researcher's own thoughts and reflections. Finally, basic record entries should always include the date and time span of each observation session.

Afterthoughts As hard as we might try, it is unlikely that we will faithfully record everything from an observation session immediately afterwards. Sometimes we will find ourselves remembering events or episodes at a later time. These lapses should not go unrecorded. Instead they should become part of the record as soon as we recall them. As the events are recalled, care should be taken to fill in details from the original time line.

Ideas for analysis   While in the process of writing up field notes, the field researcher will surely have some flashes of insight into possible patterns emerging in the data. These ideas should be recorded as they occur and reviewed as observations continue. These insights might prove to be rich fodder for more rigorous analysis.

Personal impressions and emotional reactions   Recording one's personal feelings may seem at odds with the objective mission of scientific research. Yet, making such notes part of the record is what allows the researcher to consider precisely how our subjective states may taint or color our "objective" reading of situations. The tone that characterizes a given event may be more a function of the researcher's mood than a genuine aspect of the field experience being described.

Notes for future observations   This last standard feature of field notes might best be thought of as a running "to do" list. As the researcher concludes the latest set of notes, she or he should explicitly list those things that still need to be done in future sessions: i.e., interviews with key players, observations of special events, first-hand encounters of field ceremonies or rituals, etc. Items that remain from previous lists should be carried over onto subsequent lists. As one's field work progresses, this "to do" list should grow smaller and smaller. Indeed, the size of the list may be taken as a rough indicator of the time line for a field project. When there's relatively little left to do, the researcher should be preparing to leave the field and devoting more attention to final analysis and write-ups.

The commitment to field notes must be strong. The time delay between observation and recording sessions should be kept to a minimum (we should never let more than a day go by between sessions). The Loflands have suggested that for any one hour of observation, one should be prepared to record up to 13 pages of notes (Lofland & Lofland 1984). While others may find this 13 to 1 ratio extreme, it is still widely accepted that one should spend more time writing up one's field notes than one actually spent in the field. If all of this sounds like more work than you care to do, then stand forewarned that field research may not be the data collection strategy for you.

Files

As we stated earlier, the content of field notes constitutes the raw material for data analysis. But given the fact that field notes are likely to yield pages and pages and pages for analysis, how should the field researcher proceed? One essential technique is the creation of files. There are essentially four different types of files that enable the researcher to transform field notes into meaningful and useful categories.

Chronological files organize the full record of all thick descriptions in a series of folders ordered along a logical time line. For instance, the researcher might create a series of folders organized by each week of observation. These files should help the researcher "see" the big picture of the research project. They should also help the researcher "see" any change over time. Finally, chronological files, since they contain a full listing of all thick descriptions, should help the researcher see all events in context.

Analytical files are created in order to help the researcher make sense of the data. As indicated in the previous section on field notes, ideas for analysis should be recorded for each observation period. These ideas or hunches or themes that might be productive leads for analysis should subsequently each receive their own folders. The folders would then be filled with all *pertinent* entries from the field notes. Unlike the chronological file, the analytical files will be "cut and paste" files. That is, these files will not be a source of the full record of observations. Rather, they will only contain notes that illustrate the idea or theme of a particular folder. While the specific field experience will certainly suggest some topics for analytical files, folders are often established for main concepts of sociology: norms, roles, values, conflict, interactions, groups, etc.

Mundane files organize all the information from your field notes into the most obvious categories. Bailey (1996) suggests that these files consist of the "people, places, events, and things" of one's field observations. The field researcher should consider establishing a separate folder for each major player in the field. Major events or field episodes should have their own folder. If observations varied by morning, afternoon, and evening hours, each time period should have its own mundane folder. Like analytical files, mundane files will consist of "cut and paste" entries – i.e., pertinent entries will be culled from the entire field record and filed in the relevant folder. The idea behind mundane files is to create a system that will allow the researcher to access all information about major categories as quickly as possible.

Methodological files would contain any and all notes about one's research procedures. Notes on how the researcher selected the field site, decided on observation periods, selected key informants, made sampling decisions, etc. should all be found in these files. These files will prove most relevant during the write-up phase of research when one needs to justify or explain or elaborate on various methodological strategies and decisions.

The creation of files, like the recording of notes, deserves the most serious attention of the field researcher. The good news is that in creating files, the researcher is actively involved in the analysis of field data. In identifying the various folders and thinking about the appropriate placement of entries, the researcher is doing the work of analysis. *Understanding* what one has seen in the field *requires* the researcher to engage the data in this way. In a very real sense, the more the researcher puts into field notes and files, the more she or he will get out of them. Nothing ventured, nothing gained.

The Validity of Field Research

If you are reading this book from beginning to end, you may now be wondering how field research measures up on the various validity issues: measurement, causal and external.

For some, there is no better way of empirically documenting the world around us than through natural observational methods. As the opening paragraphof this chapter suggests, much understanding can come from going to your research subjects and spending time in their terrain. Measuring parental love by watching parent–child interactions over time and under a variety of circumstances may offer a degree of accuracy that can't be matched by questions or indexes designed to measure parental love "on paper." And because of its extended time commitment and its attention to details, field work is strong on some of the essential ingredients for the process-analysis of idiographic causal research. Field researchers are present to witness the unfolding of events and outcomes. And while some might be quick to give field research low grades in terms of external validity, such judgments are really misguided. Indeed, by making careful sampling decisions – i.e., by increasing the number or the variety of observations made in one's study – the field researcher may be able to make some informed generalizations. Of course, the accuracy of such generalizations can be directly tested by careful replication. By repeating one field study in other settings or with other groups, the researcher can directly address the generalizability of a given set of research findings.

Expanding the Essentials

To find more information about qualitative research, visit Norris's QualPage on the web. In particular, see the link to "Qualitative Data Analysis" for a series of options for analysis of field data: http://www.ualberta.ca/~jrnorris/qual.html.

For another web site containing qualitative research information/links go to: http://www.communicationresearch.org/qualitative.htm.

Much will be gained by visiting the field via one of the great works. You might try William Foote Whyte's *Street Corner Society* (1955). After reading this classic, you might then see how the work has held up over the years by reading the April 1992 issue of the *Journal of Contemporary Ethnography*. This issue contains essays that offer critiques of Whyte's work as well as responses to those critiques.

For a study that may ring closer to home, you might also want to read Jay MacLeod's *Ain't No Making It: Aspirations and Attainment in a Low-Income Neighborhood* (1995). This work shows how a good research project can be born in the classroom, as MacLeod initiated the field study to complete a research requirement.

For a short but very informative introduction to field research, see Patricia and Peter Adler's "The Promise and Pitfalls of Going Into the Field" (2003).

Anyone planning on doing a field research project would be well served by reading Carol Bailey's work, *A Guide to Field Research* (1996) and John and Lyn Lofland's *Analyzing Social Settings* (1995).

Exercises

1 Practice your hand at taking field notes by providing a detailed description of a location you "know" but have never really thoroughly described (e.g., classroom, dorm room, family kitchen, neighborhood bar). Be sure to pay attention to all the pertinent categories that go into good field notes (description of physical layout, descriptions of major players and their interactions, etc.). What kinds of things did you discover once you started "paying attention"?

2 Find a public setting where you can practice your hand at field observation. Plan on spending two 30-minute sessions in the setting.

In one of the sessions, force yourself to take only *mental* notes – i.e., do not use any obvious recording tools. In the second session, go prepared with pen and paper and take notes while in the field. Afterwards, critique the two sessions. In particular, focus on how the presence/absence of explicit note taking influenced the quality of your notes as well as the quality of the interactions in the field.

12 Getting Organized: Descriptive Statistics

At this point, we are nearing the end of this brief introduction to social research methods. One major transition topic (or is it terrifying topic?) must be considered: social statistics. In this chapter, we will review the topic of descriptive statistics. In the next chapter we will kick it up a notch and introduce you to inferential statistics.

How Did We Get to this Point?

So far we have devoted most of our attention to the systematic collection of information. We have considered in some detail the issue of measurement as well as the major tools or techniques the social sciences employ in the name of measurement: e.g., questionnaires, interviews, and field research. In trying to make the connection to statistics, it is helpful to recall the definition of measurement offered in Chapter 4: measurement refers to *the process by which we attach numbers to the values of variables.* As we learned in Chapter 4, numbers don't always mesh well with the values of our variables. Indeed, we distinguish between various levels of measurement to indicate the "fit" (or misfit) between numbers and the values of variables we are measuring.

When the numbers we use merely identify qualitative differences between the values, we have a nominal measure (e.g., the variable gender where we attach the number 1 to the value male and the number 2 to the value female). When numbers indicate a rank ordering to the values of our variables, we have an ordinal level of measurement (e.g., measuring one's interest in politics as 1 = low, 2 = medium, 3 = high). When the numbers attached to the values indicate equal distance between values, we have achieved the interval level of measurement (e.g., consider measuring the daily high temperature with a Fahrenheit thermometer: the difference between 32 degrees and 33 degrees is the same as the difference between 82 degrees and 83 degrees). When the numbers we use in the measurement process are actual "counts" of some variable, we have achieved the ratio level of measurement (e.g., measuring one's community spirit by the actual number of times one has attended a community event in the past three months).

We take the time to review levels of measurement here because it helps to clearly establish the role of statistics in social research. (If you are hazy on any of the above, you may want to revisit the materials in Chapter 4 as well as parts of Chapter 9.) In the simplest sense, **statistics** can be thought of as *a set of techniques used to analyze the results of measurement.* Or to say it another way, *statistics are a set of tools for organizing data.*

What's data? **Data** is what we produce through the measurement process. When we work with statistics we are dealing with data, or more specifically with *information,* that has been *"numerically transformed."*[1] Look again at the preceding paragraph for a concrete example. Say on a survey we collect information about respondents' gender. Via the measurement process, we numerically transform this information when we record all gender data for our respondents as either a number 1 for males or a number 2 for females. Similarly, respondents' interest in politics may be reported as low, medium, or high. We take this information gathered from our respondents and create numerical "data" out of it when we record a response of low interest as a number 1, a response of medium interest as a number 2, and a response of high interest as a number 3. When we have numerically transformed all the information we have collected, we are left with a **data set.** It is this data set – this matrix of numbers – that we want to analyze. Once we have a data set, it's time to talk statistics.

For those readers who may feel intimidated by the word statistics, it is worth repeating the following: **Statistics** is merely a set of tools for organizing data. We mislead ourselves if we think they are anything more than this. They are not the goal of research; they are not truth (ergo the popular adage about levels of deceit: lies, damned lies, and statistics).[2] They are simply tools to be used in the service of research.

---

1   To be sure, not all data is numerically transformed. Field research or intensive interviewing can yield data that takes the form of words or images. For statistical analysis, however, our data must be expressed numerically.

2   The actual saying ("There are lies, damned lies and statistics") is usually attributed to Mark Twain, but Twain himself attributed it to Benjamin Disraeli.

And as is true with most tools, they really can make our work easier **if** ...
if we know which tools are right for the job. Attacking a Phillips head
screw with a hammer or even a flat head screwdriver is misguided. So
too is trying to open a corked wine bottle with a can opener. Similarly,
using the wrong statistical tool for the data at hand will produce unsatis-
factory results.

Getting Organized

Descriptive statistics are a set of techniques that organize, summarize,
and provide a general overview of our data. Perhaps the most basic way
of getting such an overview is with the tool known as the frequency
distribution. The **frequency distribution** provides an ordered listing
(from high to low) of the values of a variable along with a tally of the
number of times each value occurs. The frequency distribution allows us
to take an unwieldy set of scores and present them in a more manageable,
coherent form.

In creating frequency distributions, we usually group values of continuous variables into class intervals or ranges of values (e.g., 0–4, 5–9,
10–14, etc.). This is an important facet of getting organized. A set of 100
different values can be reduced to a more manageable number of ten 10-
point intervals (0–9, 10–19, 20-9, 30–9, etc.) or to five 20-point intervals
(0–19, 20–39, 40–59, etc.). In deciding on the size of the intervals, it's best
to use ranges that are easy to digest and that help reinforce meaningful
differences in values. Intervals of 5, 10, or 20 are commonly used.

Tables 12.1 and 12.2 show the organizing power of a frequency distribution. Table 12.1 shows a set of test scores for a group of 23 students as
they appeared on an alphabetized grade sheet. Table 12.2 shows the
frequency distribution when using a five-point class interval. The
numbers in the frequency column of Table 12.2 tell us just how many
scores fall within each range.

Summarizing Descriptions

Another way to organize data is by offering summaries of it. Such
summaries are the heart and soul of descriptive statistics. You are probably more familiar with summarizing statistics than you may realize.
Think about the last time you got a test back in one of your classes.
Chances are that you or someone in the class asked for feedback on the

Table 12.1   Ungrouped test scores

85	82
88	55
57	86
81	94
65	72
75	77
64	85
87	75
99	79
79	94
59	72
74	

Table 12.2   Frequency distribution, grouped scores

Scores	Frequencies
95–100	1
90–94	2
85–89	5
80–84	2
75–79	5
70–74	3
65–69	1
60–64	1
55–59	3

overall class performance. Generally we want this kind of "big picture" info so that we can put our own test score in perspective. By way of getting the big picture, we usually are interested in knowing the *average* test score. Someone is also likely to ask about the *range* of all scores – what was the highest grade, what was the lowest? In asking for these summaries, we are acknowledging the importance of two important descriptive statistical techniques: measures of central tendency and measures of variation.

Central tendency

Measures of **central tendency** (aka averages) provide us with a kind of statistical shorthand – i.e., they offer *one* number that best represents or summarizes an entire set of scores or values. Three different measures of central tendency are frequently used to describe data: the mean, the median, and the mode. Think about the information you want when exams are returned to you. If you want to know the *arithmetic average* test score, you are requesting the **mean**. If you want to know the score that falls in the middle of all the scores (once they are ordered), you are requesting the **median**. If you want to know the most frequently occurring test score, you are requesting the **mode**.

A **mean** is the *arithmetically derived* average of a set of scores. In saying that the mean is the arithmetic average, we are indicating that some mathematical procedure is involved in its calculation. To calculate the mean, we must *add* all the values in a set of scores together and *divide* that sum by the total number of scores. In our class test example, we would sum the scores for each and every student in the class and divide by the total number of students. The resulting number (quotient) would be the mean or average score for the entire class.

There are three important points for you to remember about the mean. First, the mean is the only measure of central tendency that is influenced by every value in a set of scores. Second, given the way it is calculated, it is totally possible to get a mean value that is different from all of the other scores in a distribution; the mean does not have to be an actual value in a set of scores. Third, given how we calculate the mean as an arithmetic average, the mean turns out to be the number that is the balancing point in a set of values. The distance between the mean *and all the numbers above the mean* is equal to the distance between the mean *and all of the numbers below the mean*. The importance of this last point will become apparent once we move onto the topic of variation.

We can also summarize data by reporting a median or a mode. The median is a "mid-way" measure of central tendency. The **median** summarizes data by identifying the value that falls in the middle of a set of values or scores that are arranged from lowest to highest. With an odd number of values, the calculation of a median is simple – the median is the value that falls smack in the middle of the list.

34, 46, 50, 52, 65
Odd: median = middle value = 50

When we are working with an even number of values, we calculate the median by taking an arithmetic average of the two middle values (i.e., we add the two middle values together and divide them by 2: the resulting number is the median).

34, 46, 50, 52, 65, 68

Even: median = average of two middle scores (50, 52) = 51

The **mode** refers to the most common or the most frequently occurring value in a set of scores. It is the simplest measure of central tendency – it can easily be gleaned from looking at a variable's frequency distribution. Find the value that occurs most often and you've found the mode. For instance, look at Table 12.3 and you'll easily see the mode for the gender composition of the US Senate serving in the 108th Congress 2003–5.

Our choice of mean, median, or mode is really one of finding the right statistical tool for the job. The mode is the *only* appropriate measure of central tendency for *nominal level* data. Remember that the numbers attached to the values of nominal measures are merely *labels* used to distinguish *qualitatively different values*. (In measuring gender, for instance, I might use the number 1 to label the value male and the number 2 to label the value female.) Ergo, any kind of mathematical calculation is off limits with nominal data.[3] The mode doesn't require mathematical calculations; we just need to find the most frequently occurring value to determine the mode. Thus it is the right tool for reporting the central tendency of nominal level data.

The median is the appropriate measure of central tendency when the set of scores we are trying to summarize contain some extreme scores (aka outliers). Extreme scores are those that are markedly different from most of the scores being described. If we calculate a mean under these conditions, the mean will be pulled in the direction of the extreme scores. (Remember, the mean has the distinction of being influenced by *every* value in a set of scores.) When this happens, the mean won't do a good job at representing the entire set of scores. It will be distorted by the

Table 12.3   Gender composition of US Senate, 2003–5

US Senators by gender	Frequency
Male Senators	86
Female Senators	14

3   Think about it: Imagine a group of 20 people – i.e., 10 men and 10 women. To calculate a mean for the variable gender, we would need to add together all the gender values for every member of the group (ten 1s for the men and ten 2s for the women) and divide by 20. This would yield a mean gender of 1.5! This value doesn't make sense when describing our gender data since there are only two acceptable values or labels for gender: 1 for male and 2 for female (or vice versa).

extreme value(s). When confronted with the presence of extreme scores, the median will do a better job of summarizing the data.

The mean is really only appropriate for use with interval and ratio level data. It is only at these levels of measurement that the numbers attached to values of the variables can be treated as "real" numbers. Only real numbers are eligible for mathematical operations like addition and division (the two operations required to calculate any mean).

Describing variation

Variety, we are told, is the spice of life. It is also an important idea for describing and summarizing data. Again, think about your last class exam. You may learn from the instructor that the class average for the exam was 75. You get your exam back and see you've scored an 85 on the test. You're way ahead of the crowd, right? Well it depends. Before knowing how you did in relation to your classmates, you really need to know how much grade variation or diversity there was in the entire class. Did most students score around 75? Or did most people score in the high nineties with a few students really bombing the exam and thereby pulling the average score down to 75? (This example, by the way, shows how outliers can pull a mean in their direction.) We really need to get this kind of information in order to have a complete big picture. We need some measure of variability. As with measures of central tendency, there are three important measures of variability in our statistical tool kit: the range, the standard deviation and the variance.

The **range** does exactly what the word suggests – it conveys the difference or the distance between the highest and the lowest values in a set of scores. The range is a quick but rather crude measure of variability. It is crude in the sense that it is calculated using only two values in an entire set of scores – the highest and the lowest. This can be misleading. Consider the following test scores:

10, 85, 85, 85, 85, 100

The range for this set of scores is 90 – i.e., the highest score (100) minus the lowest score (10). Yet to look at the entire set of scores is to see far less variability than is suggested by a range of 90. Four of the six scores are identical to each other! For a more sensitive gauge of variability, we need a measure that will use more than two scores in its calculation. Ideally, we would want a measure that takes *every* score into account when calculating a summary description of variability. The **variance** does exactly this – it uses every single score in a set of scores when calculating a summary measure of variability.

The logic of calculating the variance is fairly straightforward: to assess total variation (i.e., variance) take each score in the set and calculate its distance from the mean of the set of scores. This should give us a good overall idea of total variability in a set of scores. It all sounds good in theory, let's try it in practice. Let's try calculating the variance for the set of six scores cited above: 10, 85, 85, 85, 85, 100. Since every score needs to be considered in relation to the mean, we must first calculate the mean. Add all six scores together (you should get 450) and divide by 6. When we do this, we find the mean to be 75. (Here, by the way, is an example of how the mean need not be an actual value in a set of scores.) Now we are ready to calculate the distance between each score and the mean. To do this we simply subtract the mean from each score:

$$
\begin{aligned}
10 - 75 &= -65 \\
85 - 75 &= 10 \\
85 - 75 &= 10 \\
85 - 75 &= 10 \\
85 - 75 &= 10 \\
100 - 25 &= 25
\end{aligned}
$$

Now let's add up all of these "distances" from the mean. The average distance is 0! Did we do something wrong? No. The result really makes perfect sense if we remember the mathematical significance of the mean. It is the "balancing point" in a set of values – it is the exact point in a set of scores where all the scores above the point perfectly balance all the points below. We "see" this in the above example by virtue of the fact that the total for all positive numbers (i.e., points above the mean) is exactly equal to the total for all our negative numbers (i.e., points below the mean). Add these two numbers together (+65 and –65) and we get zero.

To calculate an "average" for the amount of variation in our set of scores, then, we must do something to accommodate this "balancing" feature of the mean. We must do something to get rid of the inevitable zero in the numerator. (Remember what we learned back in first grade math: having a zero in the numerator will always give us a zero for the quotient – zero divided by *anything* is always zero.) The solution to the zero-balance problem is to square each "distance" score before adding them together. These squared deviation scores then become the basis for calculating the variance. Again, we should try it with the above scores to help make the point. Add together the squared deviations for each of the scores and you'll see you no longer get a sum of zero:

$$-65^2 + 10^2 + 10^2 + 10^2 + 10^2 + 25^2 = 5{,}250$$

The variance is finally calculated by taking the total of the squared deviations (5,250) and dividing by the total number of scores. (Actually, the total number of scores minus 1. This adjustment reflects the conservative nature of research to which we have referred so often in this book. The $n - 1$ adjustment deflates the denominator and thereby yields a larger estimate of variation – smaller denominators always yield larger quotients. Overestimating variation is seen as the more cautious or prudent move in social research given the heterogeneity of our research populations.)

When we divide 5,250 by 5 ($n - 1$) we come up with a quotient or variance of 1,050. On one hand we know this measure *must* be better than the range since it involves every score in its calculation. Still, the number looks bizarre given that our original set of scores were numbers ranging from 10 to 100! What happened this time?

Recall that to overcome the zero-balancing feature of the mean, we squared each score's deviation from the mean. Our variance measure is expressed in these squared units. In order to get back to the original units of our test scores, we need to "undo" this squaring. We have one last statistical tool for accomplishing this: the **standard deviation**. We calculate the standard deviation by taking the square root of the variance. With this simple step, we return the variance to the original units of our original data. Taking the square root of 5,250 leaves us with a square root of 32.4 – a number much more in line with our original set of scores.

The standard deviation is best thought of as an index of the average amount of variability in a set of scores. One could say that the standard deviation takes the best feature of the variance measure – i.e., taking every single score into account when calculating variation – and goes one better. The standard deviation is expressed in the same units as the original scores we are trying to describe. One might also say that the standard deviation "complements" the mean. The mean reports the average score that best represents a set of scores. The standard deviation conveys the average distance between any one score and the mean. The standard deviation is also like the mean in that it is sensitive to extreme scores. Indeed, this characteristic is apparent in the set of numbers we have been using. Our calculated standard deviation reflects the influence of the extreme distance between the mean we calculated (75) and the very low score of 10.

It takes two to tango ... and to correlate

Up to this point, we have been considering how best to summarize the data we've collected on a single variable – e.g., reporting the "average" gender in a group (via the mode) or reporting the average test score and average variation in test scores for a group (via the mean and the standard deviation). Another important way to organize data is by reporting the overall association between two variables Is there a relationship, for instance, between test scores and amount of time spent studying for the test? As one variable increases, does the second also increase? Or perhaps as one variable increases, the second decreases. To answer such questions we need to mobilize a set of statistical tools known as correlation coefficients.

A **correlation coefficient** is a number that summarizes the degree to which two variables move together. Correlations range in value from −1 to +1. When the coefficient is 1 (either −1 or +1), the two variables are perfectly "in sync" with each other – a unit change in one is accompanied by a unit change in the other. If the variables are moving in opposite directions (one increases as the other decreases), it is a negative relationship. We indicate a negative relationship by using a minus sign before the coefficient. If the variables are moving in the same direction (both are increasing or both are decreasing together), we denote that by reporting the coefficient as a positive number. When the coefficient is 0, there is no relationship between the two variables – i.e., one variable does not have any connection with the other. Typically, coefficients fall somewhere between no relationship (0) and a perfect relationship (+/−1). The closer the coefficient is to +/−1, the stronger the relationship between the two variables. The closer the coefficient is to 0, the weaker the relationship between the two variables.

There are several correlation coefficients we can calculate to summarize the relationship between two variables: e.g., the Pearson correlation coefficient, the Spearman rank coefficient, and the Phi coefficient. As we saw when selecting the right statistical tool for reporting averages, the level of measurement for our variables must guide our selection of the right correlation coefficient to use with our data. The **Pearson coefficient** should be used when we are looking for the association between two variables measured at the interval level: the correlation between income and size of saving accounts in dollars; the correlation between height and weight; the correlation between years in school and size of vocabulary. The **Spearman rank coefficient** is appropriate when looking for an association between two ordinal level variables: the correlation between letter grades (A, B, C, etc.) and level of interest in school (high, medium, low); the correlation between birth order (first, middle, last) and self-esteem (low, medium, high); the correlation between fabric weight (light, medium, heavy) and sun block protection (low, medium, high). The **Phi coefficient** should be used when looking for an association between two nominal level variables: the relationship between gender (male, female) and party affiliation (Republican, Democrat); the relationship between marital status (married, not married) and voting preferences (Bush, Gore); the relationship between employment status (employed, un-employed) and support of welfare reform (yes, no).

Picture This

As we've tried to demonstrate in the preceding pages, we can offer a decent overview of what our data looks like via some key statistical tools: i.e., measures of central tendency, measures of variation, and measures of association. Using various visual displays of data can further enhance the big picture of our data. Graphs and charts are tools for converting numbers into visual displays. Pictures, after all, are said to be worth a thousand words. As it turns out, pictures are also worth a whole lot of numbers. According to Edward Tufte, perhaps the reigning king of graphic excellence, graphs are essential devices for effective communi-cation (Tufte 2001). Graphs and charts work well in communicating information because they take advantage of the fact that the human mind is extremely visual in nature (Bowen 1992; Tufte 1997, 2001). Indeed, Tufte reports that the human eye is capable of processing 625 data points per square inch of space (Tufte 2001).

Graphing 101

Before we start, it would help to review the basics of graphing. Most of the devices we will cover in the following section all start with the same basic model: two straight lines at a right angle to each other. The hori-zontal line is referred to as the X axis (aka the abscissa). The vertical line is referred to as the Y axis (aka the ordinate). Quantitative variables can be plotted along either the X or Y axis. Qualitative variables, on the other hand, should only be plotted along the X axis. The visual field (i.e., the area between the X and Y axis) will display bars, dots, or lines by way of communicating information about data (see Figure 12.1).

Picturing frequency distributions and central tendency

When we want to show the frequency with which values occur in a group of data we can use bar charts, histograms, or frequency polygons. As indicated above, the issue of level of measurement should guide our

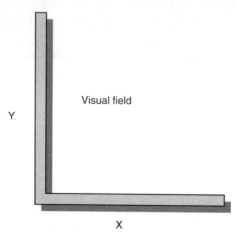

Figure 12.1   Basic line graph

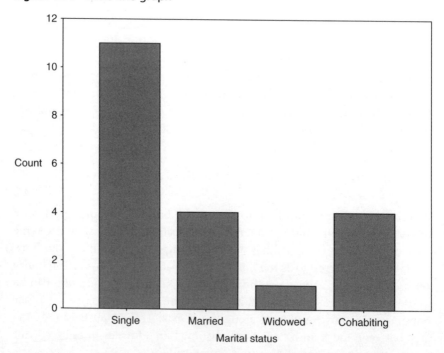

Figure 12.2   Bar chart, marital status of class of students

graphing selection. The **bar chart** is appropriate for displaying the frequency distribution of a variable measured at the nominal level. Each category or value of the qualitative variable is represented by its own bar along the X axis. The height of each bar visually communicates the relative frequency (as indicated by the Y axis) of each value (along the X axis). As indicated in Figure 12.2, the mode can be quite obvious in a bar chart.

The histogram and the frequency polygon are both appropriate visual displays for frequency distributions of quantitative variables. In both devices, the numerical categories of our variable are displayed along the X axis while frequency information is displayed along the Y axis. The **histogram** uses a series of connected bars to present frequency information. Each bar corresponds to the class intervals of the variable plotted along the X-axis. The histogram can be quite useful for spotting outliers or gaps in data. The **frequency polygon** replaces the continuous bars of the histogram with dots and a continuous line to display frequency information. The line connects the midpoints of each class interval that is plotted along the X axis. Again, either device offers quick visual feedback on averages (look for the highest bar of the histogram or the peak of the polygon). (see Figures 12.3 and 12.4.)

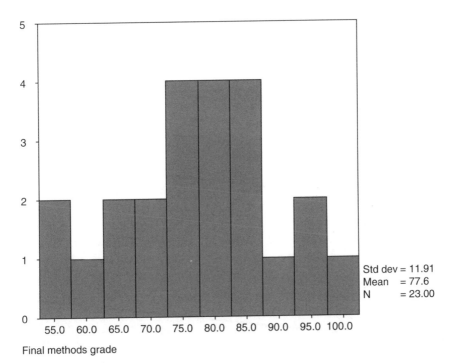

Std dev = 11.91
Mean   = 77.6
N   = 23.00

Final methods grade

Figure 12.3a Histogram of methods grades from Table 12.1

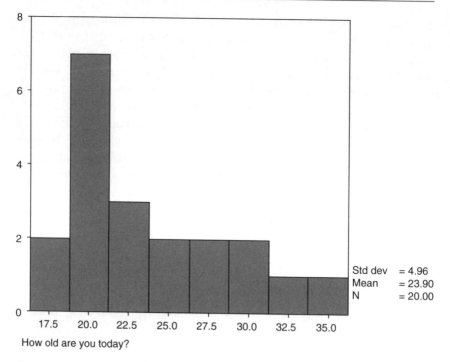

Std dev = 4.96
Mean = 23.90
N = 20.00

How old are you today?

Figure 12.3b   Histogram of student ages

Picturing variation

Histograms and frequency polygons can also show us something about variation. This is most effectively accomplished by comparing either graph of our data to three standard models for depicting shapes of frequency distributions. Take a look at Figure 12.5. In polygon A we see a visual depiction of a set of scores that have a small amount of variation between them. We "see" this by virtue of the fact that the curve is very narrow indicating that most of the scores are clumped together around the center point of the curve (the mean). Polygon B shows us the graph of a set of scores with a moderate amount of variation – the graph resembles a bell-shaped curve. Finally, polygon C depicts a set of scores that have quite a bit of variation between them, ergo the larger the "spread" of the curve around the mean. To the extent that we can "match" our histograms or frequency polygons to one of the models in Figure 12.5, we enhance our ability to communicate the variation found in our data.

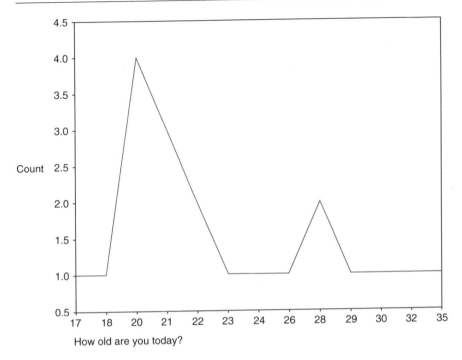

Figure 12.4 Polygon of student ages

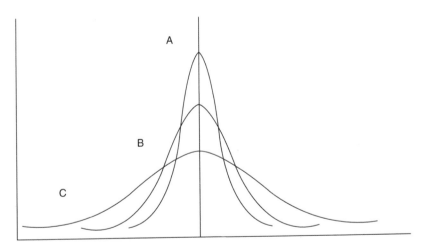

Figure 12.5 Pictures of variation

Picturing correlation

Graphing associations between variables may actually be one statistical tool you'll find both instructive and enjoyable. Tufte's praise for the scatterplot is quite high; he regards this tool as the greatest of all graphical designs. The **scatterplot** is the visual complement for the correlation coefficient. It visually displays whether there's any connection between the movements of two variables and allows the viewer to look for possible causal relationships. One variable is displayed on the X axis while the other variable is displayed on the Y axis. (If we are making a causal argument, the independent variable is placed along the X axis.) The values on either axis might be expressed in absolute numbers, percentages, rates, or scores. In the scatterplot we use dots (aka data points) to simultaneously convey information about the two variables. To figure out the exact location of the dot we first move to the right to locate the relevant value on X and then we move up to the corresponding value on Y (the use of graph paper helps in locating the exact point of intersection).

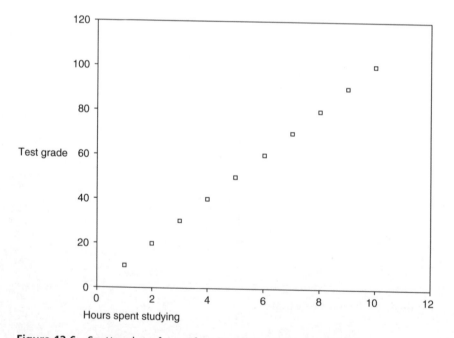

Figure 12.6   Scatterplot of a perfect (hypothetical)* correlation
* Hypothetical because there really isn't a perfect association between time spent studying and grades earned.

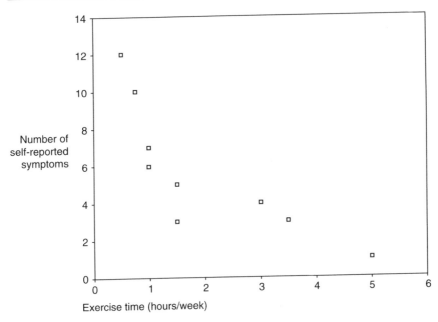

(a) A negative relationship between exercise and self-reported symptoms
(r = −0.803)

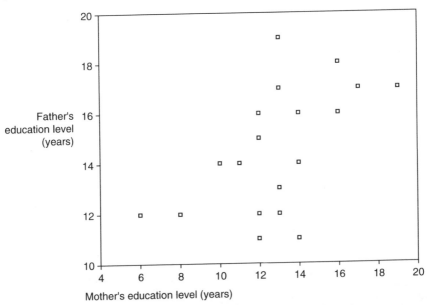

(b) A positive relationship between parents' levels of education (r = 0.607)

Figure 12.7 Less than perfect correlations

A dot is displayed for every case in our data set. Figure 12.6 shows the scatterplot for a perfect positive correlation between two variables.

This scatterplot depicts a "perfect" positive relationship because each unit of increase on the X variable is associated with a matching unit of increase on the Y variable – i.e., as we move from one unit to the next on the X variable, we see an identical movement from one unit to the next on the Y variable. Creating a scatterplot for relationships between two variables is always a good idea – it will show you if and how the two variables are related. Figures 12.7a and 12.7b show scatterplots of "less than perfect" relationships. The first one shows a negative relationship (Pearson $r = -0.803$) between time spent exercising and number of self-reported symptoms. The second one shows a positive relationship (Pearson $r = 0.607$) between educational levels for parents.

SPSS (Statistical Package for the Social Sciences)

We have covered quite a few important statistical tools in this chapter and you may be feeling like your boat is about to go down in the rough sea of statistics. The good news is that I would not put anyone in this boat without some buoyant life preservers. Every technique reviewed in this chapter is easily executed with the help of SPSS (or any other statistical package like SAS or STATA). While I have tried to give you a conceptual introduction to some very key statistical techniques, all the detailed instructions for executing these techniques can be gleaned from any number of tutorials and/or books devoted to SPSS. In fact, the latest versions of SPSS enable the user to produce averages (means, medians, modes), measures of variation (ranges, variances, standard deviations), charts, graphs, and plots with a relatively simple assortment of "point and click" operations. If you leave this chapter with a better grasp of statistics, you should take comfort from the fact that you really are on your way to being able to "do" statistics (with an assist from SPSS).

Expanding the Essentials

For those starting to tread the statistical waters take heart! There is a lot of help available online.

There are several online statistical glossaries:

Statsoft glossary: http://www.statsoft.com/textbook/glosfra. html

David Lane's hyperstat glossary: http://www.davidmlane.com/hyperstat/glossary.html
SurfStat glossary: http://www.anu.edu.au/nceph/surfstat/surfstat-home/glossary/glossary.html.
For more extended explanations, there are also several online statistics texts:

You might find the Electronic Stats textbook very helpful (see especially its link to "Elementary Concepts"): http://www.statsoft.com/textbook/stathome.html. Another online statistics text, HyperStat Online, can be found at: http://davidmlane.com/hyperstat/.
Another good online statistics text can be found at: http://www.public.asu.edu/%7Epythagor/onlinetextbook.htm.
And yet another helpful online statistics text is Gerald Dallal's "The Little Handbook of Statistical Practice": http://www.tufts.edu/~gdallal/LHSP.HTM.
For online information on graphical displays see Albert Goodman's "Graphical Data Presentation": http://www.deakin.edu.au/~agoodman/sci101/chap12.html.

There are several online SPSS tutorials available:

Einstein and Abernethy's "Statistical Package for the Social Sciences: SPSS Version 10.0": http://s9000.furman.edu/mellonj/spss1.htm
SPSS for Windows: Getting Started: http://www.utexas.edu/cc/stat/tutorials/spss/SPSS1/Outline1.html.

If you don't have access to SPSS you can still get your feet wet by visiting the Webstat site. Webstat provides a statistical computing package for Web users. By clicking on the various links found on the Webstat homepage, the visitor can get a tutorial on various statistical procedures and try his/her hand at some basic data analysis: http://www.webstatsoftware.com/.

There are also a few books that might prove useful for students without strong math backgrounds:
Neil Salkind's *Statistics for People Who (Think They) Hate Statistics* (2000),
Lloyd Jaisingh and Laurie Rozakus' *Statistics for the Utterly Confused* (2000).
For the ultimate word on graphic displays of information see Tufte's work, *The Visual Display of Quantitative Information* (2001).

Exercises

1   Consider the following set of scores in a history test. Which measure of central tendency should the teacher use when reporting the average score for the class? Why?

Scores: 81, 80, 81, 100, 75, 79, 78.

2   For the same set of test scores above, would it be a good idea for the teacher to report the range of the test scores as a way of showing the variability of the scores? Why?

3   Try your hand at SPSS. Enter the above data as values for the variable Test1.

3.1   Click on the SPSS icon on your computer screen (or click on the start column and scroll up the column until you find the SPSS option).

3.2   A window with various options will appear on the screen.

* If you are unfamiliar with SPSS, you should select the circle next to **Run the Tutorial** and click OK.
* Once you have some idea of how SPSS works, you can select the circle next to **Type in Data** and click OK.

3.3   If you are working in SPSS 10.0 or higher, you should access the "Variable View" screen by clicking on this tab in the lower left corner of the screen. In the variable view screen, each variable is represented by a row containing default information about each variable.

* Start by assigning a new variable name to replace the default name.
* Click on the first cell in the "Name" column.
* Delete the default name (if there is one).
* Type in Test1 as the name for our one variable and hit the enter key.
* At this point, we can leave the rest of the default settings as they are.

3.4   Click the tab for data view (lower left corner of screen).

* The Test1 column should be highlighted.
* Type in the first test score in the first cell and hit enter.
* Repeat this step until all 7 scores are entered.

3.5   Click "Analyze" (in tool bar running across top of screen).

- Click "Descriptive Statistics."
- Click "Descriptives."
- Click right arrow key to move Test1 into right box.
- Click "OK."

3.6   Find the Mean and the Standard deviation in the output. How do they help you understand the answers to exercises 1 and 2?

3.7   While still in SPSS, click on "Graphics."

- Select "histogram."
- Use the right arrow key to move Test1 into the right box.
- Click "OK."

What does the picture tell you about your data set?

13 Beyond Description: Inferential Statistics

Inferential statistics go beyond the descriptive tasks reviewed in Chapter 12. Inferential statistics come into play whenever we are working with samples but want to make generalizations about populations. In essence, inferential statistics support the leap from samples to populations. More specifically, they support the leap from sample *statistics* to population *parameters*. (Statistics express values found in samples; parameters express values found in populations.) To better understand how sample data can be used to say something about populations, we must familiarize ourselves with two key concepts: the normal curve and sampling distributions.

The Normal Curve

The **normal curve** provides a *visual* depiction of a distribution of scores or values on a variable. You might think of it as a "curved" version of a histogram. (See page 189 in Chapter 12.) It is worth noting that the normal curve isn't so normal. By that I mean that it is a theoretical "invention," the result of a mathematic equation. But while the normal curve is a theoretical or hypothetical device, its value as a statistical tool is quite real. For example, the normal curve is essential to testing hypotheses about group differences or about relationships between variables. It is also an essential tool for generalizing from samples to populations.

Despite its hypothetical nature, the normal curve often does match real-world scenarios. For instance, it is generally held that the normal curve accurately describes the distribution of IQ scores in the general population. Measures of memory, reading ability, and job satisfaction are also normally distributed variables. The normal curve does a good job describing the values on such variables as height and weight in the population at large. Two nineteenth-century researchers (Belgian mathematician Lambert Adolphe Jacques Quetelet and English scientist Sir Francis Galton) discovered this useful insight about the normal curve as they set about plotting the values of some common characteristics of individuals (height, weight, chest size, visual acuity, etc.). They noticed as they plotted more and more values that a common picture emerged. Across all the variables they plotted, the pattern of the frequency distribution of values resembled a bell-shaped curving line. (You will often find the normal curve referred to as a bell-shaped curve.) Researchers take advantage of this fact and apply the normal curve and its properties to the actual data they have collected. With this application, they establish a pathway for moving from samples to populations.

The normal curve has many defining and noteworthy features. In addition to its bell shape, the normal curve is unimodal – it has only one point of maximum frequency. This point of maximum frequency is at the exact center of the curve. And it is at this center point that the mean, median, and mode can all be found. The normal curve is also symmetrical – the area left of its dead-center mean is identical to the area to the right of the mean. Lastly, the area under the curve is very predictable. Let me explain.

While the term "normal curve" focuses our attention on the *curve* formed along the outer edges of the distribution, our interest is really in the area *under* the curve. If you look at Figure 13.1, the picture is meant to convey the idea that *all* of the values in a distribution (e.g., all weights, all heights, all

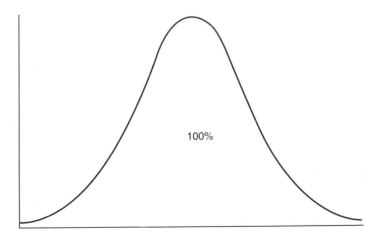

Figure 13.1   Area under the normal curve

IQs) fall *between* the curve and the baseline of the figure. And using the properties of the normal curve, researchers cast this area in the language of probabilities; they treat the area under the curve as predictable. In our everyday understanding of probability, the connection between probability and prediction is apparent. We understand that events having a high probability of occurrence can also be thought of as predictable. If your grandmother has always called you on your birthday, it is probable – indeed predictable – that she will call you again on your next birthday.

Using the normal curve, researchers can make predictions about variables that are "normally distributed." If we know (or assume) a variable is normally distributed, statisticians tell us that we can *predict* the percentage of cases for that variable that fall between set standard distances or areas under the curve. These standard areas are marked out in reference to the curve's dead center – i.e., in reference to the mean. The normal curve *always* depicts three standard distances to the right of (above) the mean and three standard distances to the left of (below) the mean. These set distances are referred to as standard deviations and are represented using what statisticians call "Z scores" or standard scores.

How does all of this translate into practice? When we know that some variable is normally distributed (like height) we can safely make predictions about the distribution of values around the mean of the variable. Figure 13.2 shows us the predictions (probabilities) that we can assume

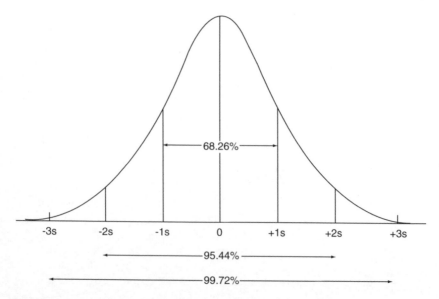

Figure 13.2 Area under the normal curve: set proportions

anytime a variable is thought to be "normally distributed." Note that 34.13% of the cases will have values (e.g., heights) that fall in the area between the mean and one standard unit of distance *below* the mean. Since the normal curve is symmetrical (the area to the left of the mean is identical to the area to the right of the mean), we can also predict that 34.13% of the cases will have values that fall in the area between the mean and one standard unit of distance *above* the mean. Adding these two areas together we can say that 68.26% of the cases of a normally distributed variable will fall between −1 and +1 standard units from the mean value of the variable. Continuing to follow the information presented in Figure 13.2, the normal curve also allows us to predict that 95.44% of a normally distributed variable's cases will fall between −2 and +2 standard units of distance from the mean. Finally, virtually all cases − 99.74% − will fall between −3 and +3 standard units of distance from the mean.

Let's go back now and illustrate the points of the previous paragraph with a concrete example. IQ is a variable presumed to be normally distributed in the population. In saying this we claim that the majority of IQ scores in a population will hover around the average (mean) IQ with only a very few people having extraordinarily high or extraordin-arily low IQs. Let's say, for the purpose of this example, that the mean IQ is 100 with a standard deviation of 10. How can we apply the normal curve in the analysis of IQ? First, anyone who has an IQ of 100 will fall exactly in the middle (dead center) of the curve. Note that in Figure 13.2 this mid-point is marked with a 0. Why? The zero indicates that there is no distance at all between the mean value and the midpoint of the normal curve. Second, the normal curve allows us to predict that 68.26% of people will have IQs that are within +/−1 standard unit of distance from the mean IQ. In our current example the value of the standard unit is equal to the standard deviation for IQ − i.e., 10. That is, 68.26% of the population at large will have IQs that fall between 90 and 110 (the mean of 100 minus one standard unit of 10 points or the mean plus one standard unit of 10 points). We can also predict that 95.44% of people will have IQs that fall within +/−2 standard units of distance from the mean IQ. And finally 99.74% of the people will have IQs that are within +/−3 standard units of distance from the mean IQ. When using the normal curve, you can bank on these "predictions" or probabilities. In fact, as we will see shortly, you can be extremely "confident" in your knowledge of the normal curve.

Think of the power of this tool! Once you assume that a group of values or scores are normally distributed, you are entitled to make predictions about the percent of cases that will be found within set distances from the mean of the group. This knowledge is key to helping us with the dilemma of inferential statistics – namely, gathering data from samples and using that data to make inferences about populations. In the next section, we'll examine why this is so.

Repeat After Me

Imagine a typical research endeavor. You are the head of a company with a social conscience. You are considering various healthcare and childcare programs for your company. You want to know what your employees think about the various plans. Your nephew, who is working as a summer intern, tells you he can help with this task. He draws a simple random sample of employees and gives them a brief questionnaire to learn about some key characteristics (age, years of education, number of children). He also questions them regarding their views on the healthcare and childcare programs. You ask if he can generalize what he has learned from the sample to your entire population of employees. Your nephew isn't so sure. Thus he decides to take another sample of workers and redo the survey with them. Much to his dismay, he finds that the two samples don't match! The samples yield different statistics with regard to average age, average income, average number of children, average number of visits to doctors in the past year, etc. A little panicked, your nephew draws yet another sample and again finds there are differences between the samples. He continues to draw samples until ... you fire him. Must things have ended this way? (At least that's what your sister wants to know!)

In the above scenario, the nephew faced the classic sampling quandary. How is it possible to use data from a sample to generalize to a population? Just because we find the mean age to be 38 in our one sample, is it reasonable to say that 38 is the mean age for the *entire population* from which the sample was drawn? Junior's experiences would seem to suggest not. What's the researcher to do? Remember the normal curve!

In his panic, the nephew started a process of repeated sampling – i.e., he continued to draw sample after sample after sample from the same population. He did this in hopes of getting closer to the true population values on key variables. In one sense, he had a good idea. If he drew enough samples from the same population and then took an average of the obtained sample data (e.g., an overall mean of the mean ages found in each sample), he would have come close to discovering the true population value. Unfortunately, researchers don't have the luxury of working this way. We don't do repeated sampling; we select only one sample. But if we take care in how we select our one sample, we can assume that it does indeed give us data that is generalizable. How is this possible? Well you should already have some idea about an answer: a probability sampling technique will give us the best crack at obtaining a representative sample. And, in turn, a representative sample does the best job at depicting an entire population. Combining good sampling with the insights provided by the normal curve will cinch our ability to make inferences from our sample to the population.

The Sampling Distribution

Let me introduce you to another extremely important hypothetical device: a sampling distribution. A **sampling distribution** is a distribution of a sample statistic – a distribution that *would* be produced through repeated sampling. For instance, graphing the means of an infinite number of samples drawn from one population would allow us to see a sampling distribution of means. If the nephew in our previous example had graphed the frequency distribution of the mean ages or mean incomes in each and every sample he drew, he would have produced a sampling distribution of these means.

The sampling distribution is a *hypothetical* distribution; in reality we never actually engage in repeated sampling. Still, this hypothetical distribution yields some important theoretical observations. First, in a sampling distribution of means, the average of all the sample means (the mean of means) is equal to the true population mean. This is an important point since we are so often trying to estimate population means from sample means. Second, if we are working with sufficiently large samples, we can assume the sampling distribution is *normally distributed*. Thus any and all properties of the normal curve can be applied to the sampling distribution. This insight will prove critical to any researcher who works with one sample but wants to use it to say something about an entire population.

Consider, for instance, using the mean age in a sample to infer the mean age in a population. Based on what we know about the normal curve, we can say that there is a 68.26% probability that our particular sample mean falls within +/−1 standard units from the mean of the sampling distribution (aka the true population mean). There's a 95.44% probability that our *one* sample mean would fall between −2 and +2 standard units of distance from the population mean. Finally there's a

99.74% probability that our one particular sample mean would fall between -3 and $+3$ standard units of distance from the population mean.

Putting It Together

If we merge two types of knowledge – empirical and theoretical – we will be in a good position to infer population values from sample statistics. By taking knowledge of our sample and knowledge of the properties of the normal curve, we can calculate the gap or the amount of error that results from collecting data from a sample rather than the entire population.

Let's consider one more time the sampling dilemma cited earlier – how can we go beyond our sample statistics and infer population values? For instance, how can we use data about a sample mean to estimate the corresponding population mean? The answer to this question is found in our calculating a **confidence interval**. A confidence interval refers to the range of values (i.e., a "correction factor") we attach to sample statistics in order to capture true population values. The formula for the confidence interval is as follows:

$$CI = \overline{X} +/- (SE \times Z).$$

As this formula indicates, a number of things go into increasing our confidence in sample statistics. X with a line above it – **X bar** – is the symbolic notation for the sample mean. The X bar in the formula indicates that our best *starting* place for estimating a population value is the corresponding sample value. The $+/-$ signs indicate that some quantity will either be added to or subtracted from the sample mean in order to bring it closer in line with a true population value. Why is it either? Well, think about the symmetrical nature of the normal curve. If our one sample and its $\overline{X}$ value falls to the left side of the normal curve, it will *underestimate* the true population value and we will have to add something to $\overline{X}$ for a better estimate of the true population value. If our one sample and its $\overline{X}$ value falls to the right side of the normal curve, the $\overline{X}$ will *overestimate* true population values and we will need to subtract an amount from $\overline{X}$ in order to bring it in line with the true population value. Finally, look at the part of the formula enclosed in parentheses. Together, the **product of SE** (standard error) **and Z** (Z score value for confidence level) will provide us with what is known as the **margin of error** of the confidence interval (see next section). This margin of error will be the exact amount that will either be added to or subtracted from the sample mean in order to bring it closer in line with a true population value.

Before moving on, let me remind you that you've no doubt already been exposed to the margin of error by the major news agencies or by major polling organizations. During election years when major news agencies report the percentage of voters supporting the major candidates, they always report the margin of error for their results. In order to zero in on true population values (and come closest to accurately calling the election), the networks will typically report their estimates of voter preferences to within a $+/-3$ margin of error. This means that if the networks report that 45% $(+/-3)$ of Americans sampled support candidate A, they are acknowledging that the support in the general population may actually be as high as 48% (45% + 3%) or as low as 42% (45% $-$ 3%). In other words, the networks are hedging their bets and will consider their estimates of voter preference to be right if the final vote falls within this 6-percentage point spread. Similarly, if you have ever read any Gallup poll results, you may have noticed that they report their findings to be accurate within a margin of error of +3 or -3 percentage points (http://www.gallup.com/).

Now that we have the logic of the confidence interval down, it's time to see how to "solve" the formula. The good news is that we really do have all of the necessary numbers to plug into the formula at our fingertips. The $\overline{X}$ will be obtained from our sample. We can easily determine the value of SE by using two additional pieces of sample information: the standard deviation (s) and the sample size (n). Finally, we can also easily determine the appropriate Z value for the formula by using our knowledge of the normal curve.

SE – The standard error

You can think of the **standard error** as the error we can expect by virtue of using a sample to learn about a population. You've already spent some time considering this idea back in Chapter 8 on sampling. Sampling is a good thing – it allows us to do research in a timely and cost efficient way. However, it is not without its limitations. Samples will seldom if ever perfectly capture the population they purport to represent. We must assume they will always contain some error. The SE is a calculation that allows us to quantify that error.

We calculate the SE using two basic pieces of data from our sample: the standard deviation and the sample size. Recall from the last chapter that a large standard deviation indicates more variation between values in our sample – e.g., more variation in variables such as income, years of education, number of children, hours devoted to community service, etc. If we've done a good job selecting a sample, the sample should reflect (albeit imperfectly) the variation in the population. The more variation in a sample, the more variation we can expect in the population.

The other key piece of sample data we use in calculating the standard error is the sample size. Recall from Chapter 8 that larger samples are more representative than smaller samples. Larger samples get us that much closer to entire populations. Ergo, our calculation of the standard error should be tempered by sample size. Consequently, we calculate the standard error by dividing the standard deviation by the square root of $n - 1$. (Again we use $n - 1$ for the same reason as given in the previous chapter – it yields a more conservative estimate of the standard error.)

Z values

Once we use our sample data to calculate the value of SE, we can move onto figuring out the value of Z. The normal curve helps us with this piece of the puzzle. **Z values** are simply another way of referring to the area under the normal curve (see pages 199–201). That is, when we talk about the normal curve and its standard units of distance from the mean, we are talking about Z scores. We've already considered three Z scores in some detail: a Z score of +/−1 encompasses 68.26% of the area around the mean; a Z score of +/−2 encompasses 95.44% of the area around the mean; a Z score of +/−3 encompasses 99.74% of the area around the mean. While we have already presented these areas in terms of probabilities and predictions, we can also talk of these areas in terms of **confidence levels** – i.e., the degree of certainty we have in claiming our assertions are accurate.

Think once again about the sampling distribution – i.e., the distribution that would occur via repeated sampling. Instead of saying that 68.26% of all samples in a sampling distribution fall within +/−1 standard units from the mean, we could express this idea as a statement of confidence. We can be 68.26% confident that our one sample falls between +/−1 standard units of distance from the mean (or between the Z scores of +1 and −1). We can be 95.44% confident that any one sample falls within +/−2 standard units of distance from the mean, and so on. In short, the Z value for our formula will be determined by the level of confidence we want to achieve when making statements about populations based on sample data. For a 95% confidence level (a level adopted by many social researchers), we use a Z score of 1.96. (This Z value should make sense to you once you recall that a confidence level of 95.44% corresponds to a Z score of 2. Being slightly less confident – just 95% – gives us a Z score just a little less than 2 – i.e., 1.96.) If we want a higher level of confidence, say 99%, we use a Z score of 2.56. Increasing our confidence level will always produce a larger (wider) margin of error – but in doing so, we increase the likelihood that the true population value will fall somewhere within our +/– range. (The Z score values for any level of confidence can be gleaned from a Z score table. Such tables are usually part of appendices of statistics books.)

Some Concrete Examples

Imagine that, based on information from a representative sample of 100 students at your college, you calculate the mean age to be 24 and the standard deviation on the age variable to be 5. Is it safe to generalize that this is the mean age for the entire student population at large? To answer this question with some confidence, we need to calculate the confidence interval. We start with the formula and plug in the relevant numbers:

$$CI = \overline{X} +/- (SE \times Z).$$

From our sample data, we know that $\overline{X}$ is equal to 24. Using our sample data we can figure out the value for SE:

$$SE = s/\sqrt{n - 1}.$$

To solve for the SE we will divide the standard deviation of 5 by 9.9 (the square root of 99):

$$5/9.9 = 0.5.$$

Next we want to multiply the SE by the Z score for our desired level of confidence. If we want to be 95% confident in our estimation of the mean age in the population, we need to plug the Z score of 1.96 into the formula:

$$CI = 24 +/- (0.5 \times 1.96)$$

$$CI = 24 +/- (0.98).$$

We can be 95% confident that the mean age in the population is 24 years give or take about one year.

Let's try one more example at a higher level of confidence. A recent survey of a sample of 100 of our sociology majors indicated that the mean GPA was 3.1 with a standard deviation of 0.5. What number should I report if I want to be 99% confident in reporting the mean GPA for all my methods students? Once again, solving the confidence interval formula will give us the answer:

$$CI = \overline{X} +/- (SE \times Z).$$

From the sample data, we know that $\overline{X}$ is equal to 3.1. Using our sample data we can once again figure out the value of SE:

$$SE = s/\sqrt{n-1}.$$

To solve for the SE, we will divide the standard deviation of 0.5 by 9.9 (the square root of 99):

$$0.5/9.9 = 0.05.$$

Next we multiply the SE by the Z score for the 99% level of confidence. To be 99% confident we must plug a Z value of 2.56 into the formula:

$$CI = 3.1 +/- (0.05 \times 2.56)$$

$$CI = 3.1 +/- (0.13).$$

We can be 99% confident that the mean GPA for all my methods students is 3.1 +/- 0.13 – i.e., the population value falls somewhere between 2.97 and 3.23.

Bringing It Home

In this chapter, we've reviewed how a few important hypothetical statistical tools – the normal curve and sampling distributions – can help us with one important task for inferential statistics: concluding something about a population based on information from a sample. In particular, we have seen how to calculate a confidence interval for sample means – an interval that has a known likelihood of including a true population value. This isn't all we can say on the topic of inferential statistics, but hopefully it will get you off to a good start. Understanding the logic of the normal curve and seeing how it factors in achieving certain levels of confidence in the conclusions we draw from sample data is vital to making a successful transition to inferential statistics.

Expanding the Essentials

For a basic review of the ideas behind inferential statistics see Richard Lowry's "Concepts and Applications of Inferential Statistics": http://vassun.vassar.edu/~lowry/webtext.html.

The following interactive tutorial should also help you grasp the principles of inferential statistics: http://acad.cgu. edu/wise/cltmodule/introduc.htm.

For an animated demonstration of a sampling distribution see David Wallace's web page: http://oak.cats.ohiou.edu/~wallacd1/ssample.html.

Some help in finding the right statistical tool for a particular data set can be found at Bill Trochim's "Selecting Statistics": http://trochim.human.cornell. edu/selstat/ssstart.htm.

Part of the reason so many people find statistics frustrating is because the numbers can be so easily "manipulated" or mis-used by those who cite them. For a very good review of how to empower yourself as a consumer of statistics, see Joel Best's *Damned Lies and Statistics: Untangling Numbers from the Media, Politicians, and Activists* (2001).

David Salsburg's *The Lady Tasting Tea: How Statistics Revolutionized Science in the Twentieth Century* (2001) is also a book worthy of your time. Salsburg organizes his work around individuals who have made significant contributions to the development of modern statistics. (He puts a face on Pearson's *r* and Gosset's (Student's) *t*.) He presents this history in a very readable and engaging style (and without relying on any mathematical formulas).

Exercises

1   In the opening paragraphs of this chapter, we identified several variables that are thought to be normally distributed. Try to identify two or three variables that you think are *not* normally distributed. Draw a hypothetical curve that best reflects the "abnormal" distribution of the variables you've selected. Defend your curve.

2   Imagine you are working with a set of "memory" scores that are normally distributed. The mean for the set of scores is 80 and the standard deviation is 8. What's the probability that a score falls between 72 and 88? How does the area under the normal curve help you "see" the answer?

3   A recent survey of a randomly drawn sample ($n = 200$) of your town neighbors discovered that residents make an average of 14 calls a year to town hall to complain about garbage/recycling services (with a standard deviation of 5). What's the mean number of complaint calls you should report for the whole town if you want to be 99% confident about your findings?

References

Adler, Patricia, and Peter Adler. 2003. "The Promise and Pitfalls of Going into the Field." *Contexts* 2(2): 41–7.

Alexander, C., Y. Kim, , M. Ensminger, K. Johnson, B. Smith, and L. Dolan. 1990. "A Measure of Risk Taking for Young Adolescents: Reliability and Validity Assessment." *Journal of Youth and Adolescence* 19(6): 559–69.

Allen, Arthur. 2002. "The Not-So-Crackpot Autism Theory." *The New York Times Magazine*, 10 November, 66–9.

Anderson, Leon, and Thomas Calhoun. 2001. "Strategies for Researching Street Deviance." In Alex Thio and Thomas Calhoun (eds.), *Readings in Deviant Behavior* (2nd edition). Boston: Allyn & Bacon.

Angrosino, Michael. 2001. "How the Mentally Challenged See Themselves." In Alex Thio and Thomas Calhoun (eds.), *Readings in Deviant Behavior* (2nd edition). Boston: Allyn and Bacon.

Babbie, E. 1998. *Observing Ourselves: Essays in Social Research*. Prospect Heights, IL: Waveland Press, Inc.

Babbie, E. 2001. *The Practice of Social Research* (9th edition). Belmont, CA: Wadsworth.

Bailey, Carol. 1996. *A Guide to Field Research*. Thousand Oaks, CA: Pine Forge Press.

Bailey, Kenneth. 1987. *Methods of Social Research* (3rd edition). New York: The Free Press.

Becker, Howard. 1963. *Outsiders*. New York: The Free Press.

Belenky, Mary, Blythe Clinchy, Nancy Goldberger, and Jill Tarule. 1986. *Women's Ways of Knowing: The Development of Self, Voice and Mind*. New York: Basic Books.

Best, Joel. 2001. *Damned Lies and Statistics: Untangling Numbers from the Media, Politicians, and Activists*. Berkeley: University of California Press.

Black, Donald. 1976. *The Behavior of Law*. New York: Academic Press.

Bourdieu, Pierre. 1986. "The Forms of Capital." In J. G. Richardson (ed.), *Handbook of Theory and Research in the Sociology of Education*. New York: Greenwood Press.

Bowen, Richard. 1992. *Graph It! How to Make, Read, and Interpret Graphs*. Englewood Cliffs, NJ: Prentice-Hall, Inc.

Braestrup, Peter. 2000. "The News Media and the War in Vietnam: Myths and Realities." http://www.vwam.com/vets/media.htm.

Bruner, Gordon, and P. J. Hensel. 1992. *Marketing Scales Handbook: A Compilation of Multi-Item Measures*. Chicago: American Marketing Association.

Burns, Robert. 1785. "To A Mouse, On Turning Her Up In Her Nest with the Plough."

Carmines, E. G., and R. A. Zeller. 1979. *Reliability and Validity Assessment*. Beverly Hills, CA: Sage.

CBS News. 2000. "Evening News." WCBS New York City Broadcast. July 19.

CBS News. 2000. "Pitfalls of the Digital Grapevine." wysisyg://8/http://cbsnews.cbs.com/now/story/0,1597,216674-412,00.shtm, July 19.

CBS News. 2000. http://www.pollingreport.com/wh2gen1.htm, released October 6–9.

Center for Disease Control. 2001. "MMR Vaccine and Autism." http://www.cdc.gov/nip/vacsafe/concerns/autism/autism-mmr.htm.

Cerulo, Karen A. 1998. *Deciphering Violence: The Cognitive Structure of Right and Wrong*. New York: Routledge.

Cerulo, Karen A. (ed.). 2002. *Culture in Mind: Toward a Sociology of Culture and Cognition*. New York: Routledge.

Chan, J., S. Knutsen, G. Blix, J. Lee, and G. Fraser. 2002. "Water, Other Fluids and Fatal Coronary Heart Disease: The Adventist Health Study." *American Journal of Epidemiology* 155(9): 827–33.

CNN.com. 2000. "Cause of Deadly Seton Hall Dorm Fire Under Investigation." http://www.cnn.com/2000/US/01/19/seton.hall.fire.04/, accessed January 19.

CNN.com. 2001. "No Link Found Between MMR Vaccine and Autism." http://www.cnn.com/2001/HEALTH/conditions/04/23/vaccine.autism/?s=8, April 23.

Cockerham, William. 1998. *Medical Sociology* (7th edition). Upper Saddle River, NJ: Prentice-Hall, Inc.

Cole, Jeffrey. 2001. *Surveying the Digital Future: Year Two*. UCLA Center for Communication Policy. www.ccp.ucla.edu.

Community Pharmacy. 2003. "The Great MMR Debate." CMP Information Ltd. February 3.

Conoley, J. C., and J. C. Impara (eds.). 1995. *Mental Measurements Yearbook* (12th edition). Lincoln, NE: Buros Institute of Mental Measurements.

Consumer Reports. 2001. "The 2001 Mitsubishi Montero Limited Not Acceptable." *Consumer Reports* 66(8): 22–5.

Daily Telegraph. 2002. "Chocolate Eaters Lick Depression. *The Daily Telegraph* (Sydney), September 9.

de Lorgeril, M., P. Salen, J. L. Martin, F. Boucher, F. Paillard, and J. de Leiris. 2002. "Wine Drinking and Risks of Cardiovascular Complications After Recent Acute Myocardial Infarction." *Circulation* 106(12): 1465–9.

Department of Energy. 1995a. "Chapter 3: The Development of Human Subject Research Policy at DHEW." In *Advisory Committee on Human Radiation Experiments, Final Report*. http://tis.eh.doe.gov/ohre/roadmap/achre/chap3.html.

Department of Energy. 1995b. "Preface. Why the Committee Was Created." In *Advisory Committee on Human Radiation Experiments, Final Report*. http://tis.eh. doe.gov/ohre/roadmap/achre/preface.html.

Diener, Eduard, and Rick Crandall. 1978. *Ethics in Social and Behavioral Research*. Chicago: University of Chicago Press.

Dillman, Don. 2000. *Mail and Internet Surveys: The Tailored Design Method* (2nd edition). New York: John Wiley & Sons.

Duneier, Mitchell. 2001. "On the Evolution of Sidewalk." In Robert Emerson (ed.), *Contemporary Field Research* (2nd edition). Prospect Heights: Waveland Press, Inc.

Durkheim, Emile. 1951. *Suicide*. New York: The Free Press.

El-Bassel, N., A. Ivanoff, and R. F. Schiling. 1995. "Correlates of Problem Drinking Among Drug-Using Incarcerated Women." *Addiction Behavior* 20: 359–69.

Erikson, Kai. 1986. "Work and Alienation." *American Sociological Review* 51 (Feb.): 1–8.

Fischer, C., M. Hout, M. S. Jankowski, S. Lucas, A. Swidler, and K. Voss. 1996. *Inequality by Design: Cracking the Bell Curve Myth*. Princeton: Princeton University Press.

Fitzpatrick, K. M. 1997. "Fighting Among America's Youth: A Risk and Protective Factors Approach." *Journal of Health and Social Behavior* 38: 131–48.

Gamson, William. 1992. *Talking Politics*. New York: Cambridge University Press.

Garraty, John, and Peter Gay. 1972. *The Columbia History of the World*. New York: Harper & Row.

Geertz, Clifford. 1973. *The Interpretation of Cultures*. New York: Basic Books.

Glaser, Barney, and Anselm Strauss. 1967. *The Discovery of Grounded Theory*. Chicago: Aldine.

Goffman, Erving. 1961. *Asylums*. New York. Anchor Books

Goffman, Erving. 1963. *Behavior In Public Places*. New York: The Free Press.

Goode, Erich. 2000. *Paranormal Beliefs: A Sociological Introduction*. Prospect Heights, IL: Waveland Press, Inc.

Grandell, Tommy. 2002. "Review of Cell Phone Studies Finds No 'Consistent Evidence' of Cancer Link." The Associated Press (B C Cycle), September 19.

Hager, M., S. Wilson, T. Pollak and P. Rooney. 2003. "Response Rates for Mail Surveys of Nonprofit Organizations: A Review and Empirical Test." http://nccs.urban.org/overhead/pretestpaper.pdf, accessed May.

Hamilton, James. 2004. "The Ethics of Conducting Social-Science Research on the Internet." In D. Wysocki (ed.), *Readings in Social Research Methods* (2nd edition). Belmont, CA: Wadsworth/Thomson.

Haney, C., C. Banks, and Philip Zimbardo. 1973. "Interpersonal Dynamics in a Simulated Prison." *International Journal of Criminology and Penology* 1: 69–97.

Harrell, W. Andrew. 1991. "Factors Influencing Pedestrian Cautiousness in Crossing Streets." *The Journal of Social Psychology* 131(3): 367–72.

Herrnstein, R. J., and C. Murray. 1994. *The Bell Curve: Intelligence and Class Structure in American Life*. New York: The Free Press.

Hirsch, M., and M. Isikoff. 2002. "What Went Wrong?" *Newsweek* (May 27): 28–34.

Hirschi, Travis, and Hanan Selvin. 1973. *Principles of Survey Analysis*. New York: The Free Press.

Horwood, John, and David Fergusson. 1998. "Breastfeeding and Later Cognitive and Academic Outcomes." *Pediatrics* 101(1): 379–85.

Humphreys, Laud. 1969. *Tearoom Trade: Impersonal Sex in Public Places*. Chicago: Aldine.

Hyman, H. 1955. *Survey Design and Analysis*. New York: The Free Press.

Independent Sector. 2001. *Giving and Volunteering in the United States. Key Findings.* Washington, DC.

Institute of Medicine. 2001. *Immunization Safety Review*. Reports and Summaries. Measles-Mumps-Rubella Vaccine and Autism http://www.iom.edu/IOM/IOMHome.nsf/Pages/mmr+report April.

Jaisingh, Lloyd and Laurie Rozakus. 2000. *Statistics for the Utterly Confused*. Boston: McGraw-Hill.

James. F. 1992. "New Methods for Measuring Homelessness and the Population at Risk: Exploratory Research in Colorado." *Social Work Research and Abstracts* 28(2): 9–14.

Jensen, A. 1973. *Educability and Group Differences*. New York: Harper & Row.

Johnson, L. 1991. "Job Strain Among Police Officers: Gender Comparisons." *Police Studies* 14: 12–16.

Katzer, Jeffrey, K. Cook, and W. Crouch. 1998. *Evaluating Information* (4th edition). Boston: McGraw-Hill.

Kimmel, Allan. 1988. *Ethics and Values in Applied Social Research*. Newbury Park, CA: Sage.

Kitsuse, John. 2002. "Societal Reaction to Deviant Behavior." In Ronald Weitzer (ed.), *Deviance and Social Control: A Reader*. New York: McGraw-Hill.

Kjaergard, Lise, and Bodil Als-Nielsen. 2002. "Association Between Competing Interests and Authors' Conclusions: Epidemiological Study of Randomized Clinical Trials Published in the *BMJ*." *British Medical Journal* 325: 249–52.

Kraut, R., S. Kiesler, B. Boneva, J. Cummings, A. Crawford, and V. Helgeson. 2002. "Internet Paradox Revisited." *Journal of Social Issues* 58 (1): 49–74.

Krueger, R. and M. A. Casey. 2000. *Focus Groups: A Practical Guide for Applied Research* (3rd edition). Thousand Oaks, CA: Sage.

Langer, Gary. 2003. "About Response Rates: Some Unresolved Questions." *Public Perspective* (May/June): 16–18.

Larry P. v. Riles, U.S. Courts of Appeals, 1984, 793 F 2d 969.

Lofland, John, and Lyn Lofland. 1984. *Analyzing Social Settings: A Guide to Qualitative Observation and Analysis* (2nd edition). Belmont, CA: Wadsworth.

Lofland, John, and Lyn Lofland. 1995. *Analyzing Social Settings: A Guide to Qualitative Observation and Analysis* (3rd edition). Belmont, CA: Wadsworth.

Lucas, A, R. Morley, T. J. Cole, G. Lester, and C. Leeson-Payne. 1992. "Breast Milk and Subsequent Intelligence Quotient in Children Born Preterm." *The Lancet* 339: 261–4.

Mabrey, Vicki. 2003. "DNA Testing: Foolproof?" *60 Minutes II*. http://www.cbsnews.com/stories/2003/05/27/60II/printable555723..., released May 28.

MacLeod, Jay. 1995. *Ain't No Making It: Aspirations and Attainment in a Low-Income Neighborhood* (2nd expanded edition). Boulder, CO: Westview Press.

Matza, David. 1969. *Becoming Deviant*. New Jersey: Prentice-Hall, Inc.

McCord, Joan. 1978. "A Thirty-Year Follow-Up of Treatment Effects." *American Psychologist* 33: 284–9.

McManis, Sam. 2002. "Perk Up: It's Not All Bad for You; Caffeine Can Get You Addicted, but a Little Bit Might Not Hurt." *San Francisco Chronicle*, December 8.

McNeal, C., and P. Amato. 1998. "Parents' Marital Violence: Long-Term Consequences for Children." *Journal of Family Issues* 19: 123–40.

McPherson, M., L. Smith-Lovin, and J. Cook. 2001. "Birds of a Feather: Homophily in Social Networks. In K. Cook and J. Hagan (eds.), *Annual Review of Sociology* 27: 415–44.

Milgram, Stanley. 1974. *Obedience to Authority: An Experimental View*. New York: Harper & Row.

Miller, Delbert, and Neil Salkind. 2002. *Handbook of Research Design and Social Measurement* (6th edition). Thousand Oaks, CA: Sage.

Monette, D., T. Sullivan, and C. DeJong. 1998. *Applied Social Research: Tool for the Human Services*. Fort Worth, TX: Holt, Rinehart & Winston.

Morgan, David. 1996. *Focus Groups as Qualitative Research*. Newbury Park, CA: Sage.

Morin, Richard. 1998. "What Americans Think." *Washington Post*, Monday August 24.

Murphy, Dean. 2002. "As Security Cameras Sprout, Someone's Always Watching." *The New York Times*, September 29.

Myerhoff, Barbara. 1989. "So What Do You Want From Us Here?" In Carolyn Smith and William Kornblum (eds.), *In the Field: Readings on the Field Research Experience*. New York: Praeger.

National Institutes of Health. 1995. Appendix 1 "Historical, Ethical and Legal Foundation for the NIH's Policies and Procedures." In *Guidelines for the Conduct of Research Involving Human Subjects at the National Institutes of Health*. http://ohsr.od.nih.gov/guidelines.php3.

National Public Radio. 2002. "Risks and Benefits of Hormone Replacement Therapy." *Talk of the Nation/Science*, July 26.

New York Times. 2002. "9 Hijackers Scrutinized." March 3, Section A:1.

Newport, F., L. Saad, and D. Moore. 1997. "How Polls Are Conducted." In M. Golay, *Where America Stands, 1997*. New York: John Wiley & Sons, Inc.

Nie, N. H., and L. Erbring. 2000. *Internet and Society: A Preliminary Report.* Palo Alto, CA: Stanford Institute for the Quantitative Study of Society.

Norris, Floyd, and Amanda Hesser. 2003. "U.S. to Allow Wine Labels That List Health Claims." *The New York Times,* March 1, Section C: 1.

O'Farrell, Timothy, and Christopher Murphy. 1995. "Marital Violence Before and After Alcoholism Treatment." *Journal of Consulting and Clinical Psychology* 42: 265–76.

Osgood, Charles. 2002. "Study Questions Gingko Biloba's Effectiveness." *The Osgood File* (CBS), August 21.

Palmer, C. E. 1989. "Paramedic Performances." *Sociological Spectrum* 9: 211–25.

Patten, Mildred. 2001. *Questionnaire Research: A Practical Guide.* Los Angeles, CA: Pyrczak Publishing.

Patton, M. 1982. "Thoughtful Questionnaires." In *Practical Evaluation.* Newbury Park: Sage.

Pfohl, Stephen. 1994. *Images of Deviance and Social Control: A Sociological History.* New York: McGraw-Hill, Inc.

Plichita, S. 1992. "The Effects of Woman Abuse on Health Care Utilization and Health Status: A Literature Review." *Women's Health Issues* 2: 154–63.

Popper, Karl. 1959. *The Logic of Scientific Discovery.* New York: Basic Books.

Powers, E., and H. Witmer. 1951. *An Experiment in the Prevention of Delinquency: The Cambridge-Somerville Youth Study.* New York: Columbia University Press.

Ranade, Supria. 2002. "New Studies Show How Waves Emitted from Cell Phones Are Hazardous." *The Johns Hopkins News-Letter* via U-Wire, November 1.

Reines, Dan. 2001. "Minute Mates: Speed Dating Has Flipped the Matchmaking Industry on Its Head, But Can You Really Find Lasting Love in Seven Minutes?" *New Times L. A.,* May.

Reynolds, Gretchen. 2003. "The Stuttering Doctor's Monster Study." *The New York Times Magazine,* March 16, 36.

Reynolds, Paul. 1979. *Ethical Dilemmas and Social Science Research.* San Francisco: Jossey-Bass.

Ritter, Malcolm. 2003. "Children–TV Violence Link Has Effect." *Associated Press Online,* March 9.

Robinson, William. 1950. "Ecological Correlations and the Behavior of Individuals." *American Sociological Review* 15: 351–7.

Ross, Emma. 2002. "Study Finds Positive Thinking Does Not Improve Cancer Survival, but Feels Better." *The Associated Press,* October 19.

Ruane, Janet, and Karen Cerulo. 2004. *Second Thoughts: Seeing Conventional Wisdom Through the Sociological Eye* (2nd edition). Thousand Oaks, CA: Pine Forge Press.

Rubinstein, J. 1973. *City Police.* New York: Farrar, Straus & Giroux.

Rudebeck, Clare. 2003. "Health: A Spoonful of Optimism; Some People Are Convinced That the Healing Power of the Mind Can Help." *The Independent* (London), February 26.

Salkind, Neil. 2000. *Statistics for People Who (Think They) Hate Statistics*. Thousand Oaks, CA: Sage.

Salsburg, David. 2001. *The Lady Tasting Tea: How Statistics Revolutionized Science in the Twentieth Century*. New York: W. H. Freeman.

Sanders, C. 1999. "Getting a Tattoo." In E. Rubington and M. Weinberg (eds.), *Deviance the Interactionist Perspective* (7th edition). Boston: Allyn and Bacon.

Schuman, Howard. 2002. "Sense and Nonsense about Surveys." *Contexts* (Summer): 40–7.

Shermer, M. 1997. *Why People Believe Weird Things*. New York: W. H. Freeman.

Sloan, A. 2003. "Will the Bosses Pay?" *Newsweek*, May 26, 43.

Smith, Tom. 1987. "That Which We Call Welfare by Any Other Name Would Smell Sweeter: An Analysis of the Impact of Question Working on Response Patterns." *Public Opinion Quarterly* 51 (Spring): 75–83.

Smith, Tom. 1990. "Phone Home? An Analysis of Household Telephone Ownership." *International Journal for Public Opinion Research* 2: 369–90.

Smith, Tom. 1992. "A Methodological Analysis of the Sexual Behavior Questions on the GSS." *Journal of Official Statistics* 8: 309–26.

Smith, Tom. 1993. "Little Things Matter: A Sampler of How Difference in Question Format Can Affect Survey Responses." *National Opinion Research Center, GSS Methodological Report no. 78*.

Smith, Tom. 1994. "Trends in Non-Response Rates." *National Opinion Research Center, GSS Methodological Report no. 82*.

Springen, Karen. 2003. "Don't Dis the Diet." *Newsweek*, June 2, 12.

Staples, William. 1997. *The Culture of Surveillance: Discipline and Social Control in the United States*. New York: St. Martin's Press.

Starr, Paul. 1982. *The Social Transformation of American Medicine*. New York: Basic Books.

Steinbeck, John. 1994. *Of Mice and Men*. New York: Penguin.

Sudman, S., N. Bradburn, and N. Schwarz. 1996. *Thinking About Answers: The Application of Cognitive Process to Survey Methodology*. San Francisco: Jossey-Bass.

Taubes, Gary. 2002. "What If It's All Been a Big Fat Lie?" *The New York Times Magazine* (July 7) 6: 22–34.

Theodorson, George, and Achilles Theodorson. 1969. *A Modern Dictionary of Sociology*. New York: Barnes & Noble Books.

Thompson, Kevin. 1989. "Gender and Adolescent Drinking Problems: The Effects of Occupational Structure." *Social Problems* 36(1): 30–47.

Thorlindsson, Thorolfur, and Thoroddur Bjarnason. 1998. "Modeling Durkheim on the Micro Level: A Study of Youth Suicidality." *American Sociological Review* 63, (1): 94–110.

Thorne, Barrie. 2001. "Learning from Kids." In Robert Emerson, (ed.), *Contemporary Field Research* (2nd edition). Prospect Heights: Waveland Press, Inc.

Torabi, M., W. Bailey, and M. Majd-Jabbari. 1993. "Cigarette Smoking as a Predictor of Alcohol and Other Drug Use by Children and Adolescents: Evidence of the 'Gateway Drug' Effect." *Journal of School Health* 63(7); 302–7.

Tufte, Edward. 1997. *Visual Explanations: Images and Quantities, Evidence and Narrative*. Cheshire, CN: Graphics Press.

Tufte, Edward. 2001. *The Visual Display of Quantitative Information* (2nd edition). Chesire, CN: Graphics Press.

Vail, D. Angus. 2001. "Tattoos are Like Potato Chips … You Can't Have Just One." In Alex Thio and Thomas Calhoun (eds.), *Readings in Deviant Behavior* (2nd edition). Boston: Allyn and Bacon.

Van Hook, Jennifer, Jennifer Glick, and Frank Bean. 2004. "Public Assistance Receipt Among Immigrants and Natives: How the Unit of Analysis Affects Research Findings." In Diane Wysocki (ed.), *Readings in Social Research* Methods (2nd edition). Belmont, CA: Wadsworth.

Vaughan, D. 2002. "Signals and Interpretive Work: The Role of Culture in a Theory of Practical Action. In Karen A. Cerulo (ed.), *Culture in Mind: Toward a Sociology of Culture and Cognition*. New York: Routledge.

Vidich, Arthur, and Joseph Bensman. 1958. *Small Town in Mass Society: Class Power and Religion in a Rural Community*. Princeton: Princeton University Press.

Whitall, Susan, and Kate Lawson. 1998. "Dr Spock's Book on Kindly Parenting Shaped Baby Boom." *The Detroit News*, Tuesday, March 17.

Whyte, William Foote. 1955. *Street Corner Society*. Chicago: University of Chicago Press.

Wilson, Gavin. 2002. "Hair Chemicals Place Stylists' Babies at Risk." *The Express*, August 1.

Wiltz, John E. 1973. *The Search for Identity: Modern American History*. Philadelphia: J. B. Lippincott Company.

Winter, Greg. 2002. "America Rubs Its Stomach, and Says Bring It On." *The New York Times*, Sunday July 7, Week in Review: 5.

Wright, T. 2001. "Selected Moments in the Development of Probability Sampling: Theory and Practice." *Survey Research Newsletter*, 13.

Wysocki, Diane. (ed.). 2004. *Readings in Social Research Methods* (2nd edition). Belmont, CA: Wadsworth/Thomson.

Zegart, D. 2000. "The Cigarette Papers: A Docu-Drama in Three Acts." http:www.pbs.org/wgbh/pages/frontline/smoke/webumentary/TEXT/ The_Cig_Papers/CP.1.

Web Resources

General Introductions/Overviews

Bill Trochim's Web Page   As I've indicated throughout the book, Bill Trochim's methods page is a great overall resource. See especially his Knowledge Base link: http://trochim.human.cornell.edu/

Research Methods Tutorials   This site takes you to tutorials written by graduate students for an audience without any methods background: http://trochim.human.cornell.edu/tutorial/TUTORIAL.HTM

Resources for Methods in Evaluation and Social Research   Another good starting place for an overview of methods topics and resources: http://gsociology.icaap.org/methods/

The Research Process   This source was written for a general audience (specifically for those working in hospitality and tourism). It covers a vast array of research topics in a straightforward, nontechnical way: http://www.ryerson.ca/~mjoppe/rp.htm

Accessing Information (*see also* Literature Reviews)

Accessing Information for Research   A general tutorial to help students get started on a research project: http://www.libraries.psu.edu/instruction/infolit/andyou/mod1/pre.htm

Finding Information on the Internet   The Teaching Library at Berkeley offers a series of tutorials for searching and evaluating web sites: http://www.lib.berkeley.edu/TeachingLib/Guides/Internet/FindInfo.html

Web Tutorial   Mayfield Publishing offers a tutorial for students conducting a web search: http://www.mayfieldpub.com/webtutor/index.htm

Applied Research (*see* Evaluation Research)

Causal Analysis

Cause and Effect   Discusses the place of causal reasoning in writing. Might be a useful place to start students of research thinking about causal analysis: http://virtual.parkland.cc.il.us/jforman/expository/Causal%20Analysis.html

Causal Analysis   Using marriage research as its base, this page examines the logic and challenges of causal analysis: http://www.utexas.edu/research/pair/causal.htm

Overview: Experimental and Quasi-Experimental Research   This site is geared to English studies but offers a series of lessons regarding the link between causal analysis and experimental designs: http://writing.colostate.edu/references/research/experiment/index.cfm

Causal Analysis: An Exercise   Offers students some practice in distinguishing background conditions and primary causes: http://mywebpages.comcast.net/erozycki/CausAnlys.html

Census Data

US Census Bureau   Everything you've ever wanted to know about the population of the US. Be sure to link to American FactFinder: http://www.census.gov/

Measuring America: The Decennial Censuses From 1790 to 2000   Offers individual histories of each census: http://www.census.gov/prod/www/abs/ma.html

Comparative Research

IDB Summary Demographic Data   International Demographic Data from the Census Bureau offers summary data on various countries of the world: http://www.census.gov/ipc/www/idbsum.html

World Wide Web Virtual Library: Statistics   The University of Florida offers a listing of links to official, government statistics for various nations of the world (you will need to scroll about three-quarters of the way through the document in order to find this info under "Government Statistical Institutes"): http://www.stat.ufl.edu/vlib/statistics.html

International Agencies and Information   An extensive list of international agencies and the data they provide: http://www.lib.umich.edu/govdocs/intl.html

Portals to the World   A Library of Congress site that offers links to electronic resources for nations of the world selected by subject experts: http://www.loc. gov/rr/international/portals.html

The State of the World's Children 2003   Provides an array of data on the conditions of children around the world: http://www.unicef.org/sowc03/tables/ index.html

Population Reference Bureau   Offers population information from around the world: http://www.prb.org

FedStats   Provides access to a wide array of federal statistics: http://www.fed-stats.gov/

Data on the Internet

Statistical Resources on the Web: The University of Michigan's Documents Center provides this collection of links to statistical data for a wide range of subjects. You can search by broad topics or via an alphabetized list of subjects. Do take a look: http://www.lib.umich.edu/govdocs/stats.html

US Census Bureau   Everything you've ever wanted to know about the population of the US. Be sure to link to American FactFinder: http://www.census. gov/

FedStats   Provides one-stop shopping for US government statistics: http:// www.fedstats.gov/

Social Statistics Briefing Room   Provides easy access to current federal statistics in areas of crime, demography, education, and health: http://www. whitehouse.gov/fsbr/crime.html

Statistical Abstract of the US   Extensive collection of social and economic indicators: http://www.census.gov/statab/www/

GPO Access   Provides access to information from all three branches of the US government: http://www.gpoaccess.gov/

Data Resources for Sociologists   A list compiled by the *American Sociological Association* of publicly available data sets for primary and secondary analysis: http://www.asanet.org/data.htm

Data on the Net   An online database of Internet sites of statistical data, data catalogues, data libraries, and more: http://odwin.ucsd.edu/idata/

ICPSR   The Inter-university Consortium of Political and Social Research at the University of Michigan provides access to an archive of social science data: http:// www.icpsr.umich.edu/index-medium.html

Finding Data on the Internet   This site (aimed at journalists) provides numerous links that put all kinds of interesting data at your fingertips: http:// nilesonline.com/data/

General Social Survey   The GSS is a biennial survey of a random sample of the US population. In accessing the GSS, students can monitor trends in Americans'

attitudes and behaviors: http://www.norc.uchicago.edu/projects/gensoc.asp; http://www.icpsr.umich.edu:8080/GSS/homepage.htm

Data Analysis (*see also* Statistics)

Data Training   A consultant for graduate students offers a "dos and don'ts" list for working with data: http://www.uiowa.edu/~soc/datarespect/data_training_frm.html

Pitfalls of Data Analysis   Clay Helberg's paper on how to avoid the misuse and abuse of statistics: http://my.execpc.com/~helberg/pitfalls/

Stats: Guidelines for Descriptive Models   Gives students an overview of the basic analysis that should be conducted for any descriptive or exploratory research: http://www.childrens-mercy.org/stats/model/descriptive.asp

Stats: Guidelines for Linear Regression Models   Useful for students wanting a concrete example of regression analysis and help in understanding the SPSS regression printout: http://www.childrens-mercy.org/stats/model/linear.asp

SPSS for Windows: Getting Started   Written for those just beginning their SPSS work: http://www.utexas.edu/cc/stat/tutorials/spss/SPSS1/Outline1.html

What is Qualitative Data Analysis?   Offers a brief discussion and typology of qualitative/quantitative data and qualitative/quantitative analysis: http://www.analytictech.com/geneva97/whatis.htm

Design (*see* Research Design)

Ethics

Protecting the Public   Offers links to numerous ethics resources: http://gsociology.icaap.org/methods/protect.html

Office for Human Research Protection's Tip Sheet on Informed Consent   http://ohrp.osophs.dhhs.gov/humansubjects/guidance/ictips.htm

Confidentiality Kiosk at the National Institutes of Health   http://grants2.nih.gov/grants/policy/coc/index.htm

Privacy, Confidentiality, and Data Security   This site is maintained by the *American Statistical Association* and offers the latest information related to privacy and confidentiality: http://www.amstat.org/comm/cmtepc/

IRB Information   This link on the ICPSR (Inter-university Consortium of Political and Social Research) web page helps clarify the role of IRBs: http://www.icpsr.umich.edu/irb/index.html

American Sociological Association's Code of Ethics   http://www.asanet.org

Evaluating Web Sites

Evaluation of Information Sources   Offers an extensive list of links for assessing information and web sites: http://www.vuw.ac.nz/staff/alastair_smith/evaln/evaln.htm

Finding Information on the Internet   The Teaching Library at Berkeley offers a series of tutorials for searching and evaluating web sites. Be sure to click on the link for Evaluating Web pages: http://www.lib.berkeley.edu/TeachingLib/Guides/Internet/FindInfo.html

Evaluation Rubrics for Websites   Provides rubrics for assessing web sites for use by students at various grade levels (primary, intermediate and secondary): http://www.siec.k12.in.us/~west/online/eval.htm

Evaluation Research

The World Wide Evaluation Information Gateway   A comprehensive database of policy and evaluation resources. In particular, see the brief online introduction to evaluation: http://www.policy-evaluation.org/

Basic Guide to Program Evaluation   Covers the basic questions and answers about program evaluation. A nice intro for anyone new to the field: http://www.mapnp.org/library/evaluatn/fnl_eval.htm

Evaluation Checklists   A resource offered by The Evaluation Center of Western Michigan University. The site offers a series of pdf documents on major issues that should be considered when conducting evaluation research: http://www.wmich.edu/evalctr/checklists/index.html

Evaluation Manual   UNESCO's offering of the basics of evaluation: http://www.unesco.org/ios/eng/evaluation/tools/outil_e.htm

W. K. Kellogg Foundation Evaluation Handbook   Written for the directors of Kellogg Foundation-funded projects, this series of pdf documents showcases evaluation research as a useful program tool: http://www.wkkf.org/Pubs/Tools/Evaluation/Pub3669.pdf

User-Friendly Handbook for Program Evaluation   A National Science Foundation resource that offers 8 pdf chapters on various aspects of program evaluation: http://www.ehr.nsf.gov/rec/programs/evaluation/handbook/

Approaches to Evaluation   Offers a number of links to such topics as action research, participatory research, empowerment evaluation and so on: http://gsociology.icaap.org/methods/approaches.html

Conducting a Participatory Evaluation   A series of tips from the USAID Center for Development and Evaluation: http://www.usaid.gov/pubs/usaid_eval/ascii/pnabs539.txt

Practical Assessment and Evaluation   An online journal devoted to assessment in field of education: http://pareonline.net/

Focus Groups

What Are Focus Groups?   One of the entries in the American Statistical Association's series "What is a Survey?" This is a very good place to start learning about focus groups: http://www.amstat.org/sections/srms/whatsurvey.html

The Use and Misuse of Focus Groups   Written for those working in computer systems development, the article warns that focus group technique is not appropriate for all research questions: http://www.useit.com/papers/focusgroups.html

Conducting Focus Group Interviews   A series of tips from the USAID Center for Development Information and Evaluation: http://www.usaid.gov/pubs/usaid_eval/ascii/pnaby233.txt

Basics of Conducting Focus Groups   Provides a very brief overview of the various stages in running focus groups from beginning prep stages to final debriefing. Could be a useful supplement once students have done some more in-depth reading on the topic: http://www.mapnp.org/library/evaluatn/focusgrp.htm

Formulating a Research Question

Using the Literature to Formulate Your Research Question   Using Becker's writings this short piece offers some guidance on how to "find" a research question in connections revealed by literature reviews: http://www.utexas.edu/research/pair/usingthe.htm

Problem Formulation   Bill Trochim gives some good tips for finding research ideas: http://trochim.human.cornell.edu/kb/problem.htm

Graphic Displays of Information

Graphical Data Presentation   Using a lecture format, this site provides an overview of the basics of graphical data display: http://www.deakin.edu.au/~agoodman/sci101/chap12.php

Data Presentation: A Guide to Good Graphics and Tables   Offers slide presentations and handouts that reflect Tufte's principles of good graphics: http://www.science.gmu.edu/~wss/methods/index.html#Graphics

Galley of Data Visualization   Gives examples of the good, the bad and the ugly of graphics: http://www.math.yorku.ca/SCS/Gallery/

Create a Graph (The National Center for Education Statistics)   Offers a rather elementary presentation but it may nonetheless be useful to those who are terrified of statistics. Allows users to work with their own data or to use data supplied by the NCES: http://nces.ed.gov/nceskids/Graphing/

Historical Data

National Archives and Records Administration   Provides access to major historical documents: http://www.archives.gov/
American Memory   The Library of Congress' site on the history and culture of the US: http://memory.loc.gov/ammem/amhome.html
American Life Histories   Manuscripts from the 1936–40 Federal Writers' Project of the WPA: http://lcweb2.loc.gov/wpaintro/wpahome.html

Hypotheses

Developing a Research Hypothesis   Written for those conducting medical research but useful for anyone trying to appreciate the essential components of good testable hypotheses: http://www.childrens-mercy.org/stats/plan/hypo.asp

Internet Research

Internet Polling   Offers a rather extensive biblio on Internet surveys (with links to some papers): http://www.wlu.ca/lispop/rres/int_poll.htm
Conducting Research Surveys via E-Mail and the Web   A RAND book (via pdf files) on Internet based surveys: http://www.rand.org/publications/MR/MR1480/

Interviewing

Introduction to Interviewing Techniques   This paper explores how interviews differ from ordinary conversations and addresses the skills required for successful interviewing: http://www.wpi.edu/Academics/Depts/IGSD/IQPHbook/ch11.ht
Qualitative Interviews in Health Care   A chapter on conducting interviews in a health care setting: http://www.bmjpg.com/qrhc/chapter2.html

Key Informant Interviews   A series of pdf documents from Program Planning and Assessment at the University of Illinois Extension that address conducting key informant interviews as part of a needs assessment: http://www.aces.uiuc.edu/~PPA/KeyInform.htm

Literature Reviews

The Literature Review: A Few Tips on Conducting It   A general introduction to any type of literature review: http://www.utoronto.ca/writing/litrev.html
Familiarizing Yourself with the Literature   While focused on the marriage literature, this site advises student on how to approach and start a literature review: http://www.utexas.edu/research/pair/literatu.htm
Writing Up Research: Using the Literature   A nicely organized discussion of literature reviews that is intended for a research audience: http://www. languages.ait.ac.th/EL21LIT.HTM
Doing Successful Literature Reviews   This George Washington University site is intended for students at the graduate level, but any serious undergraduate will find it most helpful. Includes mini-lessons on searching, assessing and integrating what is found in a review. A must visit site: http://www.gwu.edu/~litrev/
Instruction on Preparing the Literature Review   While written for a design course, this site will help anyone get a better idea of the purpose and parts of a literature review: http://anarch.ie.toronto.edu/courses/mie240/literature.html
Annotated Bibliographies   Can help students wrap their minds around a literature review. Offers guidance for writing an annotated bibliography: http://owl.english.purdue.edu/handouts/general/gl_annotatedbib.html

Measurement

The First Measured Century   This site offers a general introduction to measurement by looking at social change during the twentieth century as indicated by statistical trends in education, work, living arrangement, health, etc.: http://www.pbs.org/fmc/
State of the World's Children 2003   A site where students can see how abstract concepts are grounded in concrete measures, specifically the site offers various measures of the well-being of children: http://www.unicef.org/sowc03/tables/index.html
The US General Accounting Office   Another useful site to help students see how abstract concepts are translated into measures. In particular, click on "Useful Links" once on page: http://www.gao.gov/

Economic Statistics Briefing Room   Provides an array of economic indicators used by federal government: http://www.whitehouse.gov/fsbr/esbr.html

Sociology Glossary   This site is a useful starting place for lab exercises where students practice translating conceptual definitions into operational definitions: http://www.webref.org/sociology/sociology.htm

Stats: Establish Validity and Reliability   Offers a very down to earth explanation of measurement validity and reliability. Also offers an extensive biblio on these topics: http://www.childrens-mercy.org/stats/plan/validity.asp

General Social Survey   Accessing the GSS allows students to see the operationalization process in action. By clicking on various concepts in the subject index, users can then see the exact questions used by the GSS as measures of those concepts: http://www.icpsr.umich.edu:8080/GSS/homepage.htm

Operationalization   Offers students guidance and practice in the operationalization process: http://mywebpages.comcast.net/erozycki/Oper.html

Uncle Sam's Reference Shelf   State Rankings from the Statistical Abstract of the United States: Anyone looking for examples of ordinal level measures might take a look at this Census site which offers a series of tables showing state rankings for a variety of variables: http://www.census.gov/statab/www/ranks.html

Qualitative Methods

Qualitative Research   A good place to start since it provides many links to very useful research resources. Includes a link for an instructional guide for NUD.IST4 Classic: http://kerlins.net/bobbi/research/qualresearch/

Qualitative Methods Workbook   An e-text that presents the "insight" methods of Gestalt psychologists and others. Each chapter presents students with projects for sharpening their insight: http://www.ship.edu/~cgboeree/qualmeth.html

Qualitative Research in Health Care   An online text offering 9 chapters on various data collection options (interviewing, focus groups, case studies, etc.) and on data analysis: http://www.bmjpg.com/qrhc/contents.html

QualPage   An extensive listing of resources for qualitative methods: http://www.qualitativeresearch.uga.edu/QualPage/

Qualitative Methods   An extensive list of links to an array of qualitative methods topics: http://gsociology.icaap.org/methods/qual.htm

Focus Groups   Written for those working in computer systems development, the article warns that focus group technique is not appropriate for all research questions: http://www.useit.com/papers/focusgroups.html

Research Design

A Primer on Experimental and Quasi-Experimental Design   This paper utilizes the counseling literature to examine basic issues of design and research validity: http://ericae.net/ft/tamu/Expdes.HTM
Designing Evaluations   A GAO (US General Accounting Office) paper to guide those designing an evaluation of completed or ongoing programs: http://www.gao.gov/policy/10_1_4.htm

Sampling

Sampling   A useful glossary of sampling terms: http://www2.chass.ncsu.edu/garson/pa765/sampling.htm
Statistics Glossary: Sampling   Another glossary that presents a list of terms defined: http://www.stats.gla.ac.uk/steps/glossary/sampling.html
Sampling   Offers numerous links to papers, guides, glossaries etc.: http://gsociology.icaap.org/methods/sampling.html
Research Randomizer Tutorial   This site allows the visitor to take a ten-minute tutorial that explains the difference between a random sample and a random assignment: http://www.randomizer.org/tutorial.htm
Research Randomizer   Here one can get assistance in drawing a random sample or employing random assignment to groups: http://www.randomizer.org/index.htm
Sample Size   Any of the following sites will help you determine the right sample size for your project: **How to Determine Sample Size**: http://www.isixsigma.com/library/content/c000709.asp; **Determining Sample Size**: http://edis.ifas.ufl.edu/BPDY_PD006; **Determining Sample Size**: http://wind.cc.whecn. edu/~pwildman/statnew/determining_sample_size.htm
Telephone Sampling Questions and Answers   The Survey Research Center at Berkeley offers troubleshooting advice for executing telephone surveys: http://srcweb.berkeley.edu/res/tsamp.html

Statistics

Statistics and Statistical Graphics Resources   Michael Friendly's impressive array of statistics resources. You would do well to start here: http://www.math.yorku.ca/SCS/StatResource.html
StatSoft   Site of an easy to use electronic stats text: http://www.statsoft.com/textbook/stathome.html

Selecting Statistics   This Trochim page prompts users to provide basic information about their research analysis task (e.g., number of variables, level of measurement, etc.) and then links users to appropriate statistics: http://trochim. human.cornell.edu/selstat/ssstart.htm

HyperStat Online Textbook   David Lane's 18 chapter online statistical text. Nice clear explanations of key statistics topics: http://www.davidmlane.com/ hyperstat/index.html

David Lane's HyperStat Glossary   This site offers an alphabetical listing of statistical terms that link users to very clear explanations: http://www. davidmlane.com/hyperstat/glossary.html

StatNotes   Online Textbook by G. David Garson: Another online text that offers clear explanations of many core (and additional) topics: http:// www2.chass.ncsu.edu/garson/pa765/statnote.htm

Statistics Every Writer Should Know   A primer for journalists but valuable to anyone who wants to be an educated consumer of numbers: http://nilesonline. com/stats/

Survey Research

American Statistical Association   Once on the site, follow the Publications link to the Brochures link to the Survey Research link to access a number of useful brochures on various aspects of survey research: http://www.amstat.org

Herb Abelson's Survey Research Web Site   This is a good starting place for many relevant survey links: http://members.bellatlantic.net/~abelson/

A Brief Guide to Questionnaire Development   This article by Robert Frary does a nice job of reviewing the many considerations that go into constructing a good questionnaire: http://www.testscoring.vt.edu/fraryquest.html

Statement by Don A. Dillman on Palm Beach County Florida Ballot   Offers a considered review of how formatting of the election ballot may have produced measurement error in the 2000 Presidential election: http://survey.sesrc. wsu.edu/dillman/palmbeach_statement.htm

Conducting Research Surveys via E-Mail and the Web   A RAND book (via PDF files) on Internet based surveys: http://www.rand.org/publications/MR/ MR1480/

Public Opinion Polls   The following sites offer an array of recent public opinion polls: **Pew Research Center for the People and the Press**: http://people-press.org/; **Polling Report**: http://www.pollingreport.com/; **Public Agenda Online**: http:// www.publicagenda. org/; **Roper Center for Public Opinion Research**: http:// www.ropercenter.uconn. edu; **ABC News Polls**: http://abc.go.com/sections/ politics/PollVault/PollVault. html

How Polls Work   Here are two sites that explain how polls "work": **The Numbers Game**: http://abcnews.go.com/sections/politics/DailyNews/

POLL.EXPLAINER.htm; **Polling 101**: http://www.ropercenter.uconn.edu/pom/polling101.htm

Assessing Polls   The following sites offer tips for critically assessing polls: **How to Assess a Poll's Validity**: http://www.rci.rutgers.edu/~eaglepol/edu.htm#val; **20 Questions a Journalist Should Ask About Poll Results, 2nd Edition**: http://www.ncpp.org/qajsa.htm

Perils of Polling   This page offers a bibliography for those interested in further exploring the use and wisdom of polling: http://www.wlu.ca/lispop/rres/perils.htm

Internet Polling   Offers a rather extensive biblio on Internet surveys (with links to some papers): http://www.wlu.ca/lispop/rres/int_poll.htm

Units of Analysis

Unit of Analysis   Trochim offers a very short but informative page on distinguishing units in a study: http://trochim.human.cornell.edu/kb/unitanal.htm

Writing Resources

Guide to Grammar and Style   Great resource for reviewing many of the basics of good writing: http://andromeda.rutgers.edu/~jlynch/Writing/

Thesaurus.com   Get some help with your vocabulary (and translations): http://thesaurus.reference.com/

The Sociology Research Paper   This is a very useful link found on Michael Kearl's "A Sociological Tour Through Cyberspace" (do take the entire tour when you have the time): http://www.trinity.edu/~mkearl/research.html

Write-Up   Once again we turn to Bill Trochim's "Knowledge Base" to find a nice review of what it takes to get research down on paper: http://trochim.human.cornell.edu/kb/writeup.htm

Stats: Writing a Methods Section   This page is intended to guide those doing medical research, but it should help any student get a feel for the kind of information to include in a methods section of a research paper: http://www.childrens-mercy.org/stats/plan/methods.asp

Annotated Bibliographies   Offers guidance for writing an annotated bibliography: http://owl.english.purdue.edu/handouts/general/gl_annotatedbib.html

Index